D0279691

22₀

CA

CA

B2 €

19. MAR

INSPECTORATES IN BRITISH GOVERNMENT

Inspectorates in British Government

Law Enforcement and Standards of Efficiency

GERALD RHODES

for the
ROYAL INSTITUTE OF PUBLIC ADMINISTRATION

GEORGE ALLEN & UNWIN
London   Boston   Sydney

346.381 R

First published in 1981

This book is copyright under the Berne Convention. All rights are reserved. Apart from any fair dealing for the purpose of private study, research, criticism or review, as permitted under the Copyright Act, 1956, no part of this publication may be reproduced, stored in a retrieval system, or transmitted, in any form or by any means, electronic, electrical, chemical, mechanical, optical, photocopying, recording or otherwise, without the prior permission of the copyright owner. Enquiries should be sent to the publishers at the undermentioned address:

GEORGE ALLEN & UNWIN LTD
40 Museum Street, London WC1A 1LU

© The Royal Institute of Public Administration, 1981

British Library Cataloguing in Publication Data

Rhodes, Gerald
  Inspectorates in British government.
  1. Inspectorates in government – Great Britain
  2. Great Britain – Politics and government – 1964–
  I. Title   II. Royal Institute of Public Administration
  354.4109′1   JN451   80–41365

ISBN 0–04–351056–6

Set in 10 on 11 point Plantin by Inforum Ltd, Portsmouth
and printed in Great Britain
by Lowe and Brydone Limited, Thetford, Norfolk

CONTENTS

PREFACE

During the past thirty years the Royal Institute of Public Administration has carried out a series of research projects into significant areas of public administration. *Inspectorates in British Government* is the latest in this series.

The use of inspection by central and local government and other public-sector bodies, and the appointment of inspectorates for this purpose, has a long history going back to the early nineteenth century. For reasons which are explained more fully in the Introduction, the Institute judged that this was an appropriate time to examine the role of inspectorates which had been established for one of two purposes: either to ensure conformity with particular statutory requirements or to oversee standards of performance by other public bodies. It was hoped that a broad-ranging inquiry of this kind would not only help to put the use of inspectorates in perspective, but would also illuminate their future role. The key issues included the powers of inspectors and the use of those powers; the determination of standards; the accountability of inspectors; and the criteria for assessing the effectiveness of inspection work.

The detailed research was carried out by Mr Gerald Rhodes with the assistance of a study group under the chairmanship of Sir Arthur Peterson, a former Permanent Under-Secretary of State at the Home Office. The other members of the group were:

R. G. Fenwick, a former HM Inspector of Constabulary
A. J. Greenwell, Chief Executive, Northamptonshire County Council
R. J. Hartles, Chief Education Officer, Ealing London Borough
J. M. Lee, Reader in Politics, Birkbeck College, University of London
Miss B. M. Leighton, Directorate of Corporate Services, Health and Safety Executive
L. J. A. Merckx, formerly Engineering Manager, Head Office, Imperial Chemical Industries Limited
Mrs D. Ottley, Assistant Director, Social Work Service, Department of Health and Social Security
Dr J. J. Richardson, Lecturer in Politics, University of Keele
K. Williams, Chief Executive, Wolverhampton Borough Council

The Institute is extremely grateful to Sir Arthur Peterson and the other members of the study group for so freely giving time and energy to the project, and very much appreciates the invaluable assistance and expert advice which they provided.

The project was financed by a grant from the Social Science Research Council, to whom the Institute is indebted for support.

A project of this kind, which attempts to survey a wide area of government, naturally involves many inquiries in many different quarters. The Institute acknowledges with pleasure the ready help and co-operation of the many inspectors and other officials who patiently answered questions, provided documentary information and offered practical insights into the working lives of inspectors; thanks are also due to other bodies and individuals who contributed their views on the role of inspectors.

The sole responsibility for the views expressed in this study rests with the author, Gerald Rhodes.

INTRODUCTION

Recent developments make this an appropriate time to review the use of inspectorates in British administration in a way that has not been attempted since inspection first became an important administrative device in the middle years of the nineteenth century. As is explained in Chapter 1, the present study is concerned with inspectorates of central and local government and other public-sector bodies whose functions derive from statutes, and whose inspection work is directed to one of the two following ends:

(1) inspection to ensure compliance with statutory requirements ('enforcement inspection');
(2) inspection to secure, maintain or improve standards of performance ('efficiency inspection').

There are different reasons for suggesting that it is now appropriate to reconsider the use of inspection in these two circumstances:

(1) an increasing number of enforcement inspectorates have become the subject of political and public controversy: for the most part, controversy has arisen from the criticism that inspectors are failing to carry out the task for which they were appointed, but it will be part of the object of this study to show that it is necessary to explore beyond this criticism and examine how far traditional enforcement concepts are still appropriate to the achievement of legislative aims;
(2) little controversy has arisen over the use of efficiency inspection: inspection for this purpose within the terms of this study is in practice confined to inspectorates of central government which are concerned with services provided by local authorities, and there is a continuing debate over the use of supervision and control powers by central government in its relations with local government: the part played by efficiency inspection in central/ local relations is an essential area for examination in connection with that debate.

It is particularly important to examine the use of enforcement inspection because of its relevance to certain wider issues of public administration which are currently under discussion. In the first place, there is growing interest in and concern over problems of implementation of policy, especially the gap between legislative intentions and what is achieved in practice. The question how far statutory requirements are or can be enforced by inspection is from one point of view an aspect of the problem of implementation. Secondly, there has developed in recent years pressure for a greater degree of public participation in the decisions of government authorities. Enforcement inspection may be affected in two ways by this development:

(1) the demand for greater public participation may be expressed in dissatisfaction with the results of inspection and criticism of the methods used by inspectors to achieve those results;
(2) incentives deriving from increased opportunities for participation may offer an alternative to the use of inspection in the achievement of legislative aims.

Inspectorates established for the two purposes identified, as shown in Appendix 2, account for less than 1 per cent of the total of those employed in central and local government. But although few in number they constitute a significant and growing element in British administration. They have, however, attracted little attention or study. A few inspectorates have had notice taken of them, notably the factory and education inspectorates.[1] Recently, the work of local authority trading standards departments has been the subject of a full-length study,[2] and the wages inspectorate of the Department of Employment has been examined more briefly.[3] Even less attention has been paid to inspection as a whole and its underlying principles. A 1955 study was limited to efficiency inspectorates;[4] and a more recent brief survey, which in some sense provided the starting-point of the present study, was limited to inspectorates of central government.[5] On the other hand, thanks largely to an increased interest in the growth of government in the nineteenth century, we now know a good deal more about the origins and early history of some nineteenth-century inspectorates.[6]

Some of the reasons which have contributed to the neglect of the subject will emerge in the course of the study, but it should be noted that there has long been a general assumption that inspection is an effective means of enforcing legislative requirements. Criticisms where they have arisen have not therefore been directed at the principle of inspection but have, on the contrary, called for stricter application of the principle. Not less but more inspection has generally been seen as the answer to the failure to achieve a high level of compliance with statutory requirements. This favourable attitude to the efficacy of inspection has acted to inhibit fundamental reappraisal of its principles and methods. It is a major aim of the present study to explore the assumptions which underlie the use of inspection for both enforcement and efficiency purposes, and thus to provide background to developing a more general critique of the inspection function.

NOTES: INTRODUCTION

1 T. K. Djang, *Factory Inspection in Great Britain* (Allen & Unwin, 1942); E. L. Edmonds, *The School Inspector* (Routledge & Kegan Paul, 1962); T. R. Bone, *School Inspection in Scotland 1846–1966* (London University Press, 1968); J. Blackie, *Inspecting and the Inspectorate* (Routledge & Kegan Paul, 1970); cf. Select Committee on Education and Science, *HM Inspectorate*, HC 400–I and 400–II (HMSO, 1968); *Health and Safety at Work*, Report of the Committee, 1970–2, Cmnd 5034 (HMSO, 1972).

2 Ross Cranston, *Regulating Business* (Macmillan, 1979).

3 P. B. Beaumont, 'The limits of inspection: a study of the workings of the government wages inspectorate', *Public Administration*, vol. 57, 1979, p. 203.

4 John S. Harris, *British Government Inspection as a Dynamic Process* (New York: Praeger, 1955).

5 Owen A. Hartley, 'Inspectorates in British central government', *Public Administration*, vol. 50, 1972, p. 447.

6 See, for example, Oliver Macdonagh, 'Coal mines regulation: the first decade 1842–1852', in R. Robson (ed.), *Ideas and Institutions of Victorian Britain* (Bell, 1967); Roy M. McLeod, 'The Alkali Acts administration, 1863–84', *Victorian Studies*, vol. IX, no. 2, 1965; Jill H. Pellew, 'The Home Office and the Explosives Act of 1875', *Victorian Studies*, vol. XVIII, no. 2, 1974.

CHAPTER 1
THE INSPECTORATES

Inspection in its basic sense of

looking carefully into, viewing closely and critically, examining
something with a view to find out its character and condition[1]

can be used for many purposes and in many circumstances. The
establishment of inspectorates, that is, bodies of men and women
designated as inspectors, carries with it the implication

(1) that inspection in this general sense is not simply an incidental
part of their work but a critical element in it;
(2) that the inspection work is of such a nature that it requires to be
carried out by specified and identifiable officials; for example,
they may need particular powers to enable them to inspect.

Even so there are many kinds of inspector – factory inspectors,
inspectors of taxes, planning inspectors, meat inspectors, ticket
inspectors, inspectors of schools, staff inspectors and inspectors of
companies, among others. Their activities cover a wide range of
functions performed by public sector bodies, such as law enforcement, raising revenue, adjudicating on disputes, investigating suspected fraud, staff management and relations between central and
local government. The main arguments for singling out for particular
study enforcement and efficiency inspection are that these are the
main purposes for which inspectorates were established in the
nineteenth century and that they still constitute a major part of the
inspection work of government. Three preliminary questions will,
therefore, be examined in this chapter: *first*, how inspectorates came
to be established for enforcement and efficiency purposes; *secondly*,
what other kinds of inspectorate now exist; *thirdly*, what, if any, is the
relationship between enforcement and efficiency inspection and these
other kinds of inspection.

EARLY INSPECTORATES

Many of the inspectorates with which we are still familiar were
established in the period 1830–60, among them the inspectorates of
factories, prisons, schools, mines, railways and constabulary. How
precisely this came about, whether it was the deliberate putting into

practice of Benthamite ideas, or whether it was simply the consequence of attempts to grapple piecemeal with individual social
problems as they arose, is a question which has been much debated
by historians.[2] Much of the debate on the origin of the use of inspection is part of a wider concern with the growth of government in the
nineteenth century. The focus of this study is narrower, and is especially directed to the particular ends which inspection was intended to
serve and with the means adopted to achieve those ends by inspectors.
And here there is much more general agreement that inspection was
an attempt to regulate activities which were either new, such as the
employment of large numbers of people in factories, or at least operated on a much bigger scale than before, as in coal-mining. Although
the idea of using paid inspectors for the purpose of regulation has been
shown to go back to the eighteenth century,[3] it was in the period
1830–60 that the idea was first put into effect on any scale.

We are here concerned essentially with statutory regulation.
Broadly speaking, the mechanism was that when Parliament legislated to impose responsibilities on others it at the same time provided
for the appointment of inspectors to see that those responsibilities
were carried out. Since not every piece of legislation made this provision for inspectors, it is important to see what kind of responsibilities attracted use of inspectors.

The responsibilities were of two distinct kinds. In the first place
there were general administrative responsibilities: magistrates were
made responsible for running prisons; boroughs and local boards of
health for providing adequate drains and other sanitary measures;
county magistrates and boroughs for providing efficient police forces.
Secondly, there were responsibilities of a more limited kind for
meeting usually quite specific external requirements: shopkeepers
were to use accurate weights and measures, mill-owners were to
employ children only of certain specified ages and for a specified
number of hours, owners of merchant ships had to meet various
requirements, including employing only competent and certificated
masters and mates and providing proper stores of medicines on board
ship.

Correspondingly, there were differences in the tasks which inspectors had to perform. They might have a common element in that in
both cases they were seeing that others carried out their responsibilities, but in the first group they were primarily concerned with
efficiency of provision whereas in the second their concern was only
with whether particular requirements had been met. Furthermore, in
the first group government had a positive interest in promoting the
activity coming under the inspector's supervision, whereas in the
second government intervention was limited to the particular
requirements, and it was not seen as part of the function of govern-

ment to promote or otherwise intervene in the activity in question. Indeed, there was strong resistance to some of the early inspectorates on the grounds that even the limited intervention by them to see that specific requirements were met constituted an unwarranted interference by government in the affairs of productive industry.

ENFORCEMENT INSPECTORS AND EFFICIENCY INSPECTORS

In general, as has been claimed, two important principles were established by this early legislation relating to inspectors:

> that government might interfere in economic affairs in order to protect the individual and that Whitehall might supervise local government in order to ensure administrative efficiency.[4]

It is however characteristic of inspectorates, as of most long-standing British institutions, that these principles were not applied uniformly. Each piece of legislation, and therefore each inspectorate, was devised to meet a specific problem. When, for example, government in 1839 intervened to promote the provision of elementary education it did not do so by imposing statutory responsibilities on a set of authorities, but by offering grants to certain bodies who were willing to provide schools. The use of incentives rather than imposition of responsibilities was matched by the creation of a non-statutory inspectorate; the right to inspection was a condition of grant.[5] Again, inspectors of nuisances were concerned not so much with specific requirements as with a series of prohibitions (e.g. premises were not to be kept in such a state as to be a nuisance or injurious to health) which were to be observed in the interests of the community generally.

Nevertheless, in spite of numerous practical differences of this kind the broad picture remains of inspectorates being set up in the nineteenth century for one of two purposes, either to see that specific statutory requirements were met, or to supervise certain activities of other authorities. They differed in powers as well as purposes. Enforcement inspectorates invariably had specific powers, for example, to enter premises, inspect documents or question people, and these were laid down in the statute under which they were appointed; efficiency inspectorates sometimes had explicit powers of this kind but they were more often implicit. Enforcement inspectorates could take action through the courts if statutory requirements were not met, since contravention was a criminal matter attracting penalties laid down by statute; efficiency inspectorates operated through administrative action, their most powerful weapon frequently being the power to recommend withdrawal of government grant if standards were not satisfactory. Enforcement could be carried out either by central government inspectorates (e.g. factories, mines) or by locally appointed inspectorates (e.g. weights and measures, nuisances); efficiency inspection by its nature could only be carried out by central government inspectorates.

FIVE OTHER TYPES OF INSPECTORATE

It can be seen, therefore, that under the broad general heading of supervisory or regulatory inspection two types of inspectorate evolved. On the same basis of functional classification five other types of inspectorate can be distinguished. Although they will not be examined in this study, a brief analysis of each type (with, where appropriate, its relationship to enforcement or efficiency inspection) is given in the following pages. The five types are:

(1) *internal management inspectors*: by this is meant inspectorates whose function is part of management; for example, staff inspectors in a central department may have the responsibility of seeing that different branches of a department have the right kind and number of staff.

(2) *revenue-collecting inspectorates*: inspectors of taxes are an obvious example, but officers of HM Customs and Excise have powers in some ways analogous to those of enforcement inspectors.

(3) *checking inspectorates*: their characteristic is that they are there to check standards; for example, inspectors of the Ministry of Defence check weapons produced under contract to see that they conform to specifications laid down.

(4) *quasi-judicial inspectorates*: the planning inspectorate of the Department of the Environment hears, and in some cases decides, planning appeals.

(5) *investigatory inspectorates*: investigation of accidents (e.g. of aircraft accidents by inspectors of the Department of Trade) or of suspected fraud (e.g. by company inspectors of the Department of Trade) are examples.

(1) *Internal management inspectorates*
Of these five categories, all but the first are concerned with government relations with others, whether other authorities, individuals, companies or other bodies. For that reason alone internal management inspectorates form a quite separate subject of study. Their functioning belongs to the world of internal management and their role can only be understood in relation to a discussion of management controls, a subject of great interest but one which introduces a completely different set of issues from those involved in considering the

external relations of inspectorates. Furthermore, by definition they are inspectorates which do not need statutory designation or powers. Having said that, it is also worth pointing out that there are some rather special internal inspectorates in government. In particular, the prisons inspectorate, which was an external inspectorate until 1877 when the Home Office became responsible for prisons, has retained a distinctive identity deriving from the peculiar nature of the institutions with which it is concerned. So too in very different circumstances has the Foreign and Commonwealth Office inspectorate.

(2) Revenue-collecting

A little more needs to be said about *revenue-collecting inspectorates*. At first sight they might seem to be merely a sub-class of enforcement inspectorates since their task could be seen as securing compliance with the tax laws. That, however, is too narrow a view. Their main function is the *administration* of the tax system. Clearly, given the nature of taxes and of people's attitudes to them there is some analogy with enforcement in the sense that revenue collectors, like enforcement inspectors, are imposing external requirements. But the differences are more significant than the points of similarity. This may be seen by comparing inspectors of taxes with officers of customs and excise. Inspectors of taxes, in spite of their name, spend most of their time determining the tax liability of individuals and businesses. They were in fact known until 1919 as surveyors of taxes.[6] Customs and Excise officers, on the other hand, have power to examine goods, search vehicles and vessels (and people) and, if they have reasonable grounds for believing that evasion is taking place may, under certain conditions, enter premises, search them and seize and detain goods etc.[7] These powers have some resemblance to but are rather wider than those which most enforcement inspectors possess; but their purpose is different. Since much of the revenue with which HM Customs and Excise are concerned arises from the movement or use of goods the administration of the various duties requires a knowledge of what is physically happening to those goods, and it is for these purposes that the powers are needed. There are nevertheless some borderline cases. The Secretary of State for Social Services, for example, has the power to appoint inspectors, and such inspectors have rights of entry, of inspecting documents and of questioning people for the purpose of seeing that the Social Security Acts are carried out.[8] In practice, these inspectors are mainly used to visit employers' offices to ensure that the legal provisions relating to social security contributions are complied with.[9] They could be regarded as enforcement inspectors. On the other hand, what they are enforcing is a requirement to pay what is essentially a tax on employers. They are an integral part of the administration of the revenue-collecting side of the social security system, just as much as Customs and Excise officers are in the administration of customs duties, VAT and so on. On balance, therefore, they probably belong with revenue collection rather than enforcement.

(3) Checking inspectorates

These are also to some extent analogous both with enforcement and with efficiency inspectorates. Although a characteristic checking inspectorate is one concerned with examination of physical objects as in quality control, the main difficulties arise where inspectorates have been established to try to secure adequate control over the expenditure of public money. This may involve contracts, a notoriously difficult area in which to secure control.[10] A rather special form of expenditure where analogies with enforcement inspection are closer is, however, the giving of government grants or subsidies. Here good administration requires that there should be some check that the money has been expended for the purposes and on the conditions laid down. There is some analogy here with the use of enforcement inspection to the extent that conditions of grant may be regarded as external requirements imposed on recipients. At the same time there are obvious differences: in particular, the analogy with enforcement seems strained since government is here offering an incentive; nobody is under an obligation to take up the incentive offered but those who do are expected to conform with the conditions, a very different matter from having to conform with a purely external requirement. Again, it must be noted that those who carry out this checking work are rarely called inspectors. The Department of Industry, for example, has examiners to check on the use of regional development grants; and the Ministry of Agriculture, Fisheries and Food and the Department of Agriculture and Fisheries for Scotland have no special officials for this work but use officers of their advisory services to check on the use of grants by farmers as part of their normal work. Checking inspectorates will not be examined in detail but because in some ways they form a borderline area some reference will be made to them for purposes of comparison.

(4) Quasi-judicial inspectorates

There seems at first sight no obvious reason why planning inspectors should be so called and indeed the title has attracted comment as being anomalous, not least because in Scotland these officials are known as 'reporters'.[11] The explanation seems to lie in the tangled history of the attempt of central government to stimulate local efforts to deal with the urgent public health problems of the mid-nineteenth century. Appendix 1 sets out the salient facts but briefly one can distinguish two functions of central inspectors at that time in relation to responsibilities to be carried out by local authorities. The first was to carry out inquiries locally, part of the object of which was to give an opportunity for local views and objections to be heard; the second was to supervise the work of the authorities once they had been established. To that extent the holding of public local inquiries became bound up with inspection as a means of control of local authorities, and helped to establish the title 'inspector' for one who undertook such inquiries.

The dual function was indeed retained for many years by the engineering inspectorate of the Local Government Board and its successors. Similarly, electricity inspectors of the Department of Energy still hold public inquiries into major proposals, e.g. for power stations or overhead lines, but in their case this is combined with an enforcement function in relation to the safety aspects of electricity distribution. One consequence of the growth in the use of public inquiries generally by government has been to draw attention to the distinctive nature of the function of holding such inquiries. Thus the Council on Tribunals argued that it was wrong that engineering inspectors of the Department of the Environment should both act in a quasi-judicial capacity in the hearing of objections to schemes of works put forward by local authorities, and also be responsible for investigating and advising on the activities of those same local authorities, e.g. in applications for loan sanction. It was accordingly agreed by DOE that the public inquiry function should be transferred to the Planning Inspectorate.[12] Similarly the Council has queried the use of electricity inspectors to conduct public inquiries.[13]

The position may be summarised, therefore, by saying that whereas in the nineteenth century the holding of local inquiries was associated with the supervision by central government of the activities of local authorities and could therefore be regarded as one of the proper functions of inspectors, the purpose of holding public inquiries is now no longer supervisory, but rather to assess and help resolve disputed planning and other issues. The use of the title inspector for one who conducts such inquiries has therefore to be seen as a historical survival. The function is no longer an inspecting function except in the trivial sense that, as in much administrative work, some inspecting of documents or sites is necessary.

(5) *Investigatory inspectorates*
These provide the most difficult boundary problem of all. 'The inspectors' first job, it has been said, 'was to investigate.'[14] This is obviously true in the sense that before an inspector could take action he needed to find out what was happening. And certainly it is almost axiomatic that enforcement inspectors are sent out with the power to enter

premises, examine documents and so on, precisely because they could not know what was going on simply by sitting in an office in Whitehall examining statistical returns or other paper information. Investigation, however, goes somewhat further than this, particularly in the commonly used sense of carrying out inquiries into actions and events *after* they have occurred. Two aspects will be considered here: first, the extent to which investigations of this kind form part of the work of enforcement inspectors; secondly, the extent to which investigation forms the sole or major reason for establishing inspectorates.

Investigation of accidents forms a well-established part of the work of a number of inspectorates in the health and safety field, such as the factory, mines and quarries and nuclear installations inspectorates. Inspectors may even hold public inquiries into the more serious accidents, although the main purpose of such inquiries is fact-finding rather than the quasi-judicial one of the inquiries considered earlier.[15] Such investigations can be thought of as either having a narrow purpose of detecting possible breaches of the statutory regulations or a wider purpose of providing additional information about hazards which may help to prevent similar accidents in future. They may of course serve both purposes, but the point to be made at this stage is that investigation of accidents can in the case of these inspectorates be firmly linked with the purposes for which they were established.

Some inspectorates, however, are concerned with the investigation of accidents as a major part or even the whole of their function, and this raises the question whether one should regard such investigatory inspectorates as a separate category from enforcement inspectorates. The investigation of railway and aircraft accidents provides the main examples.

It has been argued that when, under the Railway Regulation Act 1840, inspectors were appointed to ensure that companies complied with the provisions of the Acts under which their lines were constructed, they were soon drawn into the investigation of accidents, although they had no statutory power to do so until 1871.[16] Investigation of accidents remains an important part of the function of railway inspectors, probably to a greater extent than with other enforcement inspectors, but they are nevertheless primarily enforcement inspectors concerned, for example, with safety requirements for major new works or installations, and, so far as railway staff are concerned, with the health and safety provisions of the Health and Safety at Work [etc.] Act 1974.

On the other hand, the Accidents Investigation Branch of the Department of Trade, headed by a Chief Inspector of Accidents, has virtually no other function than to investigate air accidents. Furthermore, the regulations under which such investigations are carried out make it clear that:

the main purpose of investigating accidents . . . shall be to determine the circumstances and causes of the accidents with a view to
avoiding accidents in the future rather than to ascribe blame to any
person.[17]

In other words investigation is not intended as a contribution to
enforcement through the detection of breaches of the statutory provisions. But although investigation of air accidents seems to provide a
unique example of a purely fact-finding inspectorate, the position of
the DT Accidents Investigation Branch has to be viewed in relation to
the general administrative arrangements for air safety. These regulatory functions were 'hived off' to the Civil Aviation Authority in 1971
in what was then described as 'a constitutional innovation',[18] leaving
only the accident investigation function to the department on the
grounds endorsed by the Edwards Committee that this should be
separate from the organisation administering the air safety system.[19]
Although, therefore, there are certainly some distinctive features
about the enforcement of regulations relating to air safety, they are
best examined as a whole by considering the relationship between the
functions of the CAA and the Accidents Investigation Branch of DT
rather than by treating the latter as a separate category of inspectorate.

Investigation of fraud or suspected fraud also presents difficult
problems. It is not a significant part of the work of most enforcement
inspectors, but this can be accounted for by the nature of the regulatory requirements. Building regulations, for example, are concerned
with the materials and methods of construction of new buildings, not
with whether building firms conduct their affairs honestly. One
enforcement inspectorate is, however, very much concerned with one
kind of possible fraud. Weights and measures inspectors were
traditionally concerned with the detection of false weights and
measures. Now that they have become trading standards officers[20]
they are involved much more widely with all kinds of fraudulent
trading practices such as false description of goods. Even so, the
purpose of trading standards inspection is to ensure compliance with
regulations governing trading transactions rather than simply to
detect fraud.

Some central government departments do, however, have officials
whose task is the detection of fraud. Thus the Investigation Branch of
HM Customs and Excise is solely concerned with the detection of
revenue fraud;[21] and special investigators of the Department of
Health and Social Security similarly investigate the more serious cases
of suspected fraud.[22] The Companies Investigation Branch of the
Department of Trade has power to require the production of papers
and documents of a company for inspection by an authorised officer if
there is 'good reason' for doing so; the department may also appoint

inspectors to investigate the affairs of a company in certain specified circumstances, mainly where fraud or gross mismanagement is suspected.[23]

In all these cases the procedures operate in two stages and officials with the sole task of investigating suspected fraud come in only at the second stage. For example, detection of fraud is part of the normal duty of officials of C&E and DHSS, and only the more serious and difficult cases are handled by special investigators. Similarly in company investigation inspectors are appointed for the more serious investigations. It is to be noticed that only the latter are called inspectors and they do not constitute an inspectorate in the sense of a body of officials specially designated with powers to perform a particular task since in many of the most important cases the inspectors are not permanent officials but are appointed from outside to investigate that particular case.

Although there are links between investigation of fraud and enforcement inspection, those bodies which are set up specifically and solely for the former purpose are in many ways performing a different function. By definition, they are concerned only with special cases; whereas inspection, although it may operate selectively, must keep under review the whole of its designated area. Moreover, detection of fraud, although it may make use of inspection in its basic sense (e.g. the inspection of documents) is directed primarily to two objects, the establishment of facts and the prevention of misuse of funds, whether public or private, objects which are likely to require other techniques than inspection. On balance, therefore, it is probably better to regard this as a distinct kind of activity rather than a special category of inspection.

Given, therefore, that this study is primarily concerned with enforcement and efficiency inspectorates, two questions to be answered are:

(i)   who employs inspectors of this kind?
(ii) who are the inspectors who fall into these two categories?

WHO EMPLOYS INSPECTORS?

This study is concerned with the role of inspectorates employed by public authorities. The position is clear enough so far as efficiency inspectorates are concerned, since they are all appointed by central government departments.[24] It is also worth pointing out that all these inspectorates operate in relation to services provided by local government or with strong local government involvement, e.g. the probation service. There are no central government inspectorates concerned with the efficiency of health authorities or regional water authorities or the Independent Broadcasting Authority, and still less with public corporations such as the National Coal Board. This distinctive feature was emphasised when the Water Act of 1973 transferred the responsibility for water functions from over 1,000 existing local and other authorities to 10 regional water authorities. Detailed scrutiny of individual items of capital expenditure by DOE's engineering inspectorate had been applied to local authorities under the previous system. Since 1974 regional water authorities have been required to produce only an annual plan and programme of capital works for the Secretary of State's approval. With the abandonment of detailed scrutiny of individual capital expenditure proposals the engineering inspectorate has ceased to exist; a Directorate of Water Engineering was instead established to provide the necessary professional and technical advice within the department. Nothing could better illustrate the fact that efficiency inspectorates are a feature of central government's relations only with local government and not with other parts of the public sector.

The position is more complicated with enforcement inspectorates. Both central departments and local authorities have enforcement responsibilities conferred on them by statute and these form a major part of the present study. But enforcement responsibilities are not confined to central departments and local authorities. Other public-sector bodies may also have such responsibilities. Authorised officers of the British Gas Corporation, for example, have power to enter premises and inspect gas fittings and apparatus to see that they comply with safety requirements.[25] But it is with the more recent proliferation of public-sector bodies known generically, if somewhat inelegantly, as 'quangos' that there has been a greater growth of enforcement responsibilities outside the traditional central department/local authority field.

A good example is the Civil Aviation Authority. Its operations are largely concerned with air traffic control, but it has a number of inspectorates concerned with the enforcement of specific safety requirements. For example, the flight operations inspectorate ensures that the public air transport operators conform to the various regulations relating, for example, to crew training requirements. An even more important example is the Health and Safety Executive (HSE), which has responsibility for enforcing regulations relating to health and safety at work, formerly undertaken by six separate departmental inspectorates.[26] And there are other bodies with enforcement responsibilities such as the Gaming Board.

In principle this study is concerned with inspection to enforce statutory requirements wherever this occurs in the public sector. In practice comparatively little of this kind of regulatory work has, until recently, been assigned to bodies other than central departments and local authorities. The transfer of enforcement functions from government departments to HSE, however, and the creation of regional water authorities which inherited responsibilities for the control of river pollution from river authorities originally assigned to local authorities may indicate some tendency for the balance to shift. The creation of HSE and its controlling body the Health and Safety Commission (HSC), was particularly important because at one stroke[27] a large segment of the enforcement responsibilities of central departments was transferred to another body. It must be noted, however, that HSC, although not a government department, comes under fairly close ministerial supervision; it must submit proposals for carrying out its functions to the Secretary of State for his approval, operate in accordance with those approved proposals, and carry out any directions which the Secretary of State may make in relation to its functions.[28] In addition, HSC and HSE staff remain civil servants. So far as the earlier public corporations are concerned statutory regulation responsibilities are limited in extent and generally linked to central department responsibilities. For example, the responsibility for the protection of the public in the matter of gas safety falls on the Secretary of State for Energy. The British Gas Corporation's inspectors have strictly limited powers of entry for this purpose, and any cases of contravention discovered by them must be reported to the Department of Energy who alone can undertake prosecutions, although the BGC can cut off the supply of gas in an emergency or immediate danger. For the purposes of this study, therefore, attention will be concentrated on inspectorates of central and local government and of such other public bodies as have significant enforcement responsibilities. In practice this means the CAA, HSE and RWAs and one or two smaller bodies, such as the Gaming Board.

WHO ARE THE INSPECTORS?

Inspectorates, as was said earlier, have been taken as being bodies of men and women designated inspectors for the purpose of carrying out the two specific kinds of task identified. They form the core of this study but are not necessarily the whole. Inspectorates in this sense are identified because *prima facie* they seem to provide a ready means of distinguishing those officials whose primary task is efficiency or enforcement inspection. But 'primary task' has to cover a variety of situations, in particular the problem of inspectorates which may originally have been set up with the sole task of efficiency or enforcement inspection but may since have acquired other functions. As long as inspection appears still to form a substantial part of their work they are included.

This criterion is also applied to officials who are not called inspectors. If bodies of men and women not designated inspectors nevertheless have substantial inspecting functions in the sense indicated then there seems no reason for excluding them simply because they are not called inspectors. In some cases there has been a change of name: inspectors of nuisances were later known for many years as sanitary inspectors and later still as public health inspectors: they are now called environmental health officers. Although the latter title – and indeed the earlier changes – implies some change of role or in the scope of their duties, EHOs are still the men and women on whom falls the responsibility for enforcing a variety of statutory provisions in the environmental health field. They, and others like them, one might say, are inspectors by another name.

So too are others who have never been called inspectors. Vehicle examiners of the Department of Transport, for example, carry out inspection work on public service and heavy goods vehicles to see that they comply with statutory requirements for safety purposes. They could equally well have been called vehicle inspectors from the point of view of their basic function.

A slightly different problem arises from the fact that, particularly where enforcement inspection is concerned, the statutes may provide for the conferment of inspecting powers not on inspectors as such but on 'persons duly authorised' by a minister, local authority or some other authority; or jointly on inspectors and authorised persons. Sometimes this simply means in practice that the work of enforcement is carried out by an existing inspectorate. This is particularly so in the case of local authorities. For example, the Animal Boarding Establishments Act 1963 gave local authorities power to authorise 'any of its officers' or a vet to inspect premises licensed under the Act to see whether an offence had been committed.[29] In practice this work usually falls on EHOs.

There is generally in these cases a preferred but not necessarily universally adopted method of carrying out the work. For example, the Fire Precautions Act 1971, which extended the responsibilities of fire authorities in fire prevention work, required them to appoint inspectors to enforce the Act and regulations made under it. In debate on the Bill the Home Office spokesman (Mr Richard Sharples) expressed 'our hope' that they would use officers of fire brigades for inspection purposes.[30] In the great majority of cases they have done so but they are not obliged to and could, for example, recruit inspectors specially for the job.

In the efficiency field the National Assistance (Powers of Inspection) Regulations 1948 gave any person authorised by the Secretary of State power to enter and examine residential accommodation for the elderly; and there are similar powers to inspect accommodation provided for the mentally disordered and for children.[31] These powers were originally exercised partly by an inspectorate (the Home Office children's inspectorate), and partly by officials of the Ministry of Health who were not designated inspectors. They are now all exercised by the Social Work Service (SWS) of the Department of Health and Social Security which also performs various other functions. On the criteria set out earlier, the SWS is a borderline case.

Sometimes officials not originally appointed as inspectors may be given inspecting powers. Fire prevention again provides an example. Fire prevention work has long been a part of the work of fire brigades, as under the Petroleum (Consolidation) Act 1928. But for long the work was in most cases combined with operational duties and few fire brigade officers were specialists in fire prevention work. Since 1948 there has been a steady growth in the use of fire prevention officers, whose duties include a significant amount of inspection work. Even so, much fire prevention work including inspection is still done in combination with operational duties. To talk of an 'inspectorate' in this case is therefore somewhat artifical. At the same time the volume and importance of inspection work for fire prevention purposes has grown to such an extent that it can hardly be ignored, and it is brought within the scope of this study by concentrating on the work of full-time fire prevention officers.

Finally, one may draw attention to the complex situation which can arise where more than one authority is involved. Inspection of slaughterhouses, for example, to ensure conformity with human and animal health regulations is mainly carried out by district councils using authorised officers, that is EHOs. However, certain inspection work, mainly concerned with enforcement of animal health regulations in slaughterhouses dealing with meat for export is carried out by veterinary officers of MAFF.[32] Some of these officers may spend up to one-third of their time on the work but a great many of the Ministry's veterinary officers do little or no inspecting work. Here, therefore, a specific inspecting function – of slaughterhouses – forms part of the work of an established inspectorate, and in its more specialised aspects, part of the work of a body of professional advisers of a central government department. Hence one can only look at who carries out the specific function.

INSPECTING AND NON-INSPECTING FUNCTIONS

Complications of this kind are important mainly for the possible consequences of combining inspecting and non-inspecting functions in the same group of people. It may not matter very much whether MAFF veterinary officers are included in the total of government inspectors or not, except perhaps from the point of view of pedantic accuracy about the numbers of inspectors. From the point of view of the use of inspecting powers, however, and particularly their use in conjunction with promotional and advisory functions, their methods of operation may be of significance. It seems as though inspection work may form a spectrum: at one end, 'pure' inspection – that is, inspectorates set up with the sole purpose of carrying out inspection for efficiency or enforcement purposes; at the other end, inspection powers conferred on those who have a quite different function, as a relatively small part of their work. Inspectorates form the top half of this spectrum.

In reality the picture is more complex if one takes into account the fact that changes may take place over a period. An inspectorate may start off with a single function or at least a relatively limited set of related functions. In the course of time it may acquire additional functions, some closely related to the original function but others acquired simply as a matter of administrative convenience. Thus, after the Ministry of Health assumed responsibility for the administration of the Poor Laws in 1919, the activities of the general inspectors included:

the holding of local hearings of inquiries for the purpose of eliciting information concerning proposed changes in the boundaries of parishes and other local jurisdictions, the investigation of persons being considered for the King's semi-annual honours list, the stimulation of local authorities to engage in public housing and slum clearance activities, and the supervision of local government inspection of canal boats plying the rivers and canals throughout the country. In fact, the General Inspectors were apparently used by the Ministry as liaison officers with regard to any function of the local authorities which was not already covered by some Inspectorate or other means of contact.[33]

Thus individual inspectorates may either originally or in the course of time have a range of functions of both an inspecting and a noninspecting kind. One can argue that in so far as this combination gives rise to problems in interpreting their role it can be studied within existing inspectorates. This does not, however, exclude the possibility that these problems may also be illuminated by an examination of the work of officials who are not inspectors but may have acquired inspecting powers for certain limited purposes as in the case of veterinary officers of the agriculture departments.

Some illustration of the range of inspectorates in enforcement work and of the variety of people on whom inspecting powers and responsibilities may be conferred can be judged from the work of the agriculture departments. In England and Wales [34] the MAFF has inspectorates for limited and quite specific enforcement tasks (e.g. agricultural wages, plant health and seeds); it also has inspectorates with other functions than the enforcement of statutory requirements – the sea fisheries inspectorate, for example, has a variety of tasks including general liaison with the fishing industry apart from enforcing provisions relating to the conservation of fish. In addition, authorised officers of the Ministry, in practice veterinary officers, may act as enforcement inspectors, as in the inspectors of slaughterhouses already referred to but also in the borderline area of checking that the conditions of making grants to farmers in connection with various schemes have been observed. Thus they may, for example, enter land or premises to get information, inspect animals, take samples or examine and take copies of documents in connection with schemes for the eradication of brucellosis which involve payments to the owners of herds of cattle.[35] Other officers of the Ministry's Agricultural Development and Advisory Service (ADAS) are similarly concerned in checking, for example, on payments of farm capital grants. It is not surprising, given the Ministry's close involvement with the agriculture and horticultural industries, that it should have a range of contacts varying from the formal inspectorial to the purely advisory. It is significant that the Minister in 1976 said that it was:

> not practicable to detail all the possible circumstances in which officials of my Department . . . have powers of search and entry into private property.

Even so, he listed forty-two Acts of Parliament conferring such powers, more than for any other department, without counting the powers given to other bodies for which the Minister is answerable, such as the Forestry Commission or the Meat and Livestock Commission.[36] Most of the powers listed in these Acts were for inspecting purposes. Finally, it must be noted that local authorities play a considerable part in the enforcement of statutory provisions relating to agriculture, apart from the inspection of slaughterhouses. County Councils and London Boroughs, for example, must appoint inspectors (and agricultural analysts) to enforce the provisions relating to the sale of fertilisers and feeding stuffs (e.g. on the marking of particulars on such goods for sale).[37] This work is normally carried out by trading standards officers, as also is enforcement under the Diseases of Animals Acts.

Thus, whether attention is focused narrowly on inspectorates or more broadly on the inspecting function, however it is carried out, the position is complex. For the purposes of this study inspectorates forming the main subject for examination have been listed in Part 1 of

Appendix 2 (pp. 237–270). These are identifiable bodies of men and women, whether called inspectors or not, who appear to have as a significant function inspection for either efficiency or enforcement purposes, whether that function is combined with other functions or not. Part 1 of the Appendix also gives brief factual details about each of these inspectorates.

NOTES: CHAPTER 1

1 *Oxford English Dictionary* (1901 edn).
2 A useful analysis of the wider debate with bibliography is Arthur J. Taylor, *Laissez-Faire and State Intervention in Nineteenth Century Britain* (Macmillan, 1972).
3 An act of 1810 (50 Geo. III, c. 103) made provision for a paid Inspector General of Prisons in Ireland; its origins go back to an even earlier Act of 1786 (O. Macdonagh, *Early Victorian Government 1830–1870*, Weidenfeld & Nicolson, 1977, pp. 51, 187–8).
4 David Roberts, *Victorian Origins of the British Welfare State* (Yale University Press, 1960), p. 36.
5 See Chapter 5. Inspection of schools now takes place under statutory powers contained in the Education Act 1944 and Education (Scotland) Act 1962.
6 The Income Tax Act 1952 does not appear to distinguish the two terms, and defines 'surveyor' as meaning a surveyor of taxes but including an inspector of taxes (ss. 13, 19, 526).
7 Customs and Excise Act 1952, ss. 294–8.
8 Social Security Act 1975, s. 144.
9 *Report of Committee on Abuse of Social Security Benefits* (Cmnd 5228, HMSO, 1973), paras 66, 411.
10 For a recent case where a tightening-up of administrative arrangements was recommended, see the report on alleged contractual irregularities on the Gloucester–Cheltenham section of the M5 (HC 18, HMSO, 1975). For a discussion of the difficulties generally of controlling contracts, see Chrisopher C. Hood, *The Limits of Administration* (Wiley, 1976), ch. 3.
11 R.E. Wraith and G.B. Lamb, *Public Inquiries as an Instrument of Government* (RIPA/Allen & Unwin, 1971), p. 180; J.A.G. Griffith, *Central Departments and Local Authorities* (RIPA/Allen & Unwin, 1966), p. 57.
12 *Annual Report of the Council on Tribunals, 1972–73* (HC 82, HMSO 1974), paras 94–8. With the transfer of water functions to regional water authorities under the Water Act 1973 the engineering inspectorate was in any case disbanded.
13 *Annual Report 1975–76* (HC 236, HMSO 1977), para. 93.
14 Roberts, op. cit., p. 203.
15 For example, the Chief Inspector of Mines and Quarries held a public inquiry into the explosion at Houghton Main Colliery, South Yorkshire, in 1975 when five men were killed and one seriously injured (see Report, HMSO, 1976).
16 Henry Parris, *Government and the Railways in Nineteenth-Century Britain* (Routledge & Kegan Paul, 1965), pp. 28–37, 144–7.
17 Civil Aviation (Investigation of Accidents) Regulations 1969 (SI 1969, No. 833).
18 Michael Noble (Minister for Trade), HC Deb 814, 29 March 1971, col. 1173.
19 *Report of Committee on Civil Air Transport* (Cmnd 4018, HMSO 1969), para. 877.
20 See Chapter 3 for the evolution of trading standards officers.
21 Sir James Crombie, *Her Majesty's Customs and Excise* (Allen & Unwin, 1962), pp. 169–73.
22 *Report of the Committee on Abuse of Social Security Benefits* (Cmnd 5228, HMSO 1973), paras 142–6.

23 Companies Act 1948, ss. 164–5; Companies Act 1967, s. 109.
24 Inspectors of constabulary, fire services and schools are appointed by Royal Warrant and known as 'Her Majesty's Inspector . . .'. This is now no more than an honorific title: all efficiency inspectors are civil servants serving a particular department, as indeed are enforcement inspectors of central departments whether or not they are entitled 'Her Majesty's Inspector . . .'.
25 Gas Act 1972, s. 31 and Schedule 4.
26 The six are factories, mines and quarries, nuclear installations, agriculture (health and safety), explosives and alkali and clean air.
27 Or rather at two strokes; the agriculture (health and safety) inspectorate was not originally part of HSE, but transferred at a later date.
28 Health and Safety at Work [etc.] Act 1974, ss. 11(3) and 12.
29 Section 2.
30 HC Deb 806, 20 November 1970, col. 1592.
31 SI 1948, No. 1445; SI 1960, No. 1160; Children and Young Persons Act 1969, ss. 58, 59.
32 Slaughterhouses Act 1974, ss. 19, 20, 27; Slaughterhouses Act 1958, s.9 (3).
33 Harris, op. cit., p. 30.
34 Enforcement inspection by the Department of Agriculture and Fisheries for Scotland (DAFS) has distinctive features (see Appendix 2).
35 Agriculture Act 1970, s. 106.
36 HC Deb vol. 913, 21 June 1976, WA 340–7.
37 Agriculture Act 1970, s. 67.

CHAPTER 2

THE ROLE OF INSPECTORATES

It will be clear from the discussion in Chapter 1 that it is difficult to draw precise boundaries round a study of inspectorates. People called inspectors may be appointed to carry out a wide variety of functions; equally, people who carry out an inspecting function may or may not be called inspectors, and may or may not perform this function as their sole or main task. There is no exact definition of inspection, no precise set of functions which can be collectively labelled as the inspecting function. Nevertheless, as Appendix 2 illustrates, there are a great many inspectorates which fall squarely within the field of study. Before turning to the questions which the study aims to explore it is useful to draw attention to some general indications of the nature of these inspectorates.

THE GENERAL PICTURE

The *first* concerns the balance between efficiency and enforcement inspectorates. The early inspectorates were almost equally divided between these two purposes. The great majority of inspectorates (and inspectors) today are concerned with enforcement. This has come about partly by a decline in the number of efficiency inspectorates and partly by increases in enforcement work. As to the first, some efficiency inspectorates have become internal, like the prisons inspectorate, or have disappeared altogether, like the Poor Law or DOE engineering inspectorate. They have not been matched by the creation of new inspectorates. Since 1945 only the fire services inspectorate is new. By contrast, the process of creating new enforcement inspectorates still continues; equally significantly, new enforcement responsibilities are laid on existing inspectorates. Since 1945 new inspectorates have been established for agricultural health and safety, for nuclear installations and for pipelines, among others. And local government inspectorates in particular have acquired increased enforcement responsibilities, such as the weights and measures inspectors who now function as trading standards officers. Another notable recent example of increased responsibilities derived from the Health and Safety at Work [etc.] Act 1974, which among other things brought many more people within the scope of legislation with consequential effects on the numbers of factory inspectors.

The significance of this change in the balance of types of inspectorate will emerge in the course of this study. But clearly it has been affected by two major developments which have taken place. Changes in local government since the mid-nineteenth century might be expected to affect the relations between central and local government including the position of inspectorates. It is equally a truism that the nature and extent of government regulation has changed markedly. As government involvement has grown in new or existing spheres of activity it might be expected that there would be repercussions on the extent of inspection and the number of inspectorates. In 1909, for example, government intervened to protect workers in certain low-paid trades through the establishment of trade boards (now called wages councils) to fix minimum wages. A new inspectorate was set up to enforce the payment of these minimum wages. Again, when health and safety legislation was extended to employees in offices and shops in 1963 it led not to the establishment of a new inspectorate but to an extension of the work of public health inspectors (as they were then known) and an increase in their numbers.

The *second* general point is that although enforcement inspectorates cover a bewildering range of areas of government activity, there are nevertheless certain areas which are particularly prominent in the use of inspectorates. Safety and health are the main examples. Fire prevention and building control among local authority inspectorates and railway inspection among central government inspectorates are mainly or entirely concerned with safety – that of the general public in the first two cases, and of the general public and railway employees in the third. Environmental health officers, on the other hand, and alkali and clean air inspectors are mainly concerned with health hazards affecting the general public, although now also with a significant amenity element in the work. A major group of inspectorates forming part of HSE is concerned with both safety and health, mainly of those at work but also including the general public in so far as they may be affected by hazards arising from work activities.

Certainly if one were considering the number of inspectors involved one could well argue that the device of using inspection to enforce statutory requirements was predominantly associated with government intervention to protect the health or ensure the safety either of people at work or of the public generally. In fact the only group of inspectors of any size who do not fall within these categories are the trading standards officers, who are primarily concerned with a form of economic protection.

Thirdly, there is a distinct contrast between inspection by central government, including 'hived off' authorities, and inspection by local authorities. For the most part inspectorates of central government are small and often highly specialised. There is, for example, only one inspector of anatomy, there are only five inspectors of diving and five inspectors of electrical engineering. Few have more than 100 inspec-

tors, the almost 1,000-strong factory inspectorate being quite exceptional among enforcement inspectorates, as is the education inspectorate among efficiency inspectorates. Specialisation is very obviously
associated with the relatively small inspectorates of central government, such as those for nuclear installations, drugs, or cruelty to
animals.

Local government inspectorates are of a different kind. They tend
to be large multi-purpose inspectorates. The clearest example are the
EHOs, descendants of the nineteenth-century inspectors of nuisances. Even as they were originally conceived their inspecting work
covered a wide range – food as well as drains, houses as well as
dung-heaps. It is now even wider. As numerous statutes have put the
responsibility for enforcing new legislation on district councils so
EHOs have acquired new areas of inspecting work. Shop hours under
the Shops Acts, health and safety in shops and offices under the
Offices, Shops and Railway Premises Act 1963, noise pollution under
the Control of Pollution Act 1974, animal welfare under a variety of
specific Acts including the Pet Shops Act 1951, the Animal Boarding
Establishments Act 1963, and the Breeding of Dogs Act 1973 – these
are all examples of the extension of the original inspectors of nuisances' duties. All of them may be brought under the general heading of
'public health', but that in itself covers a very wide area. Specialisation
operates *within* such a wide-ranging inspectorate so that some EHOs
are expert in meat inspection or pollution control, for example.

As weights and measures inspectors have changed into trading
standards officers they too have shown a similar tendency to acquire a
wide range of inspection duties. Apart from the weights and measures
and trade description legislation they are also concerned with enforcing the Food and Drugs Act 1955, the Diseases of Animals Act 1950
and over twenty smaller pieces of legislation. Building control officers
have a somewhat narrower sphere, and so do fire prevention officers.

Almost inevitably, all local government inspectorates are large in
comparison with central government inspectorates. There would be
little point in giving enforcement responsibilities to local authorities if
they required highly specialised knowledge and there were very few
places in the country which had to be inspected; conversely, there are
arguments against setting up a central inspectorate where inspection
is not so highly specialised and the places to be inspected are to be
found in all parts of the country. Such arguments may not provide an
entirely satisfactory explanation of the way in which inspection work
has in fact been divided up between central and local government, but
they at least show that it is not surprising that far more enforcement
inspectors are to be found in local than in central government. In
volume of work the bulk of enforcement inspection is the responsibility of local authorities. Indeed if it were not for the factory

inspectorate and the vehicle examiners of the Department of Transport the predominance of local inspection would be even more marked. And equally within local government the great bulk of inspecting work falls on EHOs and building control officers.

This leads into the *final* general point to be made here. The size of inspectorates has naturally fluctuated somewhat over the years, but there has been a tendency in recent years for the work of some enforcement inspectorates to increase sharply, leading to some (though not necessarily commensurate) increases in the size of inspectorates. The Nuclear Installations Inspectorate, for example, which began in 1960 with twelve inspectors had grown to 106 inspectors by the middle of 1979, the increase being largely accounted for by the growth in the number of nuclear power stations and by the creation of British Nuclear Fuels Limited. In a very different area of activity, inspectors under the Cruelty to Animals Act have increased from six in 1962 to fifteen today. But perhaps the most conspicuous examples of increased workload arise from the working of the Health and Safety at Work [etc.] Act 1974, and from recent consumer protection legislation, especially the Trade Descriptions Act 1968. The former has led to a 50 per cent increase in the factory inspectorate in five years. The latter has contributed to a doubling in the number of weights and measures inspectors which has taken place over the last twenty-five years or so, as well as to a change of name to trading standards officers. Both these inspectorates will be considered in more detail later in this study but this fact of increased numbers reinforces the point which was made earlier about the relative importance, in terms of numbers of enforcement as against efficiency inspectors. Some of the latter inspectorates have also increased in size; for example, the inspectorate of constabulary in England and Wales for many years consisted of two or three inspectors; there are now six together with four assistant inspectors. But the largest of these inspectorates, that for education, has shown a tendency to decline. Its peak in England and Wales was reached in 1950 when there were 558 inspectors; by 1978 this was down to 452.[1] If present trends continue efficiency inspectorates are likely to form a decreasing proportion of all inspectorates.

QUESTIONS FOR EXAMINATION

The main aim of the present study is to examine the present role of enforcement and efficiency inspectorates in British administration and to consider the implications for their future role. A broad inquiry of this kind must also take account of the fact that we are here concerned with the use of an early nineteenth-century concept in a late twentieth-century context. An underlying reason for examining the role of inspectorates is indeed the importance of establishing the extent to which the concept is still relevant. Here the contrasting developments referred to above may be significant. The use of efficiency inspectorates has declined, that of enforcement inspectorates has increased. Does this simply reflect changes in the relations between central and local government on the one hand, and increased government involvement in areas of life which were outside its scope in the mid-nineteenth century on the other? Or is there a need to probe more deeply into the reasons for the changes, to consider, for example, why it is that there is now a general assumption in favour of the use of enforcement inspectors?

The strength of the latter assumption is striking. Not only are existing inspectorates assumed to be necessary even when they have existed for a long time and were established in very different circumstances, like the Anatomy or Cruelty to Animals inspectorates; but new inspectorates are frequently set up with little or no discussion of the need for them. The Nuclear Installations Inspectorate of 1960 and the Gaming Inspectorate of 1969 are two very different examples of this tendency. What is even more remarkable is that this unquestioning acceptance of the need for enforcement inspectors is evident even when it conflicts with other strongly held views. Some Conservative MPs, for example, have long expressed uneasiness about the extent to which officials are granted powers of search and entry. Yet a great many of such powers are necessarily granted to inspectors to enable them to carry out their work.[2] Acceptance of the need for inspectors to enforce legislation carries with it acceptance of the need for effective powers. As Sir Stephen McAdden, a noted Conservative campaigner against the excessive granting of powers of entry, said in discussion of the Gaming Bill in 1968:

> for this operation, I am all in favour of people being allowed to inspect, without notice, what is going on in these gaming establishments. It departs from a principle which I have long held that the number of inspectors or others having the right of entry on to private property should be as small as possible, but exceptionally, and for this occasion only, I am prepared to take a different view.[3]

This attachment to the idea of inspection for enforcement purposes is certainly one area which requires examination. Equally the criticism which has been directed at some inspectorates, that they carry out too little inspection, fail to use their powers effectively or act too much in an advisory capacity needs to be linked to the idea of inspection. We are here concerned, first, with the aims of inspection, and, secondly, with the means employed by inspectors to achieve those aims. And both need to be looked at within the context of the factors which have contributed to changes in aims and means.

Criticisms of the kind referred to imply a certain view of the ends which inspectors should serve and more particularly of the methods they should employ, but they are frequently linked with a view that there has been a decline in the sense that the original purpose of inspection has been lost sight of over the years. The development of inspectorates, therefore, and the factors which have influenced that development are important elements in the inquiry. The work of inspectorates which may have existed for a hundred years or more is likely to have been influenced by external factors such as social, economic, and technological changes and by internal factors such as an inspectorate's own view of its role or its belief in the efficacy of using a particular method to achieve its aims. Since for the most part inspectorates have been established and have developed as separate entities one would expect the influence of these factors to have operated differently for different inspectorates, and perhaps to have contributed to the fact that some inspectorates have attracted more criticism than others.

It is not however simply because some inspectorates have been criticised that these questions are important. Those criticisms help to point more clearly to the fact that there has been little attempt to assess the effectiveness of inspection or the limits to what it can achieve. A great deal of inspecting work, particularly for enforcement purposes, is constantly being carried out and it is important to try to assess its value. In considering the role of inspectorates there is need therefore to look not only at what they do and how they do it but also at the constraints under which they operate, and hence at possible alternative ways in which the ends which they are pursuing might be achieved.

EFFICIENCY INSPECTORATES

These broad questions apply generally to both efficiency and enforcement inspectorates. Their application is however significantly different in the two cases. The use of efficiency inspectorates must be viewed in the context of relations between central and local government. That relationship is in almost every way quite different from what it was when the early Poor Law inspectors and the superintending inspectors of the General Board of Health set out on their visits. The status, organisation and functions of local authorities have been transformed. So have the means open to central government departments to control or influence the activities of local authorities. Inspectorates now form only one part of those means, and then only for certain services provided by local authorities. The question what part inspection now plays and indeed whether it really has a part to play is therefore a critical one.

ENFORCEMENT INSPECTORATES

Enforcement inspectorates must be looked at in quite a different context. Enforcement to begin with is associated not with the relationships between different kinds of public authorities but with a particular area of law, that concerned with criminal offences. It was said earlier that one of the distinguishing characteristics of enforcement compared with efficiency inspectorates was that the former had specific statutory power to take action through the courts[4] because contravention of the statutory requirements is treated as a criminal offence attracting specific penalties, usually fines. As has been pointed out,[5] the treatment of regulatory offences enforced largely by inspectors on the same basis for legal purposes as more traditional areas of crime such as theft or assault enforced by the police has created certain difficulties now that the former have become so numerous, and has led to some debate whether a distinction should be drawn between 'real' crimes and regulatory offences. One question, therefore, which the present study seeks to answer is the extent to which enforcement inspectors operate in practice in a different way from the police, and the implications which this has for the use of inspectors in enforcement work.

The point of making such a comparison between the work of the police and the work of inspectors is to focus attention on perhaps the most difficult question of all in assessing the role of enforcement inspectors, the extent to which enforcement adequately describes that role. Enforcement implies an element of compulsion backed by legal sanctions: how far that element is still essential and whether it should form a growing or a diminishing part of the work of inspectors are questions of considerable importance in considering the future of inspection work.

Thus the intention of this study is to explore, through examination of the origins, development and practical working of the two types of inspectorate which have been identified, the scope for inspection work today and some at least of the important problems which have arisen in practice. In view particularly of the fact mentioned earlier that so little work has been done on inspectorates a wide-ranging study of this kind involves certain critical questions. Three in particular deserve closer examination at this stage:

(1) the powers of inspectors;
(2) determination of standards;
(3) accountability

POWERS OF INSPECTORS

The distinctive nature of inspection lies in the fact that the inspector does not just sit in his office but goes out to make visits of inspection, that is to say, an essential part of his work is entering premises or in some cases setting foot on land in order to carry out whatever is involved in the particular inspection task. One set of powers therefore relates to this entering of premises and what the inspector does there. Just as important are the powers of the inspector to take action as a result of what he finds in the course of his inspection. For the reasons suggested in the previous chapter efficiency inspectorates are less likely to have specific statutory powers of entry and do not have statutory powers to take action as a result of inspection. Inspectors of constabulary, for example, are simply required to inspect and report on the efficiency of all police forces.[6]

Use of powers is therefore primarily important in relation to enforcement inspectorates. The wages inspectorate of the Department of Employment, for example, has power to enter premises, inspect and copy documents and question employers or workers.[7] These may be regarded as the basic powers of entry and inspection of enforcement inspectors; they may be varied in certain cases because of the nature of the inspection; there may, for example, be power to take samples of goods; or they may be elaborated as in the HSW Act 1974, which provides for a series of a dozen specific powers.[8] Thus the powers of inspectors are often on the face of it quite formidable, even granted that they have some specific limitations – they are only to be used for the purposes of the Act and may be qualified by phrases like 'at all reasonable times'. Nevertheless, it is important to examine how inspectors use these powers in practice and what bearing this use has on the relation between the purposes of inspection and the methods employed.

It is even more important to examine the use of the inspector's power to take action as a result of his inspection. Here the formal position is somewhat different as between central and local government inspectorates, and as between England and Wales on the one hand and Scotland on the other. Contravention of the statutory requirements is treated as a criminal offence in all cases; the differences relate to the administrative and judicial arrangements for dealing with such offences. In England and Wales for central government inspectorates the statutes generally provide for the institution of proceedings by inspectors; in Scotland this does not apply but the normal procedure of application to the Procurator Fiscal operates, since it is the Procurator Fiscal who has the responsibility for deciding whether to prosecute or not.[9] For local government inspectorates the right to institute proceedings in England and Wales normally rests with the local authority and not the inspector, with again the normal procedure operating in Scotland.

Whatever the formal position it is the inspector who in most cases initiates action; equally important is the fact that since he is the person who in most cases discovers any contravention of the statutory requirements it is to a large extent in his hands whether to take any action at all and, if so, of what kind. Prosecution is the legal sanction available to enforcement inspectors. It is, on the face of it, a formidable weapon; it is also one which is used to varying degrees by different inspectorates. Some inspectorates have other kinds of legal sanction available to them, usually in addition to prosecution; some activities, for example, such as the manufacture of explosives or the performance of experiments on live animals, require a licence, and although their employing authorities rather than inspectors themselves have the power to grant or withhold such licences the inspector's recommendation is usually critical if not decisive in the decision. Again, inspectorates of HSE have the power to issue 'improvement notices' requiring specific action to be taken within a specified period where there has been contravention of the statutory provisions; or 'prohibition notices' in cases where there is risk of serious injury, prohibiting specified activities until action has been taken to deal with the risk.[10] These are clearly lesser legal sanctions than prosecution but may still nevertheless be a strong weapon.

Efficiency inspectorates do not have legal sanctions of this kind available to them. They are consequently dependent for any action they may take as a result of inspection on the general administrative pressures which their employing department is able to bring to bear on local authorities which are seen as falling below an acceptable standard. There are a few specific powers available such as the power of the Home Secretary to require a police authority to retire a chief constable.[11] And in the few cases where specific central government grants remain, withdrawal of grant is another possible course open to a department which is dissatisfied as the result of an inspection report with the way in which a local authority is carrying out its responsibilities. Again, the police grant provides an example. For the most part, however, there is no specific action open to efficiency inspectors in the same way as there is for enforcement inspectors. It is true that Ministers have power to reduce the amount of rate support grant of an authority which fails to achieve or maintain a reasonable standard in discharging any of its functions, but not only is this not directly linked with inspection of a particular service but it is also hedged about with restrictions which make it a difficult weapon to use. For example, the Minister has to lay a report before Parliament stating not only the amount of reduction proposed but also the reasons, and this report has to be approved before reductions can be made.[12].

Enforcement inspectors then have strong legal powers, whereas efficiency inspectors generally have little in the way of formal powers beyond a basic right of inspection. One would expect therefore contrasts in the ways in which the two kinds of inspectorate attempt to achieve their ends. At the least it seems necessary to ask what difference the possession of strong powers makes to the operations of enforcement inspectorates. Some of these inspectorates rarely prosecute; others appear to make much more use of their powers. To explore the reasons for these differences may help to make clearer the factors which are important in determining the ways in which inspectors operate in practice. Inspectors may use their power sparingly, for example, because they believe that to do so produces better results, that people are more likely to conform to the law if prosecution or its threat are used only as a last resort; or because too frequent use of their powers may lessen their effectiveness, e.g. because the courts do not impose sufficiently deterrent penalties; or because it suits inspectors to be on reasonably good terms with those whom they inspect; or for a combination of these and other reasons. Efficiency inspectorates, lacking strong formal powers might be expected to emphasise more the persuasive approach. Whether this is so or not use of powers is one area in which the constraints within which inspectorates operate can be assessed, whether those constraints arise from external circumstances or from internal pressures.

DETERMINATION OF STANDARDS

Inspection as a means of regulation or supervision is intimately connected with the use of standards. Enforcement inspection exists at least to ensure that the minimum standards specified in statutory requirements are met. Efficiency inspection is equally concerned with standards of provision, of staffing, accommodation, equipment and so on, even though these may not be precisely specified in regulations. Inspectors may be concerned with standards in two ways, in determining them in the first place, and in applying them.

Inspectors are often experts in their particular field, and that field may require a high degree of specialised technical or professional knowledge. Nuclear installations, dangerous drugs and coal mines require highly trained people to inspect them. One would therefore expect that, for example, the question what standards of safety are acceptable in the construction, operation and maintenance of nuclear reactors would depend heavily on the views of the nuclear installations inspectors for its determination. In other cases views of inspectors may be less decisive but still influential. In what circumstances, for example, meat should be condemned as unfit for human consumption, or diseased nursery stocks of plants have to be destroyed are questions which require a technical expertise to answer which is not necessaily found exclusively in the inspectorates concerned.

A further factor which bears on the work of inspectors is the degree of specificity of standards. Some can be precisely formulated and specified in regulations. With others there is a large discretionary element. The best known example is that of the alkali works. Ever since the Alkali Act of 1874 the basis of regulating the discharge of most 'noxious gases' from these works[13] has depended statutorily on the use of the 'best practicable means' of controlling their discharge into the atmosphere. The part played by the alkali and clean air inspectorate in determining the best practicable means in any particular case, and of setting the standard to be followed is thus of considerable importance in this case.

But, quite apart from the part played by inspectors in drawing up specific rules and regulations, there will usually be a discretionary element in the way in which an inspector applies the rules. If the regulations specify a standard and this is expressed in numerical terms, then of course there is no discretion in deciding whether there has been a contravention, but only in what action should be taken. The employer either has or has not paid the minimum wages laid down by the Wages Council;[14] the ship-owner either has or has not provided beds for the crew at least 6 feet 3 inches by 2 feet 3 inches;[15] the liquid measure either does or does not completely empty when tilted at an angle of 120 degrees from the vertical.[16] These are all factual matters for the inspector to investigate, although differing in the nature and extent of investigations required. On the other hand, it is often not quantitative but qualitative standards which are being applied, or sometimes a combination of both. Motor vehicle examiners of the Department of Transport must see whether the steering is 'in good and efficient working order' and 'properly adjusted',[17] inspectors under the Food and Drugs Acts must see whether food premises have 'adequate space, suitably sited, for the purpose of the removal of waste from food . . . '[18] Building control officers must satisfy themselves that the materials used in construction are 'of a suitable nature and quality in relation to the purposes for and conditions in which they are used . . .'[19]

Some qualitative standards of this kind can be expressed in part in quantitative terms. Thus the annual testing of good vehicles by the Department of Transport to ensure that they are roadworthy is first reduced to a check list of specific items to be examined; these in turn are linked to a Goods Vehicle Testers' Manual which specifies in great detail the defects to be looked for. Even so there remain inevitably some matters which are a matter for judgment (e.g. 'excessive chafing or deterioration of hoses').

PROBLEMS OF ACCOUNTABILITY

Determination and application of standards can usefully be examined for the light they throw on how inspectors operate in practice. This in turn is important for assessing what kind of results may be expected from enforcement inspection. Two questions need to be examined here: to whom are inspectors accountable, and how effective are they in carrying out the purposes for which they are appointed? These are distinct but connected questions to which it may not be easy to provide complete answers, but which are very relevant to determining the role of inspectorates.

One important aspect of these questions is the relationship between inspectors and those whom they inspect. On a strict enforcement view of the role of inspectors this relationship is quite simple. The inspector has to do two things: first, to inspect to discover whether the regulations are being observed; secondly, if they are not, to insist on their being observed by the threat or use of the legal sanctions available to him. But how strictly an inspector in fact operates may be affected both by general factors and by specific considerations arising from the degree of discretion he possesses.

An example of the latter is the application of standards. Since there is frequently an element of judgment in deciding whether a statutory requirement is being observed, the way in which that judgment is exercised can have important consequences. A strict interpretation of the requirements may mean that the person or company subject to inspection may be involved in considerable expense in order to meet them. On the other hand, a less exacting interpretation may have serious consequences, for example in safety terms. Conflicts of interest of this kind particularly affect the work of enforcement inspectors. It is therefore important to see in what way they are resolved and the extent to which inspectors exercise administrative discretion, quite apart from any formal checks on their work which may arise in the courts.

Other considerations can also apply. Where inspectorates exist to enforce safety regulations, legal responsibility for safety rests on those inspected and not on the inspectorates. Inspecting officers of railways are entirely concerned with the safety aspects of railway operation, but the British Railways Board have responsibility for providing railway services with due regard to safety of operation.[20] HSE inspectors spend their time promoting health, safety and welfare at work partly at least through the enforcement of specific regulations, but it is the duty of employers to ensure the health, safety and welfare of their employees.[21] Whether, and if so, in what way the existence of these responsibilities affects the work of inspectors is a question to be examined. In the early days of inspectorates, for example, it was frequently argued that the use of inspectors would detract from the responsibilities of employers to ensure safety.[22] More recently the argument has been in somewhat different terms, that such responsibilities require a more positive response from employers, and not simply the carrying out of whatever the inspector suggests on his periodic visit; this argument indeed forms the basis of the more positive duty laid on employers in the HSW Act 1974. Arguments of this kind might be expected to play a part in determining the ways in which inspectors carry out their functions, and thus have a bearing on their role.

There are clearly other factors too which may be important in affecting the inspector's approach to his job. The degree to which, for example, central government inspectors are regarded simply as an operational arm of a department subject to departmental instructions in the usual way, or alternatively viewed more as a body of expert advisers, rather as lawyers or architects are viewed, may be one such factor. Similarly in the case of local government inspectorates their status within local authorities, e.g. whether the chief inspector is a chief officer, may affect the question. Another series of factors concern the degree to which an inspectorate may be subject to general or specific public pressures. Complaints or dissatisfaction with the results of inspection are obvious possible influences on inspectors. More subtly there may be more general social pressures and influences to which inspectors may respond.

In all this the aim must be to try to disentangle the complex processes which link ends, means and results; if any meaningful generalisation is to be possible about the use of inspection a clear idea of how it operates in practice now and of the factors which have contributed to the present position seems essential. There is, for example, a long debate going back to the earliest days of inspectorates about how they should set about achieving their aims and, in particular, how far they should seek to work by persuasion and by securing the co-operation of those inspected. Inspectorates which rely largely on persuasion to achieve compliance with statutory requirements may also develop an advisory role, or may even see their role as being primarily that of a professional adviser. Understanding of these developments is necessary to an assessment of the role of inspectors but more particularly to weighing the advantages and disadvantages in relation to the purposes which inspection is intended to serve. Whether too much emphasis on an advisory role is compatible with achieving a high degree of compliance with statutory requirements, or whether on the contrary persuasion and advice are more likely to achieve compliance and to promote the underlying purposes of legislation than reliance on legal sanctions are questions which are fundamental to the use of inspection for enforcement purposes. Their examination should not only help to determine the current role of inspectorates but to indicate the limits within which they operate and therefore the need for and possibilities of using other means to achieve the same ends.

The preceding pages have attempted to define the scope of this study and to indicate the questions which it will seek to answer. The following four chapters examine these questions in the context of the origins and development of a number of individual inspectorates. These inspectorates have been chosen to cover as wide a range as possible of the different types: enforcement and efficiency; central government, local government and 'fringe bodies'; large and small; multi-purpose and specialised; health and safety and other kinds of protection. As will be seen, no inspectorate is typical, and most have developed in highly individual ways. Nevertheless, the selected inspectorates do give a reasonable cross-section.

In the concluding two chapters the general questions about the role of inspectorates will be considered and an attempt will be made to set their future role in a wider context.

NOTES: CHAPTER 2

1 D.E. Regan, *Local Government and Education* (Allen & Unwin, 1977), p. 109; *Annual Report, Department of Education and Science 1977* (HMSO, 1978), p.36, para. 4.2; cf. *Education and Science in 1976* (HMSO, 1977), p. 47, para. 2.

2 See the replies given to Mr David Price, who asked each of the major departments to list their search and entry powers (HC Deb 913, 21 June 1976, WA 313–402).

3 HC Official Report, Standing Committee B, Gaming Bill, 2 April 1968, col. 493.

4 Strictly speaking, as will be seen, not all inspectorates have the power to initiate proceedings, as this is often the responsibility of their employing authority (or, in Scotland, of the legal authorities).

5 R.M. Jackson, *Enforcing the Law* (Macmillan, 1967), pp. v–vi, 5–6.

6 Police Act 1964, s. 38(2) (the Metropolitan Police are excluded); Police (Scotland) Act 1967, s.33.

7 Wages Councils Act 1979, s.22.

8 Health and Safety at Work [etc.] Act 1974, s. 20(2); in addition an inspector has power to seize and destroy or otherwise make harmless anything which he thinks 'a cause of imminent danger of serious personal injury' (s.25(1)).

9 This applies also to the police, who do not prosecute in Scotland.

10 HSW Act 1974, ss. 21,22.

11 Police Act 1964, s.29.

12 Local Government Act 1974, s.5. [New legislation (1980) will change this].

13 With the extension of legislation since the original Act of 1863, 'alkali' no longer accurately describes the type of works controlled.

14 Wages Councils Act 1979, s.15.

15 Merchant Shipping (Crew Accommodation) Regulations (SI 1953, No. 1036), Reg. 17.

16 Weights and Measures Regulations (SI 1963, No. 1710), Reg. 19.

17 Motor vehicles (Construction and Use) Regulations (SI 1973 No. 24), Reg. 95.

18 Food Hygiene (General) Regulations (SI 1970 No. 1172), Reg. 26.

19 Building Regulations (SI 1972, No. 317), Reg. 31.

20 Transport Act 1962, s.3.

21 HSW Act 1974, s. 2(1).

22 The argument was used in relation to mines inspection, among others. See Macdonagh, 'Coal mines regulation', op. cit., p.69.

CHAPTER 3

FROM WEIGHTS AND MEASURES TO TRADING STANDARDS

The Statute Book from the time of Henry the Third abounds with Acts of Parliament enacting and declaring that there should be one uniform Weight and Measure throughout the Realm; and every Act complains that the preceding Statutes had been ineffectual, and that the Laws were disobeyed.[1]

Until recently inspection of weights and measures seemed to epitomise the work of a traditional inspectorate, the unspectacular but essential routine of visiting and checking and testing, with the steady flow of prosecutions in the local magistrates' courts for those guilty of contraventions, all within the framework of statutory provisions and detailed regulations which seemed to emphasise the well-ordered routine of the work. In the past fifteen years the nature of the work has changed more rapidly than at any time since the modern system of inspection of weights and measures was established in the nineteenth century, a change symbolised by the fact that in the early 1970s the Institute of Weights and Measures Administration changed its name to the Institute of Trading Standards Administration. How change came about and how the inspectorate responded to new pressures upon them is a major theme of this chapter, but it cannot be understood without reference to the historical background.

A basic purpose of weights and measures inspection has always been the vertification of the accuracy of the weights, measures and other similar equipment used for trading purposes. But, as the quotation at the head of this chapter shows, an even more fundamental prerequisite is that there should be a uniform system of weights and measures. This was not achieved until the nineteenth century[2] but for present purposes an Act of 1824 (5 Geo. 4. c.74) which decreed that all weights and measures should conform to new imperial standards can be taken as the starting-point of the modern system. Similarly, an Act of 1835 (5&6 Will. 4 c.63) which provided for the appointment of inspectors of weights and measures by the local Justices throughout the country may be taken as the starting-point of the local inspectorate.

Nevertheless the history of the subject, particularly relating to verification, that is, the comparison of weights and measures with a standard to ensure their accuracy, goes back much further. And even inspection in the narrower sense of visiting shops to see that they were using only authorised and accurate weights and measures goes back at least to the late eighteenth century, since an Act of 1795 required Justices of the Peace to appoint examiners at quarter sessions who were to visit shops of all kinds at least once a month.[9]

There are two reasons for this long preoccupation with weights and measures. Without some uniformity in the system of weights and measures and their use trade was hampered and fraud was much more likely to go undetected. There were therefore both sound commercial reasons for government attempts at regulation, and also reasons of 'consumer protection' as they would now be called.

It is interesting in view of this to consider the characteristics of the arrangements introduced by the Acts of 1824 and 1835. They depended on two elements which were in practice distinct. The standards to which all weights and measures in use were supposed to comply were determined and kept centrally in the Exchequer, but the only means of trying to ensure that the weights and measures used by traders were accurate and conformed to the standards was the verification and inspection by the local inspectors, over whom the central government had no control.

Practically the only control exercised by the Exchequer was over the local standards, i.e. the copies of the central standards which the local inspectors used when testing and which were supposed to be re-verified at intervals to make sure that they remained exact copies. The inspectors were answerable for the performance of their duties to the magistrates who appointed them in the first place.

ESTABLISHMENT OF MODERN SYSTEM OF WEIGHTS AND MEASURES INSPECTION

Weights and measures administration in the middle years of the nineteenth century thus differed from other regulatory functions of the time. It was neither an exclusively central government responsibility like inspection of factories or mines, nor was it a responsibility entrusted to local authorities with a strongly supervisory role for the central department as happened with the Poor Law and was increasingly sought in the public health field. That it was a weakness of the system that the central government had no control over whether and how local inspection was carried out was a theme of the many committees which investigated weights and measures from 1840 onwards. The case for a measure of central supervision was acknowledged when a standards department was established in the Board of Trade under the Standards of Weights, Measures and Coinage Act of 1866, but this did not deal with three specific key issues of control: (1) the power to issue instructions to inspectors; (2) the power to lay down qualifications for appointment as inspector; (3) the power to investigate how the work was carried out in practice.

Successive Weights and Measures Acts of 1878, 1889 and 1904 established the system which was to last until the 1960s. It gave the Board of Trade considerable powers under the first two of these headings, but less under the third. As regards the first, whereas under the 1878 Act the Board was limited to approving by-laws for the duties of inspectors made by local authorities, under the 1904 Act it had the power to make general regulations. These covered specific matters such as verification and stamping, and the tests to be applied for ascertaining the accuracy of weights and measures, but also regulations

> generally for the guidance of local authorities in the execution and performance of their powers and duties under the Weights and Measures Acts.[4]

Regulations made in 1907 formed the basis of inspection work until they were replaced in 1963.

The Act of 1878 said nothing about the qualifications of inspectors, but simply put the duty of appointing inspectors on local authorities. The amending Act of 1889 for the first time gave the Board of Trade power to hold examinations to test whether inspectors

> possess sufficient practical knowledge for the proper performance of their duties.[5]

The Board had power to issue certificates to those who passed the examination. Those who were appointed as inspectors after the Act was passed could not act until they had gained the certificate. The 1904 Act went a stage further in making the gaining of a certificate a necessary condition of appointment as inspector, and the examination was to be taken by applicants nominated by local authorities. Again, this system lasted for over sixty years.

The 1889 Act also gave the Board power to hold a local inquiry into the administration of weights and measures law, but this was restricted to looking at the records and questioning inspectors, and there was no power to compel the local authority to take action if as a result of the inquiry the Board thought that improvements were needed. Similarly, the 1907 Regulations required inspectors to make an annual report to the Board but the latter had no effective power to act on this information. Thus the Board were never able to develop an efficiency inspectorate as the Home Office did in relation to the police function. Indeed they complained to the Royal Commission on Local Government in 1923 that without a proper organisation for regularly visiting and inspecting local weights and measures offices they could not compel local authorities to administer the law. With too many small authorities who were unable to provide an adequate service cases had arisen where the operation of the Acts had been in effect suspended for months through failure of a local authority to appoint a duly qualified officer.[6] Three characteristics of this system of inspection of weights and measures can be distinguished. First, it was seen primarily as a measure of protection of the public, to detect but more especially to deter and prevent fraudulent practices. Secondly, in the nineteenth century much of the work was not thought to require specialised knowledge but such knowledge became increasingly important during the twentieth century. Thirdly, it relied on a balance between central and local control. As early as 1841 an official committee tentatively suggested a nationally organised system of inspection carried out by excise officers, and the idea has been periodically revived. Inspection has remained a local authority responsibility, but subject to powers of regulation by the central department.

DEVELOPMENT OF THE SYSTEM

It is a striking fact that after the numerous inquiries and Acts of Parliament of the nineteenth century little was heard of weights and measures in the first half of this century. It had become an established part of the routine of administration, rarely arousing much controversy but partly for that reason attracting low priority from some local authorities. Inspectors themselves had a long struggle to improve their status, because for many years they lacked a separate identity.

When, for example, an official inquiry examined the position in 1866 it found that of the 731 inspectors of weights and measures in Great Britain, 476 (66 per cent) were police officers; of the remaining 255 only forty-six had no other occupation and they were therefore presumably the only full-time inspectors.[7] The inquiry itself concluded that although the verification work was a technical matter requiring special qualifications, inspection work was 'simply a police duty'.[8]

The 1889 Act and Board of Trade regulations got rid of the odder combinations of other occupations with that of inspector, but there was nothing to stop police officers taking the Board of Trade's examination and becoming qualified as inspectors. Many did, and were encouraged to do so by chief constables who saw this as a way of improving the image of the police as positively helping the poorer members of the community.[9] By 1928 there were still fifty-nine English counties and twenty-nine boroughs where weights and measures inspection was being carried out exclusively by the police.

The Incorporated Society of Inspectors of Weights and Measures, which had been trying for many years to ensure that policemen were not appointed for this purpose, in that year sent a deputation to Sir John Anderson, Permanent Under-Secretary at the Home Office, but failed to convince him of the need for change.

A major point in the Society's argument was that the work was getting more scientific and complex with the development of new measuring and weighing equipment. This development was in fact reflected in the fact that the Board of Trade examination had recently been made stiffer. The Board, although sympathising with the Society's views, was unwilling to press the Home Office, relying on the fact that events were moving in the right direction anyway; because the examination was harder fewer policemen were taking it and becoming qualified, and the result would be that in the course of time there would not be enough qualified inspectors among the police for them to maintain an adequate inspection service.[10]

Thus, although the problem was not explicitly faced at the time, it was implicity recognised that there came a point when inspection required a degree of specialised knowledge and equipment which could only be provided by a body of men specially recruited for this purpose. Because of the failure to tackle the problem directly there was a long period of overlap between weights and measures inspection as a police function and as a professional service.

It was not only the complexity of inspection work which was changing. A more important change in the long run was the development of ideas about the purpose of weights and measures inspection. Traditionally, it was concerned with ensuring that correct and accurate weights and measures were used. But in 1887 Parliament passed the Merchandise Marks Act which among other things made it an offence to apply a false trade description to goods. The Act made no specific provision for enforcement, but the 1889 Weights and Measures Act did make it an offence to sell underweight coal.

These tentative beginnings into the area of protecting the public against the giving of short weight or measure and false descriptions received a notable extension in 1926 when it became an offence to give short weight or measure in selling food.[11]

But the only general legislation, the Merchandise Marks Act, was used with varying vigour by local authorities since they were not obliged to act under it, and in any case it had drawbacks,[12] so that although it added another dimension to weights and measures inspection the traditional functions still remained by far the most important part of the work.

There is evidence however that some local authorities were unwilling to give much priority to weights and measures inspection. There was, for example, the difficulty of attracting enough people of the right calibre into the service. In 1927, for example, out of eighty-six candidates for the Board of Trade examination only fourteen passed and the Board commented that the majority of candidates 'continue to show a regrettably low standard of proficiency'.[13] For a few years there was an improvement but even in 1938 only forty-three were successful out of 189 candidates.[14] The Board could do little, since they were dependent on local authorities nominating candidates, beyond suggesting that authorities should appoint 'youths of a higher educational standard' as assistants to inspectors.[15]

But perhaps this was simply one symptom of the general lack of importance attaching to the subject of weights and measures which is illustrated more generally by the attempts to have the legislation brought up to date. As early as 1935 the Institute of Weights and Measures Administration, the professional body for local inspectors founded in 1893, had suggested to the Board of Trade the subjects which in their view should be examined, and a departmental committee was mooted, but no action had been taken when the war came. At the end of the war the Standards Department revived the idea saying that the whole system was 'in great need of a complete overhaul'. In particular, some of the authorities were too small to afford an efficient inspectorate, so that either the function should be confined to the larger authorities or it should be centralised under the Board of Trade; and 'opinions differ as to which of these courses would be better. In the meantime, there are parts of the country in which the Acts are not being administered efficiently.' Characteristically, the President of the Board (Sir Stafford Cripps) accepted the argument for a committee but added:

but we must not absorb administrative time on this to the prejudice of more urgent matters.[16]

The committee was not appointed until 1948. Its report was published in 1951, but successive governments did not find the amendment of weights and measures legislation an urgent matter, and it was not until 1963 that a new Act was passed.

THE HODGSON COMMITTEE, 1948–51, AND CONSUMER PROTECTION

Much of the report of the committee under the chairmanship of Mr E.H. Hodgson was concerned with traditional matters such as the problems of bringing under control various kinds of weighing and measuring equipment. They did, however, also make the important recommendation that there should be a general provision making it an offence to sell short weight, measure or number, and noted that there had been hardly any complaint about methods of enforcement where giving of short weight was already an offence.[17]

The committee were quite clear that such a change in the law would mean a shift in the emphasis of inspection work towards unannounced inspections and test purchases. For this and other reasons they wanted a reduction in the number of weights and measures authorities, though on a fairly modest scale.[18] They certainly did not go so far as to want a central inspectorate, but like their nineteenth-century predecessors they thought that the Board of Trade's powers should be strengthened by assuming ultimate responsibility for seeing that the local service was run efficiently, which would mean that they would themselves need an inspectorate to go round from time to time and examine the way in which the individual local authorities were carrying out their functions.[19]

At about the time that the Hodgson Committee reported there was beginning to be heard an argument for greater protection for the consumer. The various strands which contributed to this argument have been discussed elsewhere,[20] but here the main concern is with the repercussions which the 'consumer movement' had on the work of weights and measures inspectors. In 1959 the government appointed a committee under the chairmanship of J.T. Molony to review the Merchandise Marks Acts and suggest any other changes they thought desirable in the interests of protecting the consumer. Their interim report in 1960 proposed that legislation should enable requirements to be imposed on manufacturers in the interests of safety for certain classes of goods such as electrical appliances and toys. The duty of enforcing regulations should be put on local authorities, but

> we do not believe that any new inspectorate would be required; firstly, because we do not think that the power to make Regulations would need to be exercised with great frequency, and secondly because we are confident that manufacturers and traders would speedily become alive to and fully heed their legal liabilities.[21]

In fact, the Consumer Protection Act 1961, following the committee's recommendations, conferred inspecting powers on local authority officers 'authorised by them in writing', a fairly standard formula. It was the general assumption of the committee and of Parliament that enforcement would be carried out by weights and measures inspectors, although this was nowhere made explicit.[22] Of even more significance for the future was the Trade Descriptions Act 1968, which derived from the final report of the Molony Committee on consumer protection of 1962. It replaced the Merchandise Marks Acts with provisions making it an offence to apply a false trade description to any goods or to give a false indication that goods were being offered at a bargain price. The duty of enforcing the Act was put squarely on weights and measures authorities, and their 'duly authorised officers' were given power to enter premises, inspect goods, require the production of books or documents relating to the business if they had reasonable cause to suspect that an offence had been committed, seize and detain goods if they had reasonable cause to believe that an offence had been committed, and other similar powers.[23]

The Molony Committee had argued that the existing Merchandise Marks Acts were not being adequately enforced largely because there was no single authority 'to police their observance and to proceed against offenders.' The Board of Trade should not be the enforcing authority since they lacked a countrywide organisation and inspectorate, and in any case a government department was

> not well-suited, in our opinion, to supervise the application of laws affecting the every-day occurrences of normal life.

Weights and measures authorities on the other hand had the 'outstanding advantage' that they already had an inspectorate; putting the duty on them would mean some increase in establishment but avoid the need for creating a separate inspectorate. At the same time the Board of Trade should assume an 'overriding interest' in the way the law was applied.[24] These arguments were generally accepted. When legislation was eventually brought in by the Labour government the main controversy was over whether the Bill went too far in its powers to protect the consumer. There was no argument about whether weights and measures inspectors were appropriate people to enforce the new measure.[25]

If the Trade Descriptions Act 1968 marked the biggest change in the responsibilities of weights and measures inspectors since they had been established in the nineteenth century it was by no means the end of legislation on consumer matters affecting their work, but rather only a beginning. A Director General of Fair Trading with his own staff (the Office of Fair Trading) was appointed under the Fair Trading Act 1973. He has a general duty to keep under review and collect information about trade practices which might be harmful to the interests of consumers, but weights and measures authorities are required to enforce orders made under the Act relating to such practices and are likely to be involved in other provisions such as that under which the Director General can seek written assurances from a trader 'persisting in a course of conduct detrimental to the interests of consumers' that he will refrain in future.

Again, when the Crowther Committee looked at the law on consumer credit, the question of enforcement naturally received attention. One of their criticisms of the existing Moneylenders Acts, for example, was that the only means of redress open to a private citizen was to bring a civil suit, whereas it was clear to them that in the field of consumer credit

> there must also, and primarily, be provision for consumer credit administrative supervision and enforcement.

This would require a field force of inspectors in addition to a Consumer Credit Commissioner who would undertake licensing and other supervisory activities. The committee were, however, less committed to putting this inspection work on weights and measures inspectors than some of their predecessors. They found 'some attractions' in the idea put to them by the Institute of Weights and Measures Administration that they should do the work but also disadvantages – some of the work would involve intricate legal and financial questions, and there was in any case the possibility that local authorities might have difficulty in recruiting the necessary additional staff. On the other hand it was desirable to avoid having two sets of officials concerned with enforcement. They therefore finally concluded that the Commissioner should consult the Institute and the local authority associations and

> should not set about the recruitment of his own force unless and until he is convinced that no joint arrangement of the kind suggested could be made to work.[26]

Doubtless this hesitation reflected different views among the members of the committee, and the strong feeling that ideally consumer credit legislation called for central enforcement, with the dilemma that this implied setting up a wholly new nationwide organisation of inspectors. The government's response was to accept that there was a need for a central Commissioner to administer new legislation, but that weights and measures authorities 'in view of their fund of experience and local knowledge' were well fitted to undertake enforcement.[27]

Quite apart from these additional duties put on weights and measures inspectors, there was by the early 1970s a good deal of other legislation which might fall in whole or in part on them to enforce. Much of this was relatively limited in scope, but particularly important was the Food and Drugs Act 1955, which consolidated and replaced earlier legislation going back to 1875. Much of the enforcement work under this Act, concerned with the labelling and composition of food, was undertaken by weights and measures inspectors. This type of legislation did not in many cases specifically entrust enforcement to weights and measures authorities, and there was much variation in the way the work was carried out among different authorities. Rationalisation of the position was advocated by the Institute of Weights and Measures Administration[28] in a way which would bring together more effectively the work of weights and measures inspectors as a trading standards service. The emphasis in the Institute's view was not simply on the consumer protection element in the extended role of weights and measures inspectors, but on the fact that the work was also of benefit to reputable manufacturers and traders in protecting them against unfair competition, The reform of local government in 1974 brought about a drastic reduction in the number of weights and measures authorities from 241 to 98,[29] and automatically eliminated many of the previous anomalies. In England and Wales the counties are now the weights and measures authorities except in London, where under the earlier reforms this function was given to the London boroughs; in Scotland these powers are the responsibility of the region and island authorities. Many of these authorities have renamed their weights and measures inspectorate as a Trading Standards Department following the Institute's reasoning but others have chosen to call it a Consumer Protection Department. In any case the inspectors are no longer so called but are either Trading Standards Officers or Consumer Protection Officers.[30]

WEIGHTS AND MEASURES INSPECTORS BECOME TRADING STANDARDS OFFICERS

Two main features of the transformation of weights and measures inspectors into TSOs in the 1970s have been changes in the source and nature of the work. A greater volume of it under the newer legislation arises from complaints from members of the public. At the same time, TSDs have become the focus for other consumer complaints, that is, complaints on matters not covered by legislation which can only be resolved in the traditional way by negotiation between the complainant and the seller of goods or services, or, in the last resort, by civil action in the courts. The Trade Descriptions Act particularly emphasised these two changes. Consumers, becoming aware that under the Act many matters arising out of their dealings with traders or providers of services were now subject to statutory regulation, were encouraged to complain to or seek advice from TSDs about other matters not subject to statutory regulation.

This in turn led to pressures for a more effective consumer advice and protection service not simply dealing with the enforcement of matters subject to statutory regulation. From 1973 onwards the government encouraged local authorities to provide consumer advice centres with the aid of specific grants and the number of such centres rose rapidly from twenty-five in March 1974 to 120 in March 1977, but has since declined somewhat. These and other measures of consumer protection were seen as contributing to the fight against inflation.[31]

Complaints, whether related to statutorily regulated trading matters or not, have thus become a marked feature of the work of TSDs and have tended to increase rapidly. In South Yorkshire, for example, the number of complaints and enquiries received increased by 65 per cent between 1974/75 and 1976/77. Even in a predominantly rural county like Gwynedd complaints needing investigation increased by 18 per cent in the same period.[32]

The significance of these changes lies largely in the fact that they brought TSOs into contact with the general public very much more than was the case under the old weights and measures legislation. At the same time they greatly developed a change in the relationship with traders and manufacturers which had begun with earlier short weight legislation. TSOs had to devise new methods and techniques to deal with complaints which had to be dealt with under statutory provisions, especially the Trade Descriptions Act. Equally they had to learn how to handle the even larger number of complaints which did not come under the statutory provisions at all.

Complaints about non-statutory matters provided the biggest problems. Over the years weights and measures inspectors had attached particular importance to encouraging attitudes of mutual trust between themselves and traders. They saw themselves as impartial and unbiased, and therefore as acceptable to the majority of those in the trade. As a former chief inspector of Middlesex expressed it:

there is no doubt that responsible traders organisations recognise that the laws are necessary, helpful and not oppressive. This understanding is the basis of the rapport which every good authority must obtain to secure maximum effectiveness.[33]

Many viewed with alarm the prospect of TSOs becoming involved in the provision of advice and handling of complaints on matters not covered by statute, on the grounds that it would tend to make them appear too consumer-oriented, create difficulties in their relations with traders, and divert trained staff away from what was seen as the true job of TSOs in dealing with statutory matters. A number of TSDs have recruited staff with special qualifications, e.g. in home economics, to handle the work of consumer advice, leaving TSOs free to concentrate on the statutory work. Even so, it does not follow that traders and the general public always appreciate the distinction, since the work all comes under TSDs. At the same time the new situation emphasises how senior TSOs have had to develop managerial and administrative skills in a way that was not called for under the old weights and measures inspection, and these skills have centred on both the handling of an increased volume and range of work, and on the relation between statutory and non-statutory work. It is not only the source of much enforcement work which has changed but also its nature. Enforcement under the newer legislation tends to be a more complex matter than it was under the Weights and Measures Acts or, for that matter, the Food and Drugs Acts. Consider, for example what is meant by a trade description under the 1968 Act. It is an indication 'direct or indirect' of various matters specified in the Act, including the quantity of goods, method of manufacture, composition, fitness for various purposes, and testing and its results.[34]

One thing which is immediately striking is that this enormously extends the expertise which the TSO needs to have or to have access to in order to make enforcement a reality. To establish the quantity of goods being offered for sale is a relatively straightforward extension of the traditional weights and measures inspector's concern. To test the composition of textiles or wooden or metal articles goes far beyond the limited traditional concern with such things as the composition of sausages or meat pies, but still is at least analogous to them. But questions involving qualitative as well as quantitative tests, such as fitness for particular purposes, introduces a new element of judgment. Moreover a false trade description is defined as one which is false 'to a material degree' and includes a misleading description.[35] Again, the Act brings in a whole new area by making it an offence to make false statements in providing services, accommodation, facilities and the like. Not only, therefore, does the TSO have to concern himself with a much wider variety of goods and descriptions, but he must also exercise his judgment to a much greater extent and in a much more extensive context than was the case with the weights and measures inspector. A visit to a clothing shop is no longer concerned simply with whether the instruments used for measuring out cloth are accurate but with whether the bargains on offer in the window ('25 per cent reduction') really are so reduced or the description on the label ('100 per cent cotton') true. TSOs find themselves visiting people they have never visited before (second-hand car dealers for example), and investigating questions which were never remotely their concern before.[36]

The most obvious consequence of these developments has been on the nature of the work carried out. TSOs still have their statutory duties to perform under the Weights and Measures Act. The standard traditionally thought desirable by the Board of Trade was a visit of at least once a year to all premises coming under the Act. Most authorities achieved a reasonable level of inspections in relation to this standard. But the number of inspection visits to trading premises fell drastically from 450,000 in 1974/75 to 121,000 in 1975/76. The reasons for this change were largely seen by the information officer of the Institute of Trading Standards Administration as the pressure of other duties arising from the increase in legislation.[37] Certainly, the routine inspection which used to form such a large part of the work of weights and measures inspectors in many cases now forms less than half the total. One authority estimated that the fall had been from 80 per cent to 30 per cent of the total work of its TSOs and this certainly is consistent with the national picture given by the number of inspections carried out.

CHANGES IN METHODS OF WORK

Concurrently with the two changes identified – in the nature of the work and in its source – there has also been a change in the methods employed by TSOs. Weights and measures inspection was in the main straightforward enforcement work. In particular, inspectors could assume that in general traders were aware of the requirements of the Weights and Measures Act, and did not regard it as a major part of their task to explain and advise on what needed to be done.

The volume of new legislation[38] and the much greater variety of matters now covered by legislation have combined to shift the emphasis from what might be called the pure enforcement role to one in which the giving of information and advice has come to assume much greater prominence. Ignorance of the law's requirements especially among small traders was accepted as the almost inevitable accompaniment of the new legislation. The reaction of TSOs was in many cases to seek a 'sensible' enforcement policy, one which had regard to the genuine difficulties of traders but sought to enforce the law effectively when required. Thus many authorities issued explanatory leaflets which were distributed to traders in their areas; one, for example, explained to butchers what the law required when a regulation was made that the price per pound of meat was to be displayed;[39] others dealt with safety requirements for toys, nightdresses and other goods for which regulations have been made under the Consumer Protection Act 1961.

The thinking behind this approach was that the new legislation made it even more imperative to achieve effective enforcement through mutual trust and understanding between inspectors and inspected, combined with the use of sanctions in the form of prosecution where it could be seen to be justified, that is, where there was deliberate flouting of the legal requirements or a degree of negligence in meeting them which required firm handling. But it was also connected in the minds of many TSOs with the fact that they did not see themselves simply as protectors of the consumer but also as protectors of the reputable majority of manufacturers and traders against unfair competition and against dishonest suppliers of goods and services to traders. They too have to work to agreed standards, using a common language of trade terms and a uniform system of control and enforcement.[40]

It is difficult to show the practical consequences of these changes in precise terms. Since it was set up in 1973 the Office of Fair Trading has published statistics of the number of convictions obtained by local authorities under the various Acts coming under the heading of fair trading.

Table 3.1 *Convictions under fair trading legislation*

	1976	1977	1978
Trade Descriptions Act 1968	1,328	1,482	1,529
Food and Drugs Act 1955	2,400	2,221	2,113
Weights and Measures Act 1963	805	698	709
Others	674	661	723

Source: Annual Report DGFT: 1976 (HC 195, 1977), 1977 (HC 228, 1978), 1978 (HC 79, 1979).

Such figures can have very little meaning without much more detailed investigation. In particular, they give little guide to the effectiveness of the use of this, the ultimate sanction open to TSOs. Moreover, the figures published by the OFT are related to consumer and other complaints, of which there are naturally more under the Trade Descriptions Acts than under the Weights and Measures Acts. Official figures of all offences under the latter Acts for which proceedings were taken do not suggest any diminution in the activities of TSDs in this direction despite their increased responsibilities.

Table 3.2 *Proceedings under Weights and Measures Acts*

1963/64	4,170	1968/69	5,120
1964/65	3,582	1969/70	4,447
1965/66	2,143	1970/71	5,175
1966/67	6,131	1971/72	5,559
1967/68	4,848	1972/73	5,096

Source: Report on Weights and Measures by Board of Trade and Minister of Technology, HC 47, 1969; –do– by Secretary of State for Prices and Consumer Protection and Secretary of State for Industry, HC 619, 1975).

In any case, the volume of work carried out by TSOs needs to be related to other changes, such as the number of staff involved. The staffing requirements resulting from the new legislation were clearly one problem which had to be faced; it was exacerbated by both financial difficulties and the difficulty of getting suitable recruits. At the time of the Hodgson Committee's report in 1950 there were 772 inspectors of weights and measures. The number had increased to about 900 by 1963, when it was estimated that a further rise to 1100 would be needed as a result of the 1963 Act. The Trade Descriptions Act 1968 brought further revisions of establishments so that by 1974 it was estimated that an establishment of 1640 was needed simply to carry out functions already in existence although there were at that date only 1300 TSOs in post. In 1975 an estimate of the likely establishment needed in 1980 produced a figure of 1940, although this was scaled down for economy reasons (including 'frozen' posts) to 1620. Meanwhile the numbers in post had reached 1500 by 1977.[41]

Thus the doubling of the number of inspectors in a period of less than thirty years has even so failed to keep pace with the increased duties placed on them. This has contributed to developments which might in any case have become desirable. One is increased specialisation among TSOs. A number of chief officers have found it necessary to encourage individual TSOs to specialise in, for example, consumer safety questions as the legal requirements have become more numerous. The Consumer Credit Act of 1974 is likely to encourage this trend as it is a highly complex piece of legislation. At the same time such specialisation has not in general been treated as an exclusive matter and specialist TSOs also carry out general enforcement duties.

Equally important has been the trend to selective inspection. Since it is no longer possible in many cases to maintain the regular programme of weights and measures visits which used to form a major part of the work,[42] the fixing of priorities and the use of selective visiting have grown more important. In a way which never used to be the case TSOs have had to deploy their resources by deciding not only what are the essential commitments they have to meet but also specifically the premises they can afford not to inspect so frequently and those which it remains vital to visit regularly. The need for improved information on which to base more effective management of this kind has been recognised in the development through the Local Authorities Management Services and Computer Committee of comprehensive information systems now used by many TSDs as an aid to a more effective and selective use of resources.

The emphasis on priorities, clearly made more urgent by the financial crisis of the 1970s, and perhaps compounded by an unwillingness of some authorities to come to terms with the changed character of

TSD work compared with weights and measures, is a prominent theme in the annual reports of chief officers. Thus in South Yorkshire the trading standards section, whose work is most nearly comparable with that of traditional weights and measures inspection, pays more frequent visits to premises with large turnovers than to those where it is relatively small. The enforcement section, concerned with the quality and safety of goods, has had to concentrate its visits on the former because of the need to follow the order of priorities which has been established:

(1) to answer the complaints received from the public
(2) to maintain the sampling programme
(3) to carry out inspectional duties.[43]

RELATIONS BETWEEN CENTRAL DEPARTMENTS AND TRADING STANDARDS DEPARTMENTS

Selective routine inspection combined with the need to deal with a much greater volume of complaints are perhaps the most obvious changes in the way in which TSOs now go about their work. Parallel with these changes have been others which relate particularly to the accountability of TSOs. An important aspect is the relationship between TSDs and their local authorities on the one hand and central government departments on the other.

Although the Board of Trade, as has been seen, long bemoaned the fact that it did not have effective power to see that local authorities carried out weights and measures duties in the way that the Board considered necessary, it did after 1904 have power to issue instructions to both local authorities and inspectors. The regulations of 1907 not only dealt with the specific requirements to be met by traders and therefore to be enforced by inspectors, but went much further in specifying duties. Local authorities, for example, were instructed to give notice to the Board of the appointment and termination of appointment of inspectors, to provide adequate office accommodation, to see that the premises of traders were visited at least once a year and to ensure that inspectors made their annual reports in a specified form.[44] Inspectors were instructed not only in matters such as the equipment they were to use or the circumstances in which they were to obliterate stamps on weights and measures, but a 63-paragraph schedule to the regulations specified exactly how they were to carry out their duties, often in remarkable detail; for example, milk churns were to be washed out with water before being tested.[45] Moreover, it was one of the duties of local authorities under the regulations to issue copies of these detailed instructions to inspectors and see that they acted in compliance with them.[46]

The Board could issued its orders but for seeing that they were carried out it had to rely on (1) the inspector's competence and professional standards over which it had some control through examination mechanism, together with his willingness to act in conformity with the instructions, backed as they were by legal sanctions;[47] (2) such pressure as it could bring to bear on local authorities. The divided responsibility to some degree blurred the accountability of inspectors. As employees of local authorities they had to act in accordance with local priorities or pressures, but within a detailed national framework of legal responsibilities. The possibility of conflict was evident in the board's complaint that some usually small authorities were not providing an adequate weights and measures service. For inspectors the legal limits to their accountability were provided on the one hand by the fact that if they exceeded their powers they could be challenged in the courts by traders, and on the other if they 'wilfully neglected' to carry out the regulations they could be prosecuted by the Board. In practice most of them doubtless attempted to meet their legal obligations to the extent that local circumstances allowed.

Regulations under the Weights and Measures Act 1963, although still very detailed on requirements, do not go into quite the same detail of instruction. Nevertheless inspectors are still told, for example, that in testing automatic weighing machines they are to weigh consecutively 20 separate loads selected by them and then to reweigh them on another weighing instrument.[48]

The real change has come with the newer legislation. The Trade Descriptions Act 1968 gives the Department of Trade power to lay down requirements[49] but not to instruct TSOs. Legislation administered by the Director General of Fair Trading also contains little in the way of powers over local authorities and their officers and appears to depend on a high degree of co-operation with them. An example is the power of the Director General to extract a satisfactory written assurance from a trader that he will refrain from continuing in a course detrimental to the interests of consumers.[50] These novel declarations wrung from traders are publicised in the DG's annual reports. Yet the power could hardly be exercised to any effect without the co-operation of TSOs in providing the necessary information, as the DG has acknowledged.[51] There is of course a mutual interest in that a chief TSO may well find it an advantage to have these powers used where he is receiving persistent complaints about a particular trader, and a series of fines in the local court proves no deterrent.

This is only one example of the way in which the work of the DGFT depends on information which must to a large extent come from TSOs. He is indeed under statutory obligation to collect information on trading practices.[52] It is hardly therefore surprising that one of the early steps he took was to get the agreement of the local authority associations, Citizens Advice Bureaux and others that TSOs should collate information for their areas on consumer complaints and send it to OFT. The OFT also maintains a central register of convictions under consumer legislation, again largely derived from TSOs.

The Consumer Credit Act 1974, which give the DGFT a more specific executive role in the administration of the credit licensing system, and in superintending the working and enforcement of the Act, is also more akin to other legislation in the powers which it gives him in relation to local authorities. Like the Department of Trade under the Trade Descriptions Act he can call for a report from a local authority on the exercise of their functions under the Act; and can investigate by means of a local inquiry any local administration which is alleged not to be carrying out its functions properly. And, again in parallel with the Trade Descriptions Act, local authorities wishing to prosecute under the Act must first notify the DGFT.[53]

All this amounts to a good deal less formal power by central departments over local authorities and their officers, the TSOs, than used to be the case in weights and measures legislation. Clearly this change reflects in part changes in local government and the fact that trading standards are now the responsibility of larger and better-equipped authorities; in part it reflects the increased professional standing of TSOs themselves. The latter are now more demonstrably answerable to their authorities for the proper performance of their duties, with central departments in theory having power to act mainly where there is default by local authorities. And even these powers are now being called in question by the local authority associations in their attempt to diminish the controls exercised by central government generally over local authorities.[54]

THE PROBLEM OF NATIONAL STANDARDS

However, one particularly difficult question remains, that of how to secure and maintain reasonably uniform standards of administration where eighty-eight different authorities share responsibility for enforcing the Acts. The balance may have shifted since the Board of Trade tried to regulate in detail the work of weights and measures inspectors, but the attempt to influence standards can be seen in such continuing efforts by the central departments as the issue of circulars and memoranda, as well as in such statutory provisions as those relating to the notification of intended prosecutions. These efforts must be seen in the context of the fact that the choice has always been seen as lying between central enforcement of the Acts and enforcement by local government with some central oversight. Although the latter has remained the choice in practice, its continuance is likely to prove difficult as well as to raise controversy about the degree and nature of central oversight.

The traditional arguments for local control of weights and measures administration were endorsed by the Hodgson Committee. They depended largely on the view that enforcement of the law required a close acquaintance with the conditions of local trade.[55] This is clearly important and its importance has if anything been strengthened by the fact that later legislation is much more geared to responding to complaints from the public. But the difficult question is how much weight to give to considerations of localness as against other considerations, notably the need for uniformity.

Even in 1951 in relation to weights and measures administration the argument was advanced to the Hodgson Committee that the desirability of uniform administration of the legal requirements was growing in view of the fact that trade was more and more in the hands of national companies, and that therefore there should be a national enforcement system.[56] But weights and measures law and regulations, as has been seen, were relatively straightforward. Clearly, weights and measures inspectors in different areas might differ in the degree of strictness with which they enforced the law, and, particularly, in the circumstances under which they decided to prosecute, but there was comparatively little argument about what constituted a contravention.

Under the newer legislation, and particularly the Trade Descriptions Act, questions of interpretation are more difficult. At the same time the much wider scope of the legislation has made a greater impact on traders; for example, they themselves need to be much more alert to the possible implications of their activities. Bodies like the Retail Consortium have expressed anxiety about the fact that in some of the matters covered by the new legislation there is no agreed standard of what constitutes an acceptable practice, with consequently different interpretations by different local authorities. Some national companies with retail outlets in all parts of the country have pointed out that it makes nonsense of their activites if a trade description which is acceptable in Southampton is not accepted in Oldham.

In 1974 a working party of officials under the chairmanship of the Director General of Fair Trading began a review of the Trade Descriptions Act. Their report dealt with this point and suggested that local authorities should themselves take steps to develop consultative arrangements between themselves and traders to try to minimise these problems. They also but mainly for other reasons suggested that the OFT should have power in exceptional cases to exercise enforcement powers, and take prosecutions since they thought that prosecution by a central authority in special (though unspecified) cases might have a greater impact, although they rejected any idea of a power of veto over local authority prosecutions.[57]

Local authorities and the ITSA are well aware of the problem of national standards, and not least of the fact that unless local authorities can demonstrate that it is possible for them to achieve a reasonable degree of uniformity the pressure for the work to be taken over by a central body will grow stronger. Increasing involvement with EEC regulations, for example, emphasises the fact that in many countries it is assumed that there will be central enforcement. Informal exchanges between TSDs have long existed and the ITSA has produced guidance for its members on a number of questions of interpretation. More formally, the local authority associations have formed the Local Authorities Co-ordinating Body on Trading Standards (LACOTS) to act both as a forum for discussion of such issues and as a channel of communication with central departments on trading standards matters.

However, given the increasing scale and complexity of legislation affecting the work of TSOs there seems to have been considerable reluctance to face squarely the problems arising from divided responsibility. The Consumer Credit Act in particular, as has been shown, is essentially a measure of central control in which the role of TSOs is one of acting as agents of central government. Yet this is not how the legislation was framed in spite of the overriding responsibility of the Office of Fair Trading.

What has happened is that at each succeeding stage – revision of weights and measures legislation, introduction of consumer protection and trade description legislation, introduction of consumer credit legislation – the question whether there should be central or local enforcement has been raised, and each time it has been answered only in relation to that particular stage and without taking into account the total effect of changes in the legislation in making a cumulative change in the position of TSOs. Thus it has seemed easier to adapt on each occasion an existing institution rather than face the problems which would undoubtedly arise in creating a new central inspectorate, including the strong opposition of the local authorities.

The present position is thus a somewhat uneasy one. The local authorities have done as much as they can to minimise the disadvantages of enforcing locally legislation concerned with national trading activities, at the same time stressing the advantages of local knowledge and control, and insisting that a body like LACOTS can effectively deal with problems like the avoidance of duplication in prosecutions.[58] Central government, although denying that it has any desire to take over the work, from time to time makes threatening noises about the need for greater consistency in standards.[59] Despite rumblings of discontent from certain sections of the retail trade the attempt to combine the advantages of local control with the application of uniform standards has not obviously been a failure; but life is more difficult for TSOs than in the quieter days before 1960.

THE RELATION BETWEEN INSPECTORS AND INSPECTED

Nor are inspectors' relationships with those whom they inspect quite so straightforward as they once were. In 1968 the then Minister of State at the Board of Trade (Mr George Darling) saw TSDs as establishing

> friendly relations with the reputable traders in the area to get matters put right outside the courts, but also working with local traders to put dishonest operators out of business by quickly reporting offences.[60]

This conventional view of an inspector combining advice and persuasion with tough enforcement where necessary has not been so easy to put into practice. There is no doubt that many traditional weights and measures inspectors preferred the comparative certainty of the regular work and routine inspections under weights and measures legislation to the uncertainties of the newer legislation. Equally others have responded to the challenge – and incidentally seen the advantage to their own status – in the new responsibilities. But just as the TSO is caught between his local responsibility for enforcement and the national implications of much of what he is enforcing, so his new duties create a dilemma in determining the degree to which he should exercise an advisory role, particularly in circumstances where so much of the work is responding to complaints rather than carrying out routine visits. The dilemma is at the root of the argument about trading standards *v.* consumer protection. Many TSOs and local authorities have preferred the former title precisely because they see themselves as neutral, as not being either for traders or for consumers, and wish to emphasise that neutrality, whereas they see consumer protection as at least suggesting that they are primarily acting on behalf of one group, consumers. Yet from the time of the 1870 Commission which explicitly drew attention to the advantage to the poorer classes of inspection of weights and measures 'acting as a preventive of fraudulent and negligent practices' to the post-war movement in favour of strengthening the position of the consumer in relation to the supplier of goods,[61] the emphasis has been on the value of inspection as protection for the public. Clearly a corollary of this is that conscientious and honest traders have benefited from the checking of their careless and dishonest competitors.

But the inspector has always emphasised the need to work with the local traders, to get 'friendly relations with the reputable traders'. Can he still do this and maintain his function of protecting the consumer against false or misleading trade descriptions? Alternatively, will a tough policy against traders not only make relations difficult but in the long run make enforcement difficult? The consumer organisations tend to the view that too many offences under the Trade Descriptions Act escape being dealt with because local authorities are either unable or unwilling to take action. Retailers' organisations on the other hand see the pressures on TSOs leading to their being less helpful than they might in guiding the shopkeeper through the mass of new legislation which he can so easily contravene inadvertently.

TSOs themselves generally see themselves as taking a helpful line, that is, they aim first to enlighten traders on the legal requirements; where contraventions are discovered, the use of legal sanctions is a last resort in cases where traders, after being warned, fail to put matters right. These seem sensible enough principles on which to work particularly given the general assumption of most TSOs that the majority of traders are honest and that therefore contraventions are generally due to ignorance or mistakes rather than malice.[62] But it is not surprising that differences of view have arisen as to how far TSOs have carried out their aims in practice, and equally how far they are effectively enforcing the law. For the whole area of trade descriptions is inevitably controversial in a way that for the most part traditional weights and measures inspection was not. Most TSOs have tried to deal with the new situation by building on their previous knowledge and experience. Hence they have been reluctant to move too far away from the routine inspections and well-tried methods of the past. Most outside observers would agree that in the circumstances they have tried well to cope with the new responsibilities. Doubt remains because of the ambiguity of precisely what is expected of them in this new situation. For although enforcement of statutory provisions remains the primary function of TSOs, the nature of the enforcement work and the relation between it and advisory work raise difficult questions.

WHAT KIND OF ENFORCEMENT?

Consider, for example, how the operations of TSOs under the Weights and Measures Act compare with those under the Trade Descriptions Act. From the nature of the former one would expect a very large number of inspections carried out routinely to result in a small proportion of errors or contraventions and an even smaller number of prosecutions. In other words, the assumption was that what weights and measures inspectors were doing was to keep a check on the functioning of a basically accepted system. There are in fact few national statistics until recent years to demonstrate this. The Board of

Trade put out annual reports until 1939 but then suspended publication, first because of the war and then in anticipation of a revision of the law which did not in fact take place until 1963. In any case the main national figures were of prosecutions but these were not related to the number of inspections.

Some more recent but incomplete national figures compiled by the ITSA tend to support the general inference. They show, for example, that in 1971/72 of over 13 million items of food examined under the Weights and Measures Act (that is, to check quantity) 1.4 per cent were found to be incorrect; and of over 1 million weights examined 9 per cent were incorrect. However, the more than 700,000 visits which were carried out for the purpose of this Act resulted in 4,312 prosecutions.[63] Clearly this information in itself does not make it possible to say whether TSOs are making a reasonable use of their powers and effectively ensuring compliance with the Act. For one thing, the figures for 1975/76 tell a startlingly different story – visits down to less then 121,000 but prosecutions just over 3,000, weights examined up to over $3\frac{1}{2}$ million but the percentage incorrect down to 0.8.[64]

Again, one of the most conspicuous changes in the work of TSDs, as has been suggested, is the fact that complaints, especially from the public, form a large and growing source of investigatory work. Complaints from the public in fact rose from just over 20,000 in 1971/72 to nearly 280,00 1975/76. For reasons which have already been discussed by no means all these complaints relate to matters coming under the various Acts administered by TSDs. Indeed as far as the Trade Descriptions Act is concerned only 27,000 investigations resulted from complaints from the public.[65]

The limitations of these figures would in any case make it difficult to draw any general conclusions from them. What they do is to draw attention to two different approaches to enforcement, the reconciliation of which is at the heart of the TSO's dilemma. The traditional approach is systematic, carrying out large numbers of examinations and tests from which one does not expect to find many defects and certainly very few which merit the ultimate sanction of prosecution.[66] The other approach relies less on the routine check and is more concerned with identifying the *prima facie* problem areas.

Quite different problems arise from these two approaches. The first depends on an implicit view of what constitutes a reasonable degree of enforcement. For example, the traditional standard laid down by the Board of Trade for weights and measures inspection was an annual visit to each trader's premises. There is no evidence that this was based on any exact analysis or calculation, for example, of the effect of visits paid only every other year; still less, of the effect of a system of priorities. Necessity, as has been shown, has forced TSOs to adopt measures of this kind, but with considerable uneasiness about the consequences. The ITSA's information officer, for example, took a pessimistic view of the consequences in the longer term of a reduction in inspector/trader contracts, seeing this as leading to a lowering of standards and an increase in complaints.[67] On the other hand it might be argued that it is not necessary to carry out the vast amount of inspecting and testing which has been traditional in the weights and measures field. Might not a reasonable and acceptable degree of enforcement be attainable with less inspection?

In response to the problem of frequency of inspection under the changed circumstances, several TSDs have recorded and analysed information which shows not only the effect of intensified inspection in lowering the rate of infringements discovered at inspection but also the variations which occur in different types of trading activity; in addition, it can be shown that beyond a certain point, on average when the rate of infringement has been reduced to about 5 per cent the use of additional resources on enforcement becomes much less cost-effective.[68] Such information is clearly essential for TSOs wishing to direct their resources in the most effective way but it still leaves unanswered what standard of compliance is acceptable.

In the past this question did not attract much attention because weights and measures raised scarcely any public concern, and certainly were not a matter of political controversy. It is likely to be of increasing concern in the future both because of the more controversial nature of the newer legislation and because the great increase in the volume of enforcement work is likely to focus more attention on the amount of resources needed to carry it out.

The second approach raises equally awkward questions. Complaints may indicate areas where something is wrong e.g. second-hand car dealing under the Trade Descriptions Act. But should enforcement concentrate on these areas – and indeed on specific traders within these areas who give rise to most complaints – at the expense of routine inspections? If the main aim is to protect the public then complaints – or at least well-founded complaints coming within the statutory provisions – give some measure of the things which the public want put right and where they feel that they have been unfairly treated. Some of the newer legislation can indeed only be enforced on the basis of complaints after the event (for example, misdescriptions of holidays). On the other hand, only to deal with complaints would not only tend to put TSOs into the position of being exclusively for consumers and against traders, but might also mean that undesirable trade practices which less easily or less frequently came to light were not investigated properly. And if some mixture of regular inspection combined with investigation of complaints is to be preferred, then again the question of what level of routine inspection should be aimed at to ensure a reasonable degree of enforcement becomes prominent.

Certain themes stand out in the discussion in this chapter, but ultimately leave a question-mark over the future. The three most prominent are:

(1) the difficulties of maintaining a balance between local and national control;
(2) the increased professionalism of TSOs, encouraged both by central government desire to improve standards and the attempts of inspectors themselves to improve their status;
(3) greater public pressures on the work of TSOs.

One of the main purposes of this chapter has been to show the influence of these factors in transforming weights and measures inspectors into TSOs. But they also affect what view is taken of the success of inspection work in this field. When, under the original weights and measures legislation – and to a large extent under current weights and measure legislation – the need was to ensure the observance of specified and detailed requirements, the use of inspectors was an effective method. The questions which arose were mainly about the mechanisms for improving the application of the method. In particular, there was, first, the problem of keeping the requirements up to date; it has been claimed, for example, that after 1904 the failure of the legislation to keep pace with technical developments in weighing and measuring apparatus led to 'inadequacy and absence of control in an ever growing field of apparatus'.[69] Secondly, there was the problem of ensuring that numbers of inspectors, their qualifications and the organisation of inspection work were adequate; this essentially depended on the part played by factors (1) and (2) cited above. The fact that the principle of accurate weights and measures was generally accepted in some ways made the effective use of inspection easier; at the same time the lack of political impetus was a disadvantage in ensuring that sufficient resources were devoted to weights and measures inspection. But it is probably true that a reasonable degree of accuracy of weights and measures was achieved and maintained; whether the results justified the resources devoted to it is a more open question and one which was hardly discussed.

The broadening of the work under the impact of the consumer movement has had both advantages and disadvantages for TSOs. The greater scope and interest of the work, and its increased status, have to be set against the greater difficulties in meeting the needs of the job, and the greater liability to public criticism.[70] Whether enforcement inspection is still the best means of dealing with some of the problems now raised in the trading standards field, and if it is, in what way it should be carried out, are questions requiring an answer. The first may not arise immediately, given the great faith which still exists for insisting on specific requirements and seeing that they are met. The second provides the more immediate question marks over the future, mainly in relation to:

(1) the balance between enforcement and advice and how the two should be linked;
(2) the ability to achieve acceptable national standards.

The first of these arises partly over the place of consumer advice in the work of TSDs. Bodies which have been in the forefront of the consumer movement, such as the Consumers Association, see it as a logical development that there should be an obligation on local authorities to provide consumer advice centres and other similar facilities, but the problems of blending this work with the more traditional enforcement work are not easily resolved. There remains the more fundamental problem confronting all enforcement inspectors of how strictly that enforcement should be carried out, and of the extent to which they should seek compliance with statutory requirements by means of persuasion and advice. In theory it should be possible to assess how effective the present methods of inspection have been in ensuring that the aims of legislation are met; but in practice it is by no means easy to do this.[71] The question of national standards equally lies in the future, in the sense that it may prove harder as the work of trading standards develops to maintain the present somewhat uneasy balance.

One may perhaps sum up by saying that the considerable changes in the work of TSOs over the last few years are likely to make increasingly necessary a critical self-examination of the role of TSOs.

NOTES: CHAPTER 3

1 *Report of Select Committee on Weights and Measures*, 1814, p. 3; among other things they were required to recommend 'the most effectual means for ascertaining and enforcing uniform and certain standards of weight and measure for the future'.
2 According to the standard work on the legislation (John A. O'Keefe, *The Law of Weights and Measures*, Butterworth, 1966) it was not finally achieved until the twentieth century; he quotes *The Grocer* of 1862 to show the variety of measures in use at that date (p. 48).
3 See *Final Report of Commissioners appointed to consider the subject of Weights and Measures* (House of Commons Paper 565, 1819).
4 Section 5(1)
5 Section 11.
6 Royal Commission on Local Government, Minutes of Evidence, 21 June 1923, questions 4337, 4338.
7 *Report of Standards Commission* (C 147a, PP 1870, XXVII), XIV and Appendix III, Abstract F; some of the occupations listed are curious – Colchester employed an ironmonger (at £50 a year), Bath a journalist (at £150) and Cromarty a grocer (at £15).
8 ibid., XX.

9 cf. T.A. Critchley, *A History of Police in England and Wales* (Constable, 2nd edn, 1978), p. 123.
10 This account is taken from PRO BT 101/956.
11 Sale of Food (Weights and Measures) Act 1926.
12 For example, it did not apply to oral descriptions; there had to be a written or printed document such as a label or invoice.
13 *Report by the Board of Trade on their proceedings and business under the Weights and Measures Act during the year 1927* (HMSO, 1928), p.4.
14 *do. year 1938* (HMSO, 1939), para. 10.
15 *do. year 1929* (HMSO, 1931), p.6.
16 PRO BT 101/1149.
17 *Report of the Committee on Weights and Measures Legislation* (Cmd 8219, 1951), paras 221, 225, 226.
18 ibid., paras 411, 414–18.
19 ibid., paras 425–7.
20 Ronald Wraith, *The Consumer Cause* (Royal Institute of Public Administration, 1976), ch. 1.
21 Cmnd 1011 (1960), para. 45.
22 There was, for example, much discussion on the committee stage of the Bill of whether the powers proposed for the secretary of state were too wide, but no discussion of inspectors and their powers.
23 Trade Descriptions Act 1968, ss. 26–8.
24 *Final Report of Committee on Consumer Protection* (Cmnd 1781, 1962), paras 679–85; they qualified these recommendations with the assumption that only the largest units of local government would exercise the new responsibilities (para. 682).
25 There was, however, some argument over the extent to which the Board of Trade should exercise powers of prosecution (see especially committee stage, House of Lords, HL vol. 287, 4 December 1967, col 473–5).
26 *Consumer Credit, Report of the Committee* (Cmnd 4596, 1971), paras 7.4.1–6.
27 *Reform of the Law on Consumer Credit* (Cmnd 5427, 1973), para. 104. In fact the Director General of Fair Trading administers the Act.
28 In a memorandum *Proposals for a Trading Standards Service* (July 1971)
29 A number of authorities (especially in Greater London) have made joint arrangements so that the effective number of separate authorities is eighty-eight.
30 For convenience, in the remaining part of this chapter references to the new departments and their officers will be in the form of the abbrevations TSD and TSO, these being the commonest designations.
31 Cmnd 6151 (HMSO, 1975), para. 32.
32 Information from annual reports of chief officers.
33 O'Keefe, op. cit., p.70.
34 Trade Descriptions Act 1968, s.2; the list of matters extends to ten items.
35 ibid., ss. 3, 14.
36 For example, the Chief Trading Standards Officer of Gwynedd records the investigation of an alleged false statement in connection with a computer dating system. (*Annual Report*, 1974/75).
37 J.J. Corfield in *Municipal Year Book 1978*, p. 95; cf. Chartered Institute of Public Finance and Accountancy, *Local Government Trends*, 1978, p. 49.
38 Including, now increasingly, EEC regulations.
39 The regulation was made under the Prices Act 1974, another piece of legislation enforced in part by TSOs.
40 *Proposals for a Trading Standards Service* (Institute of Weights and Measures Administration, 1971).
41 I am indebted for these staffing figures to Mr D.W. Johnson, chairman of the Policy and Research Committee of the Institute of Trading Standards Administration.
42 Among examples taken from annual reports, Gwynedd in the three years 1974/75 to

1976/77 never achieved an annual rate of inspections higher than 41 per cent of the total number of premises to be visited, South Yorkshire 55 per cent and Enfield 62 per cent.

43 South Yorkshire CC, Consumer Protection Department, Annual Report 1975/76, pp. 14, 18.
44 SR & O 1907, No. 698, regs 4, 8, 9, 10.
45 ibid., Schedule, para. 43.
46 ibid., reg. 22.
47 Under section 5 (4) of the 1904 Act an inspector refusing or wilfully neglecting to act in compliance with the regulations was guilty of an offence.
48 Weights and Measures Regulations 1963 (SI 1963, No. 1710), reg. 136. The general power to regulate the duties of inspectors under s.47 of the 1963 Act was, however, repealed by the Local Government Act 1972, and SI 1963, No. 1710, is covered by more specific powers, e.g. s. 14(1), which gave the Board power to regulate the inspection, testing, etc., of weighing and measuring equipment.
49 For example, s. 8 on the information to be marked on goods.
50 Fair Trading Act 1973, s. 34.
51 First AR, Director General of Fair Trading (HC 370, 1975), p. 16
52 Fair Trading Act 1973, s.2(1)
53 Trade Descriptions Act 1968, ss. 26 and 30; Consumer Credit Act 1974, s.161.
54 Review of Central Government Controls over Local Authorities (Local Authority Associations, 1979), pp. 148–9.
55 Cmd 8219 (1951), para. 407.
56 ibid., para. 406.
57 Review of the Trade Descriptions Act 1968 (Cmnd 6628, 1976), paras 269–77.
58 See Review of Central Government Controls, op. cit., p. 146.
59 For example, speech of Mr Fraser (Minister of State, Department of Prices and Consumer Protection) to ITSA (The Times, 21 June 1978).
60 HC Deb 759, 22 February 1968, col. 685.
61 cf. Ronald Wraith, The Consumer Cause (RIPA, 1976), p.10.
62 cf. Ross Cranston, Regulating Business (Macmillan, 1979), pp. 5, 33.
63 See Local Government Trends (Chartered Institute of Public Finance and Accountancy, 1978), table 10.5.
64 ibid. The figures for the two years are not directly comparable since they do not relate to exactly the same number of authorities.
65 ibid. In the previous year this figure was over 93,000.
66 It may also serve other purposes, e.g. to ensure that TSOs have up-to-date knowledge of traders, products, etc.
67 J.J. Corfield in Municipal Year Book 1978, p. 65.
68 Information kindly supplied by Chief Trading Standards Officer, Northamptonshire CC.
69 O'Keefe, op. cit., p. 60
70 For example, to the extent that a TSD may be accused of being corrupt by aggrieved members of the public (A.R. South Yorkshire Consumer Protection Department 1976/77, pp. 24–5).
71 cf. Cranston, op. cit., pp. 8, 173.

CHAPTER 4

INSPECTION IN FACTORIES AND MINES

———————◆———————

The primary object of the appointment of inspectors is to promote and enforce the uniform observance of the legal obligation cast upon owners and managers of mines, and upon all persons employed in mines to carry on their operations in conformity with the statute. (Instructions of the Secretary of State for HM Inspectors under the Coal Mines Regulation Act 1872 etc; C 1987, 1878)

It is not enough to think in terms of 'ensuring compliance' with minimum legal requirements. Whatever the means adopted, this concept is too narrow and restrictive. Inspectors should seek to raise standards above the minimum levels required by law. They should advise on better organisation. They should be concerned with the broad aspects of safety and health organisation at the workplaces they visit, as much as with those narrow aspects which may have been made the subject of detailed statutory regulations. (Report of the Committee on Safety and Health at Work: Cmnd 5034, 1972)

There is so much wrong with the enforcement system and the attitudes of those who run it that many workers have written off all inspectors as stooges of the employers. (Patrick Kinnersly, *The Hazards of Work: How to Fight them*, 1973)

ORIGINS OF FACTORY AND MINES INSPECTION

This chapter is concerned with two central government inspectorates, the factory inspectorate and the mines inspectorate.[1] Both now have responsibilities under the Health and Safety at Work [etc.] Act 1974.[2] But apart from their common concern with safe and healthy working conditions the two inspectorates in almost every way present marked contrasts. The factory inspectorate has much the broadest range of responsibilities of any central government enforcement inspectorate. Before the 1974 Act it was concerned with the problems of industries as diverse as petrochemicals and textiles, electronics and steel, as well as taking in building sites and docks. The HSW Act extended the list to include health and safety hazards in hospitals, schools and refuse collection, among others. The mines inspectorates has always been much smaller and more specialised, concerned mainly with coal mines, and, since 1894, quarries.

Again although both inspectorates originally began in the Home Office,[3] the circumstances of their origins differed. The history of both has been discussed elsewhere.[4] Here it is sufficient to note that the Factories Regulation Act 1833, under which the first inspectors were appointed, was limited to imposing conditions under which children could be employed in mills and factories, whereas the corresponding Mines Act 1850[5] was directed to improving the arrangements for ensuring the safety of those who working in the mines. Much of the agitation which preceded the 1833 Act was linked with the belief that restrictions on the hours worked of children employed in factories would lead to a reduction of the hours worked by adults.[6] Mines legislation on the other hand derived from the concern of the public and the miners over a series of mining disasters which resulted in heavy loss of life. However, questions of safety and general welfare were not entirely neglected in 1833,[7] and a series of amending Factory Acts during the remainder of the century gradually extended regulation to adults as well as children, to workshops, docks and warehouses as well as mills and factories, and, above all, to safety and especially the guarding of machines, as well as health and welfare.[8] Mines legislation too was extended to regulate the employment of women and children, but the predominant concern with safety remained.

There was another notable contrast in the early history of the two inspectorates. The mines inspectorate required a much higher degree of specialised knowledge. The resolution of many safety problems, such as those caused by the explosion of gases or by roof falls, called for the skill of mining engineers and could not be effectively carried out until the necessary scientific and technical knowledge was available. The factory inspectorate, on the other hand, did not in the early days need a great deal of specialised and technical knowledge, although clearly as the work extended and as industrial processes became more complex, such knowledge became more necessary. Nevertheless the contrast has persisted. Mines inspectors were and still are qualified mining engineers with experience in the industry. Of factory inspectors, on the other hand, over 40 per cent in 1972 were graduates in non-scientific and non-technical subjects,[9] although a majority of new recruits now have scientific or technical qualifications.

In spite of these contrasts, there was one great similarity between the Acts establishing factory and mines inspectorates. Both were bitterly opposed by mill and mine owners respectively as unwarranted interference by government in productive economic activities.

THE WORK OF NINETEENTH-CENTURY INSPECTORS

The 1833 Act laid down specific requirements to be followed by mill and factory owners (nobody under 18 to be employed at night, for example, no child to be employed more than twelve hours a day). The Act established the principle that the job of the inspectors was to see that the Act was observed, and gave them powers both to enter premises and obtain information for this purpose and to apply legal sanctions in the case of failure by owners to observe the provisions of the Act. These three elements – specific requirements, powers of entry and powers of action – continued to form the basis of subsequent factory legislation. The original mines legislation depended less on specific requirements, but subsequent legislation brought in many such requirements, and the job of the inspector did not in principle differ from that of the factory inspector.

But although the task of the inspector seemed to be quite clear and unambiguous there was from the beginning much debate about how it should be carried out. Among the first four inspectors under the 1833 Act there was apparently a difference of view over whether they should prosecute every time they found a breach of the law, or whether they should first try to persuade employers to comply with the act, using prosecution only as a last resort.[10] By the 1870s the issue seemed in no doubt. Alexander Redgrave, who became the first chief inspector of factories in 1878, told the Factory and Workshops Act Commission:

it is our object to be the friend of the manufacturer as much as the friend of the *employé*.

Acting with 'the very greatest leniency and discretion', the aim was:

that we should simply be the advisers of all classes, that we should explain the law, and that we should do everything we possibly could to induce them to observe the law, and that a prosecution should be the very last thing that we should take.[11]

To some extent this attitude might be seen at first as a response to the intense opposition to the employment of inspectors in the early days, the desire to conciliate powerful manufacturers as a means of inducing them to comply with the Acts. A similarly conciliatory approach was stressed in the early instructions to mines inspectors.[12] This approach persisted, however, even after the initial opposition to the use of inspectors had declined. The 1876 Factory Commission, for example, claimed that there was 'general acceptance and even popularity of factory legislation' as compared with the initial resistance.[13] And a later chief inspector saw a vindication of the approach not just in overcoming the original opposition but in positively assisting in the successful extensions of the Factory Acts, so that by 'quiet work' and 'the avoidance of undue friction' they had largely been able to apply successfully special rules relating to dangerous trades.[14]

There was a further argument in favour of the conciliatory approach. The instructions to mines inspectors quoted at the beginning of this chapter stress that what is being enforced is the obligation on those owning or working in mines to observe the statutory provisions. Nothing, it is pointed out, should be done to weaken the responsibilities of owners and managers for the safe operation of the mine since these provide 'the best security for the observance of the law'. Equally inspectors were to impress on those employed in the mines that they also have a duty to observe the statutory provisions and that 'their safety in a great measure lies in their own hand'.[15]

This stress on the limited nature of the inspector's responsibilities is a theme running through much of the history of factory and mines inspection. In theory, inspectors were there simply to see that the law's requirements were met, not to take responsibility for health and safety. Yet, as will be seen, it was not always easy in practice to draw such an unambiguous line, particularly when legislation went beyond laying down specific requirements.

It was not only the approach of inspectors which was an issue. Since the purpose of inspection was to see that statutory provisions were carried out, some attempt had to be made to decide on the frequency and nature of inspection visits which would achieve this. By 1899 general instructions to factory inspectors had established that every factory or workshop should be visited once a year with more frequent visits where, for example, the inspector 'has reason to suspect irregularities'[16] The instructions to mines inspectorates of 1878 were less precise on frequency of inspection. They did, however, contain an important statement of the justification for routine inspections without notice:

the liability to official inspection at any time without warning may be a most effective guarantee against abuse, and an unexpected visit from an Inspector is not the less beneficial because he finds nothing of which to complain.[17]

THE EFFECTIVENESS OF INSPECTION IN THE NINETEENTH CENTURY

One may sum up the way in which inspection in factories and mines had evolved by the end of the nineteenth century by saying that it relied on persuasion rather than prosecution, and on prevention of breaches of the law rather than their detection. To a large extent these developments were due to inspectors themselves. Moreover, their increasing professionalism was also evident in the fact that they did not confine themselves simply to ensuring that specific legislative requirements were being complied with; increasingly they saw themselves, and were seen, as promoting the underlying purposes of the legislation, that is the safety, health and welfare of those working in factories and mines. This has an important bearing on the question of how to assess the effectiveness of the work of inspectors in the nineteenth century.

The 1876 Factory Commission saw the value of the inspectors' work in

the great amelioration which has taken place in the condition of the protected workers, effected as it has been, in the main through their instrumentality.[18]

This, however, seems to raise two questions neither of which can be answered with much precision: (1) whether one can measure the success of inspectors in improving conditions; (2) even if one could, whether one can determine how much of that success was due to the particular approach adopted by inspectors.

The first question appears at first sight to be easier to answer for the mines inspectorate than for the factory inspectorate. Since the origin of the inspectorate was in the public concern over the high rate of accidents and particularly fatal accidents in the mines, the accident rates should provide a broad measure or progress. The following figures show that the numbers of fatal accidents (there are no figures for non-fatal ones) did indeed decline following the appointment of an inspectorate:

Table 4.1   *Accidental death rates in mines*

Years	Annual average death rates per 1,000 employed
1853–62	3·90
1863–72	3·14
1873–82	2·24
1883–82	1·81
1893–1902	1·39

Source: Report of Committee on Safety and Health at Work, Vol. 2: Selected Written Evidence (HMSO, 1972) p.419.

It is reasonable to assume that some part of this decrease is attributable to the activities of inspectors, but impossible to put even an approximate figure on how large a part. Still less is it possible to judge whether even better results might have been obtained if inspectors had taken a firmer line, or whether on the contrary the figures show that inspectors were right to stress the value of a conciliatory approach and a very sparing use of the weapon of prosecution. In practical terms the critical fact was that as long as the safety position in the mines continued to improve there was unlikely to be any serious challenge to the methods used by the inspectors.

A rather different approach is needed with the factory inspectorate since it operated on a much broader front. Even at the end of the century the protection of women and children remained an important part of the work. In 1895, for example, 55 per cent of the 2,993 prosecutions initiated by factory inspectors concerned the employment of women and young persons, mostly relating to hours of work.[19] There is no measure of the extent of compliance with such specific requirements as those relating to hours of work; and it is even less easy to measure broad improvements in conditions. We do not know how many contraventions of the statutory provisions were discovered by inspectors and dealt with without recourse to prosecution. We certainly do not know how many escaped the attention of inspectors altogether.

Very largely we have to fall back on impressions and expressed views to form any idea of what factory and mine inspection had achieved by the end of the nineteenth century. Broadly, it was generally accepted that much has been achieved in terms of the object of legislation, and that without inspection this achievement would not have been possible. Beyond that it was difficult to go. In particular, it left open questions for the future: how far it was possible, for example, to approach the ideal of 100 per cent observance of the statutory requirements for 100 per cent of the time; or how far one should go in pursuing observance of specific requirements as against other means of making progress.

INSPECTION WORK, 1900–45

Four themes run through the history of inspection in factories and mines in the twentieth century: (1) the changed conditions in which the work was carried on; (2) ways of ensuring that those who had responsibilities for health and safety carried them out; (3) frequency of inspection and numbers of inspectors needed; (4) use of specific regulations or a more broadly-based approach. All these themes interconnect, and one object of the following pages is to trace these interconnections and their consequences for the developing role of inspectors.

A number of official reports drew attention to the growth in the amount and complexity of matters requiring the attention of factory inspectors. Already in 1904 one report referred to the growing 'intricacy, variety and speed' of factory machinery, and the greater knowledge which inspectors therefore needed in inspecting for safety requirements.[20] By 1920 the stress was on such factors as the greatly increased use of electrical power. In addition, workers were claiming an increased say in the conditions of their employment, which might in the end lead to:

what may be called the police duties of the Inspectors becoming less and less important and the technical and advisory sides of their work more and more important.[21]

In 1929, apart from the greater use of machinery and electricity there was also the tendency towards an increase in very large factories and the development of new processes each presenting special problems. Moreover, there had been an intensification of efforts to improve health and safety, for example through the encouragement of the Safety First movement which had led to 'repeated visits to works for the discussion of safety arrangements'.[22]

By 1956 the pre-war changes in industry were seen largely as increasing existing hazards but not as adding new ones whereas since 1939:

developments in plant, machinery and materials accelerated the speed of development of these hazards and introduced completely new ones.[23]

This growth in the work of inspectorate was to some extent counter-balanced by the 'much more co-operative attitude in industry' and its growing realisation of the value of good working conditions. However, on balance developments in the previous thirty years were thought to have increased the volume and complexity of the work, partly because more co-operation meant more emphasis on advice which was time-consuming although 'what may be called the inspectorial as distinct from the advisory function has been made less onerous by this development.'[24]

One of the ways in which the work of the factory inspectors conspicuously changed was in the much greater attention paid to safety questions this century and also to the subtler and more long-term hazards to health in place of the more limited concern with the conditions of employment of women and children which had characterised the nineteenth-century approach. There was for example, a diminution in the number of prosecutions relating to employment matters and an increase in those relating to safety, although it was not until after 1939 that the number of the latter exceeded the former.[25] Changes in the conditions of inspection work drew attention to the fact that there might be limits to what inspectors could achieve by enforcing specific statutory requirements. Already in 1908, when an increase in the number of factory accidents led to suggestions that changes might be needed in the system of inspection, the Home Secretary (Herbert Gladstone) argued that although inspectors had done a lot to ensure that machinery was properly fenced 'there came a point when their power failed.'[26] The departmental committee which was set up in response to these pressures elaborated on this view. It was impossible to have enough inspectors to see that all machines were both properly guarded when they were installed and well maintained subsequently. It was primarily the duty of the occupier to secure the safety of the factory; all the inspection could do by periodic visits was to see that he was doing this and give him advice. Moreover:

> there are many dangers in factories which can only be avoided by constant daily care in carrying out a number of small precautions, the omission of which can seldom be detected by the periodic visits of a factory inspector.[27]

This seemed to set definite limits to what could be expected from inspectors. At the same time the committee touched on another twentieth-century theme. They were concerned about the number of visits paid by inspectors. They produced figures to show that approximately 25 per cent of factories were not visited in any one year, and although many of these were probably 'small and unimportant' they thought that the staff of 200 inspectors should be increased so that the minimum standard of inspection could be attained.[28]

These views seemed to give more prominence to the shift in emphasis in the work of inspectors noted earlier. Originally appointed to ensure that certain specific requirements were met they were now concerned with the much broader question of how to improve safety in factories through advising and stimulating the efforts of employers and workers. This presented something of a dilemma. As the chief inspector complained in 1913, many employers did only the minimum required by law, many employees treated safety devices as an unnecessary nuisance, and yet it was estimated that 25–40 per cent of industrial accidents could have been prevented if all practicable means had been taken.[29]

This seemed to raise two questions: how inspectors could best ensure that statutory requirements were observed; and what, if anything, could or should be done about other health and safety matters. The first alone represented a great deal of activity. Again taking 1913 as an example, the 217 inspectors in that year paid 406,000 visits, issued nearly 196,000 contravention notices and undertook nearly 3,900 prosecutions.[30] Even so, this activity only touched part of the problem of health and safety in factories. The chief inspector pointed out in his report for 1926 that a comparatively small proportion of the accidents reported resulted from unfenced machinery; to achieve a reduction in the large number of 'human failure' cases required proper organisation within the factory; inspectors tried to stimulate such activity, but

> have found it curiously difficult to arouse interest among either employers or workers. Progress in the establishment of safety organisations has in fact been disappointingly slow.[31]

However, to many people outside the factory inspectorate it seemed self-evident that adequate and frequent inspection was the key to safety in factories. In the early 1920s for example there was frequent Parliamentary questioning of the adequacy of the inspectorate. Lord Henry Cavendish-Bentinck asserted that a large proportion of accidents were due to the fact that there were not enough inspectors to enforce the regulations and could not be attributed simply to carelessness.[32] Mr Rhys Davies, a former junior Minister at the Home Office, saw 'a distinct and intimate connection' between the visits of inspectors and the number of accidents.[33] The departmental committee which was set up largely as a result of these pressures was less inclined to accept such a simple view of the matter, even toying with the idea that the development of voluntary safety organisations in factories would lessen the need for inspection, although they hastened to add that this development had not yet gone far enough to affect the immediate question of the standard of inspection.[34] The committee paid a great deal of attention to the question of priorities in the use of inspectors' time, and drew up detailed guidelines which for the first time attempted to give some precision to the idea of concentrating the efforts of the inspectors where they were most likely to be effective. Thus the more important factories and workshops, they recommended, should be visited at least once a year, the less important once every two years and all to be given a thorough inspection within an average period of four years, warehouses once every five years, and so on.[35]

But there continued to be a divergence of emphasis between enforcement of statutory provisions and pressure on employers or employees to take action on safety matters. In 1932 in a review of a hundred years of factory inspection the chief inspector summed up the work of an inspector as

> instruction (on matters within the law), and advice (on matters outside the law), rather than compulsion.[36]

A recurring theme in the 1930s, however, was the need for educating people to have a proper regard for safety, to overcome 'ignorance, obstinacy and misguided zeal', and for employers to provide proper supervision if the 'appalling' number of accidents cause by lack of ordinary care or forethought was to be reduced.[37]

Somewhat similar arguments were used in the 1930s in relation to mines inspection. A royal Commission was appointed in 1935 to examine safety in coal mines. It saw scope for reducing the accident rate, but this would require a change of attitude on the part of those in the industry; they based this view largely on the fact that inspectors were reporting many accidents which ought not to have happened.[38] There were however still echoes of the nineteenth-century controversies, with the miners' representatives pressing for more frequent inspections as against the view that too much inspecting would undermine the responsibility of management for safety.[39]

THE BACKGROUND SINCE 1945

It is in the period since 1945, however, that tendencies which were evident earlier in the century and even before have grown stronger and raised even more acutely questions about the role of the factory inspector in particular. On the one hand, the past thirty years have seen great changes in both the organisation of industry and the nature of its operations; on the other, greater public concern has developed about questions of safety and health. Together, these have caused the inspectorate to examine more closely its own role and methods. In a broader context, more general changes in society have among other things affected the status of inspectors and at least in certain ways given more prominence to the question of their accountability. Some of these changes were reflected in the work of the committee which under the chairmanship of Lord Robens examined the subject of safety and health at work between 1970 and 1972, and in the subsequent legislation which created an entirely new administrative structure for the work of not only the factory and mines inspectorates but also a number of other inspectorates.

The most obvious changes in industry generally since 1945 have been the tendency to concentrate manufacturing operations in a comparatively small number of companies, many of them multinational; and the development of new processes, often using new materials, as in the petrochemical industry. In addition, and partly connected with these changes, there has been a great extension of certain methods of working – among them increased mechanisation, continuous-process working and automation. So far as organisational change is concerned, perhaps the most immediately obvious example affecting the work of inspectors is the nationalisation of the coal mines, which at once reduced the number of employers with whom the mines inspectors had to deal from several hundred to one,[40] and at the same time changed the nature of the relationship between inspectors and employers in that the National Coal Board was, like the inspectorate itself, created by and ultimately responsible to Parliament.

The annual reports of the Chief Inspector of Factories have increasingly since the war dealt with the general problems of the inspectorate as well as with the more detailed analysis of industrial hazards which had traditionally formed the bulk of such reports. In part this reflects the varying personalities of the chief inspectors themselves, but in part also the increasingly more public character of the debate about safety and health at work and the part which the factory inspectorate should play. In 1951, for example, a review of half a century of inspection concluded that the basic principles of inspection had not changed; and in 1951 as in 1901 inspectors still spent much time advising manufacturers on the guarding of machinery. There had however been over the years much more emphasis on accident prevention particularly through the encouragement of voluntary action.[41]

But the theme of industry's responsibility for improving standards became increasingly prominent. The complaint of the chief inspector in 1913 found its echo in his successor's report for 1961:

> too many firms still have no safety organisation whatever, or where it exists it is ineffectual . . . in many places standards are still deplorable and much inadequately guarded machinery is daily being used. Many employers appear to rely on HM Inspectors to deal with the safety problems in their works.[42]

In 1962 'a complete change in the climate of opinion' in many parts of industry was being called for.[43] In 1963 a special chapter was devoted to the responsibilities of those in industry. With this went a greater stress on the causes on accidents. In 1963, 66 per cent of reported accidents fell in five categories, and although some of these accidents might be connected with breaches of the factory legislation, the majority

> occur in circumstances which cannot readily be controlled by legislation, for example, lack of attention to good industrial housekeeping and to general tidiness, ignorance of proper methods of lifting, failure to make use of protective clothing . . . and above all lack of knowledge and application of safe methods of work.[44]

Moreover, legislation could only lay down minimum standards in certain matters where requirements could be precisely specified and enforced; beyond that it was up to those who owned, managed or worked in factories to take steps to prevent accidents and eliminate disease.[45] The same theme was repeated in the following years.[46]

Less prominently, but still with increasing emphasis over the years, the theme of the changing nature of hazards in industry was developed. In 1963, for example, it was pointed out that changes in factory processes had practically eliminated some hazards but had greatly increased others; for example, automation and mechanisation were reducing the contact between the worker and dangerous processes and substances but increasing the hazards of maintenance work.[47] In 1966 attention was drawn to the 'profound effect' on the work of the inspectorate of technological developments and the increased scale of industrial operations.[48] Examples were given the following year of the hazards which might arise from new processes and the storage of large quantities of potentially dangerous materials and the problems this posed for inspectors who were called on to give advice:

> which must be realistic, having regard to the often extreme remoteness of the risk, the scale of disaster which could ensue, and the cost of remedial measures.[49]

REAPPRAISAL IN THE 1960s

It will be evident that these themes were not new. What was new was that they were pressed with more urgency in the 1960s and led to a more profound questioning than anything attempted previously of the inspectorate's methods and approach. Certainly for a body which was concerned with the promotion of safety and health in factories, the accident figures gave no grounds for complacency.

The figures were affected by many factors, including the factory inspectorate's own efforts to improve the reporting of accidents in the 1960s, as well as the level of industrial activity and its nature. But, whatever the limitations of the figures, in the 1960s as in the early 1900s they were one piece of tangible evidence on which critics could seize to argue that more should be done about safety at work, and, especially, that more vigorous action should be taken by factory inspectors.[50] The inspectorate's insistence on the need for industry itself to take steps to prevent accidents was in part an answer to this, but its plausibility depended on being able to show that many if not the majority of accidents could not be prevented by any action on the part of the inspectorate. The chief inspector might declare boldly: 'no increase in the size of the inspectorate would make important inroads into the gross figures' (of accidents),[51] but there was an uneasy awareness in the annual reports from the late 1960s onwards that what was lacking was reliable information on the underlying causes of

Table 4.2 *Accidents reported to the factory inspectorate, 1950–69*

Year	Total reported	Fatal
1950	193,059	799
1951	183,444	828
1952	177,510	792
1953	181,637	744
1954	185,167	708
1955	188,403	703
1956	184,785	687
1957	174,713	651
1958	167,697	665
1959	174,071	598
1960	190,266	675
1961	192,517	669
1962	190,158	668
1963	204,269	610
1964	268,648	655
1965	293,717	627
1966	296,610	701
1967	304,016	564
1968	312,430	625
1969	322,390	649

Source: AR 1960: Robens Report (Cmnd 5034, 1972), Tables 1 and 2. Figures for 1960 and later years not comparable with those for earlier years because of a change in definition.

accidents.[52] The establishment in 1970 of an Accident Prevention Studies Unit, later renamed Accident Prevention Advisory Unit (APAU,) was a response to this need, seeking reasons for differences in the incidence of accident rates in different industries, areas and factories. Its tentative association of a good health and safety record with efficiency in management is clearly of considerable importance in the continuing debate over the inspectors' role.[53] Even so, the inspectorate was vulnerable to criticism on the question of frequency of inspection. For even if they could argue that a great many accidents were not due to breaches of the Factory Act, it was still necessary, as it always had been, to relate the amount of inspection work to the need for securing a reasonable degree of compliance with the Act. But again the problem was that there was no way of measuring the success of the inspectorate by objective means. In 1967 it was conceded that with the increased work-load provided by the Offices, Shops and Railway Premises (OSRP) Act 1963 it was not possible to make a general inspection of all premises under the Factories and OSRP Acts more often than once in four years. In the chief inspector's view this was inadequate. He argued that insufficiently frequent inspection resulted in a fall in safety standards, because many managements needed fairly frequent reminders if standards were to be maintained.[54] Again, this was hard to reconcile with the insistence that the prime responsibility for health and safety lay with those who worked in industry. For if many managements needed to be reminded of their statutory responsibilities if the minimum standards required by law were to be maintained, there was surely little likelihood that they would accept the voluntary responsibilities which, according to the inspectorate, were necessary if any real progress was to be made in reducing the number of accidents.

The fact that chief inspectors now felt it necessary to put forward these general arguments in their annual reports was partly due to a sense that the time had come to re-examine some of the long-held assumptions on which the Factories Acts had been built, and partly to the need to justify the work of an inspectorate now subject as perhaps never before to public comment and criticism.[55] There had indeed been comment and criticism before, as has been seen, but it was mostly limited in extent, finding expression characteristically in Parliamentary questioning. In the 1960s comment and criticism became more intense and came from a variety of sources – from workers on the shop-floor, for example, whose concern was more likely to be with immediate issues such as the ventilation, temperature or sanitary facilities than with the prevention of accidents which occupied so much of the inspectorate's attention, or from the trade unions, who took an increasing interest in health and safety questions.

It was significant that in 1960 there appeared a full-scale study of the problem of health and safety at work by John Williams, inspired in the first place by the Labour Party research department. He was critical of many government policies. In particular he claimed that there was a failure to relate policies on the extent and method of factory inspection to the need to reduce accident rates.[56] But the study went much wider in providing a comprehensive review and making proposals which later became prominent themes in debate.[57] This study reinforced the arguments of those in Parliament and elsewhere who wanted to see a strengthening of the factory inspectorate and an increase in the frequency of inspection.[58] But perhaps the most significant development of the 1960s was the increased trade union concern and activity in health and safety matters. Much of this was directed at the question of effective safety organisation in factories with participation by representatives of those working there, but increasingly trade unions pressed for a strong inspectorate and strict enforcement.[59]

ENFORCEMENT POLICY OF FACTORY INSPECTORATE

However, on the critical question of enforcement policy, the inspectorate stood firmly on what had by now become a long-established tradition. In his 1969 report the chief inspector repeated the argument that inspection, being a process of sampling, could not ensure rigid compliance all the time, and that generally better compliance could be obtained:

if one persuades the occupier of the need for compliance as a matter of good practice, rather than to avoid conflict with the law.

The emphasis on persuasion and on goodwill between the inspector and the inspected was balanced by the need for prosecution for those who were careless, dilatory, inefficient or ineffective:

one well merited case may encourage management to review its organisation for compliance and bring about improvements in areas other than those for which the information is laid.[60]

Striking evidence of how these attitudes worked out in practice was provided by a study of a sample of inspectors' files covering the period 1961 to 1966. These disclosed 3,800 contraventions of the Acts and regulations, a large proportion of them (38 per cent) being for lack of proper fencing of dangerous machinery. In the great majority of cases (nearly 75 per cent) the inspector took action by means of a formal notification of matters requiring attention, and in less than 4 per cent did he either threaten prosecution directly or actually institute proceedings. Even in the comparatively few cases where it was the third or more occasion on which the firm had been found to be contravening the regulations, prosecution or its direct threat was only used in just over 10 per cent of the cases.[61]

Another study, also based on 1960s experience, by members of the Sub-Faculty of Law at the University of Kent, summed up the position:

it is extremely rare for a general inspection *not* to result in a 'discovery' and formal notification of a number of breaches of the law for which criminal proceedings could be instituted. But in the vast majority of cases such matters are not regarded as criminal offences in any ordinary sense either by the Inspectorate or by the employers concerned.[62]

To the critics this approach of the factory inspectorate carried the danger that they might be too closely identified with management and might consequently fail to act as vigorously and effectively as they should against breaches of the statutory provisions. One case which throws interesting light on this question was reported on by the Parliamentary Commissioner for Administration in 1976, but relates to the activities of the Factory Inspectorate in the 1950s and 1960s. It concerns an asbestos factory at Acre Mill, Hebden Bridge, which closed in 1970. A former employee who contracted asbestosis claimed that this was in part due to inadequate enforcement by the factory inspectorate of the Asbestos Regulations.[63] The PCA's report did indeed find that the district inspectors were not

> sufficiently decisive either in conveying to the management the sense of urgency that was appropriate or in pursuing the question of a prosecution when, over a period of years, improvements were not forthcoming.[64]

To a large extent the PCA's criticism rests not so much on the enforcement policy followed by the inspectorate as on deficiencies in organisation and co-ordination of different branches. Nevertheless his detailed narrative highlights the problems presented by a policy which seeks to maintain a balance between advice and persuasion on the one hand, and strict enforcement on the other. To proceed largely on the basis of goodwill means taking into account and balancing against one another many different factors and matters of judgment – the degree of co-operativeness of the management,[65] for example, or the extent to which technical developments permit reasonable solutions to health or safety problems, or the extent to which a company's temporary difficulties should be permitted to defer their attainment of the required standards. As the chief inspector of factories put it in his 1968 report:

> the Inspector is fully aware that there may be three sides to a problem – the management's and the workers' as well as his own. The management has to run a successful business in a competitive world and must constantly experiment with new processes and materials. The worker must be allowed to behave as a human being may reasonably be expected to behave, and not as an automaton.[66]

But because the inspector's first concern was with management, especially given his insistence that primary responsibility for health and safety in a factory lay with management, there could easily arise the suspicion that too little attention was paid to the workers' views and too much to those of management. Again Acre Mill provides a good example. Among the specific complaints made were:

Inspectors never saw conditions at Acre Mill as they really were because there was always warning of visits, accompanied by instructions from management to clean workplaces and have all machinery working properly in accordance with regulations, and in any case inspectors did not make close inspection but merely walked through the factory . . . and they never had an opportunity to discuss working conditions with them.[67]

What is important in the present context is not whether these allegations were true – the PCA did not find in them cause for complaint against the inspectors – but that they were almost inevitably bound to arise from the particular way in which the inspectorate saw their role. Increased public pressure on the factory inspectorate to justify its methods of securing compliance also compelled closer attention to the wider question of the extent to which it could be expected to secure safety in industry. However, these questions were merged in the late 1960s into a wider review of health and safety at work.

In June 1967 the Minister of Labour announced a review of the Factory and OSRP Acts. A consultative document was issued in December of the same year setting out the department's main proposals.[68] From the point of view of the present discussion the most interesting proposals were that the new legislation should have 'more of an enabling character' than existing legislation, with much more detail put into regulations; and that more specific obligations would be put on occupiers and employers for health and safety. But neither these nor other improvements proposed would have fundamentally altered the work of the inspectorate.

However, a variety of factors contributed to a new approach in the course of lengthy discussion on the consultative document. One factor was doubt whether revision of these two Acts alone was adequate in view of the increased concern with safety and health at work. There was in particular the fact that quite separate legislative provision had grown up notably for mines and quarries and for agriculture, in each case with separate inspectorates. One question, therefore, was whether the existence of separate legislation and inspectorates was still the right method, given the piecemeal growth which it reflected.[69] Another factor was increased public concern during the 1960s about environmental safety and amenity for the general public. Hitherto the factory and mines inspectorates had been reluctant to become involved in questions of public safety despite certain pressures on them to do so.[70] On the other hand, other legislation which was primarily concerned with hazards to the public was enforced by separate inspectorates, in particular the alkali inspectorate and the nuclear installations inspectorate.[71] One question therefore was whether the division between safety at work and safety of the general public was still meaningful, and this necessarily involved looking at the work of these other inspectorates.

Immediately before the general election of 1970 the Secretary of State for Employment and Productivity appointed a committee under the chairmanship of Lord Robens to examine the whole question of the provision for safety and health at work (except in transport). Apart from examining existing statutory and voluntary arrangements the committee was asked to consider what more needed to be done to protect the public from hazards arising from work activities, although 'general environmental pollution' was excluded. Not only was this therefore a much broader enquiry than any previous government enquiry into matters affecting the inspectorates concerned with health and safety at work, but by its very nature it was bound to raise the fundamental questions about the role of such inspectorates and about the responsibilities of those in industry for dealing with health and safety hazards.

ROLE OF MINES INSPECTORATE SINCE NATIONALISATION OF THE COAL MINES

One difficulty was that different inspectorates saw their roles rather differently. This was certainly true of the factory and mines inspectorates. The mines inspectorate had followed a very different course from that of the factory inspectorate since 1945. In one sense it had an easier task in defining its role since from 1948 it was operating largely within a single unified industry with only one employer and one major union. However, the mines inspectorate did not come under public pressures in the same way as the factory inspectorate. On the other hand, it had to make a considerable adjustment in practical terms, not simply to the fact, especially in the 1960s, of a declining industry, nor to technological change. These were challenges which the inspectors would have had to face in any case. What was completely new was the fact of dealing with an employer who was not dedicated to the pursuit of private profit and who had at the same time the resources to employ professional and technical staff of equal competence to that of the inspectorate.

Thus there could hardly have been a greater contrast with the situation which existed when the mines inspectorate was first established. It had been established against the fierce opposition of the mine owners because it was clear that the latter would not pay sufficient attention to safety matters unless they were compelled to do so by effective outside pressure. And part of the way in which that pressure was made effective was through the professional competence of the mining inspectors, who could demonstrate that safety precautions were feasible. The creation of the National Coal Board might have been expected to lead to the questioning of the need for an inspectorate. As a responsible public body the NCB could be expected to have a regard for safety which could not be so obviously assumed when the mines were under private ownership, and it could certainly employ safety engineers on a sufficient scale to ensure this.

The question was not raised directly, but was answered by implication in the way in which the inspectorate developed in the twenty years after nationalisation. This was in the direction of putting even greater emphasis on its advisory role. Inspectors were told that by establishing good relations with both management and workers, and acting as helpful advisers, they could often succeed in improving health and safety standards beyond the legal requirements, using their own knowledge and experience.

The approach and arguments are not too dissimilar from some of those being expressed at the same time by the factory inspectorate but there is no doubt that the mines inspectorate took them much further in practice, and that this was in continuation of a long-established tradition. The use of the weapon of prosecution provides a good indication. The 1938 Royal Commission commented on the tradition of using prosecution sparingly and, although not disagreeing with it, pointed out that there were dangers of allowing slackness in supervision and discipline if it were carried too far. They showed that prosecutions, which had averaged thirty-two a year in the period around the beginning of the First World War had fallen to nine a year in the 1930s.[72] In the period from 1948 to 1975 prosecutions practically ceased altogether.[73]

A further distinguishing feature of the mines inspectorates has been its relationship with the unions and in particular the National Union of Mineworkers. There is a long history of union concern for safety and support for the inspectorate,[74] and this has certainly not diminished since nationalisation. There has therefore been less tendency to criticise the inspectorate for being too closely concerned with management's problems. On the other side, there has been little general public interest from outside the industry in the work of the inspectorate. These various factors have contributed to the fact that there had not been up to the time of the Robens committee any great pressure for the inspectorate to re-examine its role in the way that the factory inspectorate had begun to do. Furthermore, the statistics did not suggest that traditional methods might have reached a point of stalemate. Between 1947 and 1967 the death rate per thousand employed in coal mines fell from 0.85 to 0.36 and the rate for serious injuries from 3.4 to 2.4, although the total injuries rate rose from 223 to 399.[75] To some extent this improvement was due to factors peculiar to mining rather than to industry generally. Whereas modern technology was creating additional hazards in industry, it was in mining helping to solve some traditional problems. For example, the accident rate from falls of stone or earth has been dramatically reduced since 1945, although previously this had been the main source of accidents.[76]

ROBENS COMMITTEE, 1970–72

It is not surprising that the Robens committee found a good deal of uncertainty about the role of the inspectorates which came within their terms of reference. 'The government departments', they said,

and inspectorates talk about enforcement, about compliance, and about the provision of advice and assistance with varying degrees of consistency.

They saw the reasons largely in historical developments which had changed the context in which they operated but had not led to any conscious reappraisal of objectives. To remedy this 'fudging of basic policy' they developed the more explicit advisory role set out in the quotation at the head of this chapter:

we believe that, as a matter of explicit policy, the provision of skilled and impartial advice and assistance should be the leading edge of the activities of the unified inspectorate.

To this end the inspectorate should develop new techniques, e.g. safety audits in depth, and should have much more frequent contacts with workers and their representatives.[77]

This view of the inspectorate needs to be set against the committee's general conclusion that the existing system was too much and too rigidly tied to statutory regulation by Acts and detailed regulations whereas what was needed was a more flexible statutory system and above all 'more effective self-regulation'.[78] Accordingly much of the report is concerned with what should be done by industry itself, and with the nature of the proposed new legislation. A crucial argument in this context was that a new authority should be set up with exclusive responsibility for safety and health at work, and that within it should be created a single unified inspectorate by a merging of six existing inspectorates.[79]

The committee thus rejected the argument that all that was needed was a strengthening of the inspectorates combined with a greater willingness to prosecute. At the same time they proposed strengthening the administrative sanctions open to inspectors by the addition of improvement notices, that is, notices which the inspector could send to an employer requiring him to put right specified faults within a stated time; and prohibition notices, that is, notices requiring particular machines, processes, etc., to be stopped unless action was taken to deal with specific hazards either immediately or within a stated period.[80]

Although the committee's discussions and recommendations went much wider, on the specific question of the inspectorate's role they were clearly much influenced by the preoccupations and view of the factory inspectorate. The emphasis on self-inspection and on the advisory role of the inspectorate marked the direction in which the inspectorate's thinking had been moving. Other inspectorates, and particularly the mines inspectorate, had not had similar problems and had not been seeking change. Correspondingly, neither they nor the mining industry generally were in favour of a unified inspectorate. Since they were quite content with existing arrangements, they saw only the possibility of these being weakened by the merger of the mines inspectorate with the factory and other inspectorates. Before the Robens proposals could be translated into the Health and Safety at Work [etc.] Act 1974, the Secretary of State for Employment had to make quite explicit promises to the NUM that the separate identity of the mining inspectorate would be preserved under the new legislation.[81]

THE HEALTH AND SAFETY AT WORK [etc.] ACT, 1974

The legislation was not achieved without a 'prolonged and intensive period of interdepartmental consultation' – 'a first-class Whitehall row' and one which was 'a classic in Whitehall history'.[82] One of the stumbling-blocks was the question of a unified inspectorate to which Robens had attached importance. Another was how wide the new legislation should go. The Ministry of Agriculture, Fisheries and Food fought successfully to have the agricultural health and safety inspectorate excluded; but it was a Pyrrhic victory, for the following year, under a less tenacious Minister, agriculture was brought in.[83]

Clearly the organisational question and the whole concept of bringing together a number of inspectorates with differing histories and traditions were important matters. Equally important for the work of inspectors was the question of the balance between voluntary effort by industry and statutory regulation, and between a further strengthening of the advisory role of inspectorates and an increased emphasis on enforcement of law. The Robens Committee in each case put their main emphasis on the first alternatives, in spite of the new proposals for improvement and prohibition notices. To that extent they followed the CBI more than the TUC. For although both organisations recognised the importance of action within industry itself (although differing on how this was to be achieved), to the TUC this was 'not an alternative to strong safety legislation, strictly enforced'.[84] The CBI on the other hand wanted the legislation to be simplified, with much detail put into codes of practice and a specific recognition of inspectors as expert advisers to industry.[85]

Much discussion of the Robens proposals centred on these questions. As the government spokesman on the 1974 Bill put it, even among those who accepted the scope of the new proposals for legislation and for a unified inspectorate,

> there was anxiety and apprehension about the general philosophy of the report which, to many, seemed to call for a regression from rigorous statutory responsibilities firmly enforced. The Robens message seemed to be too permissive for some of us to stomach . . .[86]

Nevertheless the HSW Act 1974 drew heavily on the Robens philosophy, particularly in proposing that existing legislation and regulations on safety and health at work should be 'progressively replaced by a system of regulations and approved codes of practice', which together with the general provisions of the 1974 Act would aim at maintaining or improving standards of health, safety and welfare established by existing legislation.[87] At the same time the Act put emphasis on the duties of employers, both generally and in particular; for example, they had to prepare written statements of their policy on health and safety and the arrangements for carrying it out.[88] There were also important provisions relating to the involvement of employees in health and safety matters, notably the appointment of safety representatives and committees.[89] Two new bodies were set up by the Act, the Health and Safety Commission (HSC) and the Health and Safety Executive (HSE) and were made responsible for implementing the Act. The HSE in particular had the duty of making adequate arrangements for the enforcement of the legislation.[90]

INSPECTION SINCE 1974

The HSW Act came into force at the beginning of 1975. Its consequences for inspection in factories and mines may be considered under three headings: (1) organisation; (2) nature of the work; (3) accountability.

(1) *Organisation*
An immediate problem was that of the relationship between the different inspectorates now brought together in HSE. Robens had argued for a unified inspectorate, and indeed the logic of the estab-

lishment of HSE seemed to call for such an arrangement. It was, however, ruled out by the terms of the political compromise over the mines inspectorate, as well as by subsequent arguments over the position of the alkali inspectorate.[91] According to the Director General of HSE, it was decided instead to keep 'for the time being' the separate identity of the inspectorates, but to provide for closer working arrangements.[92] The structure of HSE devised to meet this aim was, perhaps inevitably, complex. It was mainly based on functional divisions (hazardous substances, research and planning, etc.) together with divisions representing each of the four major inspectorates (factories, mines and quarries, nuclear installations, alkali and clean air),[93] The heads of all the divisions together with the Director General and his deputy constituted the management board to consider major policy questions and co-ordinate the work of the different divisions.

At the level of day-to-day working arrangements there were increased opportunities for the exchange of expertise and information between different inspectorates, and for rationalisation of visits to avoid duplication. Such opportunities have to be seen in the context of the fact that the largest inspectorate was already in process of a major reorganisation at the time of the HSW Act, occasioned both by the Robens report and by the changed emphasis on priorities referred to below. The essence of this reorganisation was the grouping of the inspectorate in the field into a smaller number of area offices with stronger support from scientific and specialist teams. At the same time, inspectors were to become more expert in the problems of particular industries through the setting up of National Industry Groups for each major industry or group of industries in which they would concentrate on the specific health and safety problems of those industries.[94]

Other inspectors might be housed in the same area offices, but in accordance with the decision to retain separate inspectorates, continued to be responsible to their own chief inspector and not to the area director of the factory inspectorate. Moreover, although they had available to them the specialist advice of the factory inspectorate it was left to them how much they used such facilities. Although therefore there have been closer working arrangements than existed before, the inspectorates have on the whole continued to operate mainly independently of each other.

The difficulties of combining in one organisation bodies with such separate and distinctive traditions is perhaps best illustrated by the attempts to devise common policies on the use of sanctions. Such attempts come up against the further difficulty of trying to lay down general rules and at the same time maintaining the ability of the inspector to use his discretion when confronted with a particular situation in the field. The following table indicates the use made by factory and mines inspectors of the traditional weapon of prosecution as well as the newer improvement and prohibition notices.

Table 4.3 *Number of prosecutions*, improvement notices and prohibition notices, 1962–77*

		Factory			Mines	
Year	Pros.	Imp.	Pro.	Pros.	Imp.	Pro.
1962	1134	—	—	0	—	—
1963	1210	—	—	0	—	—
1964	1496	—	—	0	—	—
1965	1502	—	—	0	—	—
1966	1471	—	—	0	—	—
1967	832	—	—	0	—	—
1968	937	—	—	0	—	—
1969	1058	—	—	0	—	—
1970	1196	—	—	0	—	—
1971	1330	—	—	0	—	—
1972	1547	—	—	0	—	—
1973	1782	—	—	1	—	—
1974	1826	—	—	0	—	—
1975	1433	4189	2208	2	0	0†
1976	1150	4123	1977	0	0†	0
1977	1478	4833	1927	0	0	0†

* For factories, numbers of persons or firms prosecuted, 1962–71, number of cases heard, 1972–76: for mines, figures refer only to coal mines.

† One prohibition notice issued 1975, two improvement notices 1976, one prohibition notice 1977, all in relation to quarries.

Sources: Annual Reports, Chief Inspector of Factories; Divisional Inspectors of Mines and Quarries; HSE, Manufacturing and Service Industries.

Thus in spite of the fact that one of the earliest actions of HSE was to issue general guidelines to inspectors on the use of prosecution there has so far been no noticeable change in practice in the two inspectorates. Furthermore, the factory inspectorate, but not the mines inspectorate, has made considerable use of the new notices.[95]

(2) *Nature of the Work*
As might be expected, the factory inspectorate in particular has been affected by the problems of 'new entrants' that is, the 8 million people brought within the scope of health and safety legislation for the first time by the HSW Act, and by the increased attention paid to the effects of modern technology, as seen for example by the setting up by HSC of an advisory committee on major hazards. Its work has also been much affected by the new and more specific obligations imposed on employers and employees by the HSW Act. The Mines inspector-

ate has been much less affected by these developments. For the factory inspectorate there have been consequences both for the manner of carrying out the work and for the staffing requirements. Even before the Robens Committee had reported, the chief inspector of factories had instituted a new programme of inspection based not on regular inspection at stated intervals, but on a more selective approach which would take into account the numbers of employees, the level of risk and the known performance of the company in health and safety matters. The result was that more time was being spent on inspection of large, high-risk factories and correspondingly less on visiting smaller factories.[96] This tendency to selective inspection has been reinforced by the new legislation.

For example, HSC has suggested four criteria on which the basic inspection programme should be based – present standards of health, safety and welfare; the size and nature of the worst problem which could arise in a particular factory; the ability of management to maintain acceptable standards; and the length of time since the previous visit.[97] An attempt has been made to plan much more systematically than before priorities in the work programme, particularly through five-year rolling programmes. Such attempts encounter the basic difficulty of reconciling different objectives of the inspectorate, especially the specific task of enforcing legal provisions which still remains an important part of the work and the more general provision of advice towards raising standards. Moreover the nature of the legal provisions has changed in view of the more general obligations now imposed by section 2 of the Act, and this is reflected in the fact that a high proportion of the improvement and prohibition notices include a reference to section 2 (1).[98] At the same time many employers find the idea of safety policies backed by an effective safety organisation altogether too novel and continue to see their legal obligations as being to comply with specific requirements.[99]

The factory inspectorate has not only therefore needed more staff, but also a different approach, simultaneously trying to convey the different philosophy behind the HSW Act as compared with the Factories Act, and to develop new techniques for monitoring what the employer does, appraising safety organisations rather than simply seeing that employers conform to specific rules. It means, as a recent report acknowledges, that the inspector will be increasingly drawn into balancing what is appropriately on safety grounds against the degree of risk and the cost of preventive measures.[100]

(3) Accountability
Accountability can be considered from a number of angles. Central inspectorates like those for factories and mines have long been characterised by considerable independence and discretion in the field.

There are therefore problems associated with checks on the use of that discretion, for example by employers who consider that inspectors have exceeded their powers. There are also problems arising from the need for management accountability, that is, for chief inspectors to ensure that individual inspectors carry out a proper and effective programme of work. Finally, there are questions arising about the accountability of the inspectorate as a whole. Once more, these questions arise more acutely in the case of the factory than the mines inspectorate.

As is generally the case with enforcement inspectorates, any person who thinks that an inspector is imposing unreasonable requirements can refuse to act and defend himself in court if as a result the inspector prosecutes him. The HSW Act has made two important changes. Improvement and prohibition notices which require action to be taken by administrative means and not a court order are open to challenge by appeal to an industrial tribunal. On the other hand, where, as is frequently the case, statutory requirements are framed on the basis of something being done 'as far as practicable' or some similar wording, the onus is now on the defence in any court proceedings to show that action was taken as far as practicable.

In practice, there are various constraints on inspectors' actions. So far as prosecutions are concerned, for example, the effort involved in preparing and presenting a case needs to be weighed against the likelihood of its leading to effective action. The case may be dismissed or a fine imposed which is a good deal less than the cost of compliance with the Act.[101] Again, the fact that hardly any appeals are made against improvement and prohibition notices[102] tends to support the view that inspectors are more concerned to take action where they have a strong case than to act too harshly and risk being challenged on the grounds of having acted unreasonably. But the system clearly relies a good deal on the professional integrity and good sense of inspectors.

Similarly, internal accountability has always been a difficult problem because of the need to reconcile administrative discretion in the field with the responsibility for ensuring that the work is carried out adequately and effectively. The new rolling programmes will provide the framework for the use of inspectors' time in relation to the resources available, but the problem is to relate this specifically to work in individual areas. It has proved impossible to do this in precise terms such as a specified work-load for each area.

The HSW Act also made changes in a wider context. Previously, each inspectorate formed part of a government department, but with a good deal of autonomy in its practical operations. The formal position is more complex now. The HSE management board is itself responsible to the HSC on matters of general policy, and the latter is responsible to the Secretary of State for Employment; for example it must submit proposals for carrying out its functions for approval by the Secretary of State and must act on directions given by him.[103] However, probably the main change at the practical level centres on the HSE management board in that each inspectorate may now have to justify its general policy in relation to that of other inspectorates. It cannot assume, for example, that an extreme reluctance to prosecute will go unchallenged. Although, therefore, it is difficult to see that major changes have taken place, some modifications have been made. This is exemplified in the fact that following a serious explosion at Houghton Main Colliery in 1975 the mines inspectorate instituted prosecutions which it almost certainly would not have done before 1974. That the NCB's chief safety engineer was led to comment 'it is difficult to believe that a subsequent prosecution such as Houghton will contribute in any way to safer mines'[104] brings the subject of accountability in its narrower sense into the wider setting of the effectiveness of inspection. Since inspectors are there to act in the public interest we need to examine not only to whom they are directly accountable for the performance of their duties, but whether they are effectively performing the task for which they are appointed. For in a sense that is the ultimate test of their accountability.

EFFECTIVENESS OF INSPECTION

Recent developments, and not just the HSW Act, have not made it any easier to judge the effectiveness of the work of the factory and mines inspectorates. The fact, for example, that the former are using 6,000 to 7,000 improvement and prohibition notices a year does not in itself indicate whether a greater degree of compliance with the Acts is now being achieved, still less whether there has been an improvement generally in health and safety at work. Because of this, arguments for a stronger enforcement policy have by no means ceased. The different philosophy which lies behind this demand as compared with that of HSE can be judged from the comment of two critics who argue that tougher enforcement with substantial fines and a realistic chance of being prosecuted

> would surely lead most firms to pursue a more positive policy of accident prevention, and also to seek the advice of the inspectors more readily.[105]

In practice the views of those who think that too little use is made of the sanctions open to inspectors (or too much)[106] are balanced by inspectors' own judgment of their appropriateness and effectiveness. And in any case qualitative judgments are more necessary, given the fact that we are no longer concerned simply with specific statutory requirements.

The one quantitative measure that exists tends to raise more questions than it answers. Just as it was seen earlier that the fatal accident rate in mines dropped sharply during the nineteenth century, so it can be shown that the fatal accident rate in factories is only a quarter of what it was at the beginning of the century.[107] It is still declining, and the number of deaths in 1977, at 357, was the lowest for a century.[108] Such figures are inadequate as a general measure of the effectiveness of inspection work.

Nor on the other hand do specific instances of the inspectorate's influence help very much in the general assessment. The introduction of the Power Presses Regulations in 1966, for example, led to an immediate reduction in the number of accidents from their use, which would not have happened without the intervention of the factory inspectorate.[109] Similarly the work of the inspectorate in Stoke-on-Trent in demonstrating the possibility of making china without the workers running the risk of contracting silicosis provides another example.[110] But specific examples like this would have to be put alongside the daily routine of inspection, and the consequences which that has had on levels of performance in safety and health matters. Hardest of all to estimate is the influence of inspectorates on changes in the climate of opinion. If trade unions in the 1960s generally showed more interest in health and safety questions, how far was this due to the work of the factory inspectorate and how far to more general considerations, for example, that at a time of full employment and rising prosperity trade unions became more attracted to such questions? If employers in 1970 were more aware of and responsive to safety considerations than they were in 1900 how much has this been due to the efforts of the inspectorates and how far to changes in the structure of industry and to a general spread of ideas of social responsibility?

Although questions like these do not permit precise answers there is no doubt that the inspectorates have acted and continue to act in the belief that they do have a part to play in influencing attitudes. This is particularly evident in the enforcement of the HSW Act. The annual reports now lay stress on the fact that what the ·inspectorates are seeking is a more positive commitment within industry to safety and health questions. But this raises the difficult question of how effectively an inspectorate can achieve what HSC has described as

creating the conditions for more effective interaction between management and workpeople to reduce hazards.[111]

The strategy for promoting these more positive attitudes to health and safety in industry relies heavily on the provision of information, on extensive consultation with both sides of industry by HSC and HSE on new proposals, draft regulations, etc., and on greater involvement in health and safety matters by those who work in industry, especially through the appointment of safety representatives and committees. There is the further question whether, if these methods proved successful, the role of the inspectorate would diminish or become almost exclusively promotional and advisory. The history of the mines inspectorate in the last thirty years offers a partial answer. The creation of the NCB brought an increase in the resources devoted to safety. For example, whereas in 1936 there were only 42 safety officers in the industry serving 1,200 mines, by the 1970s safety staff numbered 400 for 240 mines with a headquarters branch under a chief safety engineer.[112] At the same time, the system of workmen's inspection, first introduced in 1872, was also extended by the NUM and the other unions in the industry. Here then was an industry with a strong concern for safety on the part of both management and unions. What part if any was there in the changed circumstances for an outside inspectorate?

The theoretical answer to this question lies in the fact that the inspectorate by its very nature has a different attitude to safety. Management may be committed to achieving a high level of safety but it has an overriding obligation to produce coal as efficiently and cheaply as possible, whereas the inspectorate's sole concern is with a high standard of safety. To that end mines inspectors are professionally trained, whereas safety staff may well not be.[113] Again the unions' first concern is for the protection of their members and to that end they may well press for safety measures to be taken which go beyond what seems practicable to the inspectorate. The role of the inspector thus becomes akin to that of an arbiter, liable to be criticised sometimes by management for insisting on measures which to them seem unnecessary or at least too costly in relation to the benefits; and sometimes by unions for not pressing hard enough for improvements which to them seem to be called for in the interests of their members.

Behind these theoretical arguments lie unanswered questions. How important is safety in relation to other considerations affecting the running of an industry? Where management is responsible and the unions strongly geared to safety questions could not these questions be left to be largely or entirely settled between them with little or no intervention from an inspectorate? How much influence can an inspectorate now exert on standards of safety in an industry like coal-mining? These questions might have been but were not raised when nationalisation transformed the coal industry. Both the NCB and the unions have remained content with the system, largely because of a strong belief that it has worked and continues to work. Thus not only has there been no incentive to ask fundamental questions about it, but there has been strong resistance to any suggestion of change, as was evident in the negotiations preceding the HSW Act. This resistance extends not simply to the fact of having a separate inspectorate but crucially to the way in which it operates. That safety questions are a matter for negotiation and discussion within the industry between management, the unions and the inspectorate and that they should only in very exceptional circumstances give rise to prosecutions are unquestioned assumptions, as was evident at the time of the Houghton Main prosecutions.

The view that further progress in promoting health and safety at work depends on changing attitudes of employers and employees is not new. It was, for example, a theme of the 1938 Royal Commission on Mines and of annual reports of the chief inspector of factories in the 1920s and 1930s. But the increased emphasis now put upon it raises more sharply the contrast with other approaches to health and safety as well as directing attention to the difficulties of assessing the contribution of inspectors. As long as the work consisted mainly in seeing that specific requirements were met it had a definite and limited content. Progressively it has expanded into less definite areas and laid more stress on the use of persuasion and advice. Correspondingly, it is likely to face greater argument over the direction in which it is going, from those, for example, who believe that there is an incompatibility between the needs of production and safety which cannot be resolved by efforts to promote a change of attitude[114] Inspectors on the other hand frequently stress the preventable nature of many accidents if employers and employees adopt different attitudes.[115] Such fundamental differences of view are made harder to resolve by the absence of any measures of progress beyond the crude figures of accidents. They do emphasise, however, the fact that the onus is much more on inspectors now to demonstrate the effectiveness of their approach. The establishment of the APAU is in a sense a symbol of this changed situation; it is seeking the answers to questions which the inspectorate was not under challenge to answer before.

This latter point perhaps provides the clue to much of the discussion in this chapter. In the long history of the factory and mines inspectorates their effectiveness was unchallenged as long as they were seen to be seeking to ensure that specific statutory requirements were met. The doubts which arose in the case of the factory inspectorate led to two different and incompatible pressures, for more inspectors enforcing the law more strictly, or to a different approach to health and safety. That both pressures arose from the same cause, a feeling that more ought to be done about health and safety, in fact shows how little had been done to try to demonstrate how effective existing measures were. The inclination of the inspectorate itself towards placing great reliance on industry itself taking more positive steps to secure health and safety was in part a response to the pressures, and especially the increasing concern and dissatisfaction about the situation expressed by the trade unions; but it needed the endorsement of the Robens Committee to make it effective.

However, the combination of increased public concern over health and safety at work and the much broader responsibilities of inspectors in promoting it through the endorsement of safety policies and organisation will increasingly put on them the onus to explain and justify their activities to a far greater extent than was necessary in the past. It will also be harder for them to do this than it was when their concern was largely limited to the enforcement of specific statutory requirements. It is significant that the Director General of HSE recently posed the question:

How far and, more important, in what circumstances is the most effective way of dealing with hazards: to strengthen legislative controls, to increase workplace visits by inspectors, to invest more in research or in our publicity campaigns drawing attention to the risks and giving guidance on how to overcome them?

And even more significant is the answer he gave:

At present our decisions must be based largely on subjective judgments but we hope progressively to develop the study of techniques for evaluating the effects of what we do.[116]

In the past the lack of any effective measure of the work of factory and mines inspectorates hampered judgment of the extent to which they were successful in carrying out the tasks which legislation put on them. Faith in the use of inspection together with, especially in the mines, some generally favourable statistics about death rates seemed largely to satisfy critics who in any case put their trust for the most part in more inspection. It would have been difficult to be precise about the contribution made by inspectors to improvements in health and safety conditions, but in any case it was not necessary to be precise since there was no fundamental challenge to the principle of inspection.

All that is no longer true. We need to be satisfied that what the inspectors are doing measures up to the needs for improved health and safety, and is having an effect in proportion to the effort devoted to it. In that sense we cannot be sure at present that inspectors are being made ultimately accountable to the public interest which they must serve. We have to rely too much on subjective judgments. They will not be adequate in the future when so much reliance is being placed on action within industry rather than external controls.

NOTES: CHAPTER 4

1 Strictly speaking, their titles are 'Her Majesty's Factory Inspectorate' and 'Her Majesty's Inspectorate of Mines and Quarries'. The somewhat inaccurate titles in the text are used throughout for brevity, and because, in the case of the latter inspectorate, the distinctive problems of inspecting quarries are not dealt with.
2 Subsequently referred to for brevity as 'HSW Act'.
3 The mines inspectorate was transferred to the Mines Department, Board of Trade, in 1920, the factory inspectorate to the Ministry of Labour in 1940. Both, under the HSW Act, became constituent parts of the Health and Safety Executive in 1975.
4 See, for factories, B.L. Hutchins and A. Harrison, *A History of Factory Legislation* (London, 1902); M.W. Thomas, *The Early Factory Legislation* (Thames Bank, 1948); for mines, MacDonagh, op. cit., and Sir Andrew Bryan, *The Evolution of Health and Safety in Mines* (Ashire Publishing, 1975).
5 An inspector was appointed under an earlier Act of 1842 but he had a limited role.
6 Cf. Hutchins and Harrison, op. cit., p. 109.
7 In the report of the Factories Inquiry Commission which preceded the 1833 Act (PP 1833, XX), pp. 68–9.
8 See T.K. Djang, *Factory Inspection in Great Britain* (Allen & Unwin, 1942) for a brief account of these developments.
9 *Report of the Committee on Safety and Health at Work* (Robens Committee) (Cmnd 5034, HMSO, 1972), para. 226.
10 Thomas, op. cit., p. 259.
11 Minutes of evidence (C 1443–I, PP 1876, XXX), question 495.
12 See MacDonagh, op. cit., p. 76.
13 *Report of Factory and Workshops Acts Commission* (C 1443, PP 1876, XXIX), para. 251.
14 *Report of Chief Inspector of Factories and Workshops for 1895* (C 8067, PP 1896, XIX), p.5.
15 C 1987, PP 1878, LXI, ss.2 and 3.
16 The instructions are in PRO Lab 15/8, general instructions 8.
17 C 1987, s.2.
18 C 1443, para. 251.
19 C 8068, 1896, appendix 3A.
20 Unpublished report of committee on factory staff, 1904 (copy on PRO Lab 14/173.).
21 Unpublished report on the staffing and organisation of the factory inspectorate 1920 (copy on PRO Lab 14/333).
22 *Report of the departmental committee on the factory inspectorate* (HMSO, 1929), paras 24 and 25.
23 *Staffing and organisation of the factory inspectorate* (Cmd 9879, 1956), para. 40.
24 ibid., paras 41–3.
25 In 1938 prosecutions relating to employment still formed 48 per cent of the total, those relating to safety only 27 per cent but by 1950 45 per cent related to safety and a further 29 per cent to offences under special regulations (i.e. mainly safety questions), but only 18 per cent to employment.
26 HC Deb 4th series, vol. 190, 3 June 1908, col. 147.
27 *Report of Departmental Committee on Accidents in Places under the Factory and Workshop Acts* (Cd 5533, 1911), p.28, 51.
28 ibid., p.51.

29 *Report of Chief Inspector of Factories and Workshops for the year 1913* (Cd 7491, 1914), p. 18.
30 ibid., pp. 163, 184.
31 Cmd 2903 (1927), p. 14.
32 HC Deb 173, 15 May 1924, cols 1592–4.
33 HC Deb 187, 28 July 1925, col. 347.
34 *Report of committee* (HMSO, 1929), para. 28.
35 ibid., para. 42. These standards continued to be the ones at which the inspectorate aimed until they were modified in the mid-1950s.
36 Annual report for 1932 (Cmd 4377, 1933), p.9.
37 cf. annual reports for 1930 (Cmd 3927, 1931), p.5; and for 1936 (Cmd 5514, 1937), p.22.
38 *Report of Royal Commission on Safety in Coal Mines* (Cmd 5890, 1938), pp. 6, 7.
39 ibid., p.112; cf. HC Deb 187, 28 July 1925, cols 265–83.
40 There were and still are a number of small coalmines worked under licence from the NCB by private owners, but for most practical purposes the industry can be regarded as being under one ownership (excluding the problems of mines working minerals others than coal).
41 *Annual Report of HM Chief Inspector of Factories* (AR) 1951 (Cmd 8772, 1953), pp.13, 14, 16.
42 AR, 1961 (Cmnd 1816, 1962), p.8.
43 AR, 1962 (Cmnd 2128, 1963), p.8.
44 AR, 1963 (Cmnd 2450, 1964), pp. 8, 9.
45 ibid., p. 47.
46 e.g., AR 1966 (Cmnd 3358, 1967), p. 7, 8; AR 1967 (Cmnd 3745, 1968), p. x.
47 AR 1963, p. 25
48 AR 1966, p.7.
49 AR 1967, p. xiii.
50 See, for example, *Occupational Accidents and the Law* (Fabian Society Research Series, 280, 1970).
51 AR 1967, p.xi.
52 AR 1966, p.9.
53 AR 1969, p. xiv; 1971, pp. ix–x; 1973, p. xi.
54 AR 1967, p. xii.
55 AR 1968 (Cmnd 4146, 1969), p. xviii.
56 John L. Williams, *Accidents and Ill-Health at Work* (Staples Press, 1960), ch. 8, especially pp. 141–3.
57 For example, the need to extend the legislation to bring in those not covered by it.
58 See, for example, HC Deb 619, 14 March 1960, col. 902; 644, 12 July 1961, cols 372–3; 648, 8 November 1961, WA 61; 654, 26 February 1962, WA 97.
59 For a forceful expression of this view see the evidence of W.H. Thompson to the Robens Committee (Written Evidence, pp. 656–69).
60 AR 1969 (Cmnd 4461, 1970), pp. xii, xiii.
61 This information is taken from W.G. Carson, 'White-collar crime and the enforcement of factory legislation', *British Journal of Criminology*, October 1970, pp. 383–98.
62 The Law Commission: Published Working Paper No. 30, *Strict Liability and the Enforcement of the Factories Act, 1961* (Law Commission, 1970), p.21.
63 *Third Report of the Parliamentary Commissioner for Administration, Session 1975–76* (HC 259, 1976), pp. 189–211.
64 ibid., p.209.
65 The fact that management were regarded as generally co-operative at Acre Mill was a factor in influencing attitudes to prosecution, as indeed it was generally in the inspectorate (HC 259, p. 205, para. 44; p. 206, paras 46–7).
66 AR 1968 (Cmnd 4146, 1969), p. 9.

67 HC 259, p. 199, para. 31.
68 It was entitled 'Ministry of Labour, New Safety, Health and Welfare Legislation: First Consultative Document'.
69 Williams (op. cit., p.481) had advocated a single government department respon sible for health and safety; the Fabian report (op. cit., p.10) a single safety code enforced by a single inspectorate.
70 For example, the report on the crane accident at Brent Cross in 1964 (Cmnd 2678, 1975); similarly, the report on the Aberfan disaster in 1966 (HC 553, 1967) suggested that the mines inspectorate should be concerned with the safety of people living near mine tips.
71 The NII was (and is) concerned with hazards to workers as well as the general public arising from the operation of nuclear reactors.
72 Cmd 5890, 1938, pp.84, 86.
73 Report of the Committee on Safety and Health at Work, Vol. 2, Selected Written Evidence (HMSO, 1972), p. 377. There were twenty-three prosecutions in the ten years 1948–57 but only nine in the seventeen years 1958–74.
74 cf. Bryan, op. cit., pp. 61–5.
75 Robens Committee, vol. 2, pp. 419–20. This latter figure was a cause of concern, although more attention tended to be paid to deaths and serious injuries (cf. Williams, op. cit., pp. 31–6).
76 Bryan, op. cit., p. 101.
77 Cmnd 5034, paras. 209–13.
78 ibid., ch. 1.
79 ibid., ch. 4 and paras 204, 205; the six were factories, mines and quarries, agriculture, explosives, nuclear installations and alkali and clean air.
80 ibid., paras 269–77.
81 Mr Michael Foot on Second Reading of the HSW Bill (HC Deb 871, 3 April 1974), cols 1292–4.
82 ibid., col. 1287.
83 The Bill was originally prepared under the Conservative administration and reintroduced by the Labour government after the election of February 1974; the agricultural inspectorate was transferred to the Health and Safety Executive under the Employment Protection Act 1975.
84 Written Evidence, Committee on Safety and Health at Work, p. 671.
85 ibid., p. 111.
86 Mr Harold Walker (Under Secretary, Department of Employment), HC Deb 871, 3 April 1974, col. 1393.
87 Health and Safety at Work [etc.] Act 1974, s. 1(2).
88 ibid., s. 2(1), (3).
89 ibid., s. 2(4)–(7).
90 ibid., s.18.
91 See below, Chapter 6.
92 Health and Safety Commission Report 1974—76 (HMSO, 1977), p. 24, para. 9.
93 The explosives inspectorate was for practical purposes absorbed into the factory inspectorate; the agricultural inspectorate became a sub division of the safety policy division.
94 AR 1974 (Cmnd 6322, 1975), pp. ix–xi.
95 Mines inspectors already had power to impose restrictions or prohibitions in cases of danger (Mines and Quarries Act 1954, s. 146) but there is no reference to the powers being used in recent annual reports. It is also worth noting that local authorities have made considerable use of the new powers; for example, in 1977 local authorities initiated 94 prosecutions under the 1974 Act and issued 3020 improvement notices and 464 prohibition notices (HSE: Manufacturing and Service Industries 1977, appendix 1, table 7).
96 AR 1973 (Cmnd 5708, 1974), pp. ix–x.

97 *HSC Report 1976—77* (HMSO, 1978), paras 97, 98.
98 *Health and Safety: Manufacturing and Service Industries 1977* (HMSO, 1978), p.3.
99 *Health and Safety: Manufacturing and Service Industries 1976* (HMSO, 1978), p. 5 and ch. 2: 1977, p.4, para. 19; p.5, para. 33.
100 *Health and Safety: Manufacturing and Service Industries 1976* (HMSO, 1978), p.vi.
101 cf. Law Commission, Strict Liability and the Enforcement of the Factories Act 1961, paras 61–3.
102 *Health and Safety: Industry and Services 1975* (HMSO, 1977), p. 8.
103 HSW Act 1974, ss. 11 (3), 2.
104 J.L. Collinson, 'Managing health and safety in a period of change', Institute of Mining Engineers, Symposium on Health, Safety and Progress, 1976.
105 Denis Gregory and Joe McCarty, *The Shop Steward's Guide to Workplace Health and Safety* (Spokesman Books and Ruskin Trade Union Research Unit, 1975), p. 43.
106 cf. CBI Evidence to Robens (Selected Written Evidence, p. 126).
107 AR 1973 (Cmnd 5708, 1974), p.xiii.
108 *Health and Safety: Manufacturing and Service Industries 1977* (HMSO, 1978), p.1, Table B. Similarly death rates in mining are still declining (*Health and Safety: Mines and Quarries 1977*, HMSO, 1978, appendix 2, table 1).
109 The number of accidents was: 1964 – 503; 1965 – 450; 1966 – 353; 1967 – 230 (AR 1967, pp. 22–4).
110 I owe this example to Mr Bryan Harvey, former Chief Inspector of Factories.
111 *HSC Report 1977–78* (HMSO, 1978), p.1.
112 J.L. Collinson, op. cit.
113 ibid. In fact the whole article is a plea for a more professional approach to the management of health and safety.
114 See Theo Nichols and Pete Armstrong, *Safety or Profit* (Falling Wall Press Ltd, Bristol, 1976).
115 A particular case is the construction industry (see, for example, *Construction: Health and Safety 1976*, HMSO, 1978, pp. 30–4).
116 *Health and Safety Commission Report 1976—77* (HMSO, 1978), p. 16.

CHAPTER 5
INSPECTION IN SCHOOLS

More perhaps has been written about the inspection of schools than about any other kind of inspection. Partly this is because the history of education in this country has attracted much interest and inspection is very much a part of that history: partly it is because inspectors and ex-inspectors are highly articulate and have contributed their own writings on the subject ever since the days of H.S. Tremenheere and Matthew Arnold. Nevertheless, for reasons which will become apparent, this does not necessarily make it any easier to chart the changing role of the inspector of schools than that of the weights and measures or factory inspector. Two general points need to be made at the outset about the scope of this chapter. It deals only with inspection of schools as opposed to other institutions such as technical colleges, and it is restricted to England and to some degree Wales, rather than Scotland. This emphasis is simply to make the discussion manageable. Inspection of Scottish schools in particular would require a separate chapter.

THE AIMS OF SCHOOL INSPECTION: THE NINETEENTH CENTURY

It seems easy enough at first sight to establish the purpose for which schools inspectors were originally appointed. Government in 1839 offered grants towards the building of schools: inspection was the means of controlling the use of such public funds, of seeing whether they were being used for the purpose and in the manner intended by government. From the beginning this was a true but an inadequate description of what inspection was intended to do. The grants were at first administered by a committee of the Privy Council, and inspectors were, and still are, formally appointed by Order in Council and therefore known as 'Her Majesty's Inspectors' (HMI). The instructions from the committee to the first two inspectors in 1840 made it clear that although they were to visit the schools 'to ascertain that the grant has in each case been duly applied' they were also to provide information on the work of the schools and to give:

> the promoters of schools an opportunity of ascertaining, at the periodical visits of inspection, what improvements in the apparatus and internal arrangements of schools, in school management and discipline, and in the methods of teaching, have been sanctioned by the most extensive experience.[1]

Thus three elements seem to be present in these original inspection arrangements:
(1) a check on the use of public funds; (2) provision of information to the central authority; (3) provision of advice to those responsible for running the schools. The importance of this third element as against the idea of supervision and control present in the other two was stressed in the instructions, since inspection

> is not to be regarded as operating for the restraint of local efforts, but for their encouragement.[2]

The role of the inspectors in those early days has to be viewed against the background of government intervention in education. The government grant was a device for the encouragement of education without direct government involvement in the running of schools. The latter was left to the churches, largely acting through the National Society (Church of England) and the British and Foreign School Society (nonconformist). It was therefore, an open question at the beginning how far government encouragement should go, and, correspondingly, what part the inspectors should play. If government had simply been content to leave the initiative to the societies, providing money in response to their requests, the inspectors could have been limited to, first, seeing that applications for grants were justifiable in accordance with the rules governing their provision; and, secondly, verifying, by later visits, that the grants had been properly spent. That the role of the schools inspectors was from the outset broader than this is generally attributed to the influence of the first secretary of the Committee of Council on Education, Dr Kay (later Sir James Kay-Shuttleworth), who saw grants as a means to achieving greater efficiency in education and looked forward to a time when education would be universal.[3]

Nevertheless, given that there was no statutory basis for these early government grants or for the appointment of inspectors, the basic justification for the use of the latter was regulatory; the right of inspection was insisted on from those seeking grants

> in order to secure a conformity to the regulations and discipline established in the several schools.[4]

This was emphasised even more when to the original capital grants were added annual grants for books and equipment. Inspectors' reports became the basis on which such grants were paid.

However, the further development of inspection in schools was affected by external pressures concerned with the state of education. The (Newcastle) Royal Commission appointed in 1858 as a result of dissatisfaction with the state of education recommended a system of grants directly related to such things as the attendance record of pupils, and the results of examinations in reading, writing and arithmetic, as a means to achieving greater efficiency in the provision of education.[5] It was on this basis that Robert Lowe, Vice-President of the Council, introduced in 1862 new rules for the giving of grants for elementary education, the well-known Revised Code,[6] and its system of 'payment by results'.

From the point of view of the role of school inspectors, the main change introduced by the 1862 code was in the annual grants. The greater part of such grants now depended on the results of an annual examination of all children over the age of 8, and since these examination were to be conducted by the inspectors this now became their major task. The effect was to make more prominent the functions of control and provision of information and to make less prominent the function of advice and encouragement.

After 1862, and more especially after the Elementary Education Act 1870 established school boards, there was a rapid increase in the number of schools, with consequences for the size of the inspectorate. The original two inspectors of 1840 had become twenty-three by 1850 and sixty-two by 1860. Thereafter the increase for elementary education alone was very rapid.

Table 5.1 *Numbers of inspectors and children and students in institutions inspected*

Year	No. of inspectors elem. schools and training colleges	No. of children in public elem. schools ('000s)	No. of students in training colleges
1864–5	84	1,240	2,106
1869–70	98	1,693	2,097
1879–80	245	3,896	3,112
1889–90	306	4,804	3,294
1899–1900	351	5,686	5,234

Figures relate to England and Wales, and exlude inspectors in other branches of the Education Department (27 in 1899–1900).
Source: Board of Education Report 1922–3, p.45.

Not surprisingly, one of the most obvious consequences of the introduction of the Revised Code was its effect on the relationship between the inspector and individual teachers. Before 1862 the relationship had been on the whole a good one, with teachers welcoming the advice inspectors were able to give. It was difficult if not impossible to maintain this when so much turned on the individual examinations after 1862. As a later Secretary of the Education Department put it:

imagine the feelings of the unfortunate teacher when he looked over the inspector's shoulder and saw the failures being recorded wholesale, and knew that his annual salary was being reduced by two and eightpence for each failure.[7]

THE INSPECTORATE, 1902–44

The Revised Code continued to operate until 1895. In the following years the annual examination was abandoned. According to the Board of Education the system was breaking down under its own weight, and it would have been impossible to continue it without a large increase in the number of inspectors.[8] But there were other changes taking place which combined to establish the inspectorate on a new footing from the end of the nineteenth century. The most significant change was the establishment of local education authorities under the Education Act 1902 who took over the work of the School Boards and also became responsible for ensuring that there was adequate secondary education in their areas. The Board of Education was itself established in 1899 bringing together the work of the Education and Science and Art Departments, each with its own inspectorates. Thus almost simultaneously there had to be faced the problems of what kind of inspection should take place in elementary schools to replace that under the Revised Code, and what kind of inspectorate was appropriate to the changed circumstances of the scope and administration of education.

The answers which were evolved to these questions in the early years of the century effectively determined the role of the inspectorate for over half a century. The Department has always stressed the continuity of aims in inspection. The Board of Education's 1922–23 Report quoted with approval the 1840 statement of the inspector's tasks;[9] the Ministry of Education in 1950 said of the aims of inspection:

they differ hardly at all in essentials from those envisaged by the great man who was the first to hold the position of Secretary to the Committee of Council on Education, Sir James Kay-Shuttleworth.[10]

And in 1976 the Senior Chief Inspector told the House of Commons Expenditure Committee that the role of HMI had not changed but only its 'style' and 'mode of operation'.[11]

Yet even if it is true that there has been continuity of aims, this does not mean that each aim has always had the same degree of priority, still less that the way in which the aims have been viewed in practice and the methods of achieving them have remained the same. The main questions which therefore need to be considered are not only what the inspector was expected to do and how, but also what were the factors making for change.

The formal position did not change greatly. Under the 1870 Act one of the statutory conditions had been that elementary schools were to be 'open at all times to the inspection of any of Her Majesty's Inspectors'.[12] The 1902 Act was less explicit, and the inspectors' authority stemmed from the fact that local education authorities (LEAs) now had specific duties laid on them and could obtain central government grants only by complying with the Board's requirements. The basic justification of employing inspectors, therefore, was, as it had always been, to see that value for money was being obtained for the expenditure of taxpayers' money. The circumstances were, however, different now that grant was paid to LEAs rather than to individual schools. Although inspectors still had to certify that specified requirements had been met when they inspected schools, the direct link between payment of grant and standards in that school no longer applied. Inspection of individual schools gradually became less a matter of seeing whether the way in which that school operated justified central government in using taxpayers' money to support it, and much more a matter of seeing, first, whether standards in a particular LEA area were satisfactory; and secondly, by implication, whether the country was getting value for the money spent on education.

The existence of LEAs was particularly important in its effect on the work of schools inspectors. One illustration is the fact that some of the larger LEAs developed their own inspectorial and advisory services, as indeed some of the School Boards had done. A Board of Education survey in 1922, inspired largely by Treasury criticism of the risk of overlapping and waste in having two sets of inspectors, concluded that for the most part LEA inspectors had quite a different job, mainly administrative or concerned with organising particular subjects such as physical training.

However, where, as in London and a few other large authorities, there was a comparatively large inspection staff, fewer HMIs were needed and systematic detailed inspection of elementary schools was not carried out by them.[13] In this the Board seemed to be acknowledging that inspection of standards in individual schools was not necessarily or exclusively a function for a central inspectorate. The practical implications for the role of HMIs was not very great in 1923, when few authorities had large well-staffed inspection services, but their existence nevertheless emphasised that the educational system now had three main elements – the central department, the LEAs and the individual schools and teachers.

Inspectors of schools did not, however, become inspectors of education services. The Board of Education and its successors did not have or seek the power to lay down what education authorities should do and how they should do it. On the other hand it had considerable power to influence what was done, notably through its use of the grant system. Specific grants in particular were seen as a means of promoting educational development and were for this reason long preferred to block grants.[14] It was clearly essential to the Board's view of its relationship to LEAs that it should have some regular means of contact with them. This task was one of those entrusted to inspectors, 'intermediaries' between central department and local authorities, as one Permanent Secretary called them, keeping the Board informed on important matters of local administration and policy.[15] The district Inspector having this function was to be the 'eye and ear of the Board' but 'must be neither meddlesome nor stand aloof'.[16]

It remained true, however, that a large part of the inspectors' work was the visiting of schools. One change here was the growth in the number of secondary schools after 1902, with the consequent need to devise suitable methods of inspection for them. One method was the 'full inspection' in which a number of inspectors (two to eight) spent several days on the inspection of a single school, at the end of which they produced a detailed report. According to the Board, the object was to examine the circumstances and aims of the school, to see what measure of success it had had and to find what could be done to help it. Full inspections were supposed to take place at intervals of about five years.[17]

More explicitly, inspection of schools served two purposes:

> to see that a standard, and a rising standard, of general efficiency is being attained, and that the sums voted by Parliament for the purpose . . . are fruitfully expended.

and to make known 'what was being done throughout the whole country' and as far as possible to improve it.[18] The concern with standards thus lies at the heart of inspection whether conceived narrowly in value-for-money terms or in more broadly promotional terms.

Inspection work in schools and liaison work with LEAs were major elements contributing to a further distinguishable activity of inspectors. They were the expert educational advisers of the Board of Education. Their experience and knowledge of what was happening in the educational world led to their being asked for information and advice on educational questions.

The advantages to the Board of having a field force or 'outdoor staff' both for liaison purposes with LEAs and for providing information on and giving assistance to the schools was made clear in the Board's

UNIVERSITY COLLEGE LIBRARY CARDIFF

evidence to the Royal Commission on the Civil Service of 1929–31.[19] Yet again we also need to know the relative importance of these various functions at different times as well as how they were carried out. The problem confronting anyone looking at the rôle of the inspectorate in the twentieth century is twofold; not only to answer these questions but to discover how answers to them were arrived at, to decide not only what inspection policy was at any given time but how it was determined.

The second part is the more difficult to answer. The inspectorate was part of the Board of Education but like other central inspectorates it had a large part in determining the scope of its work, just as inspectors in the field had a good deal of discretion in interpreting their duties. That the Board's administrators could however hold firm views and put pressure on the inspectorate is illustrated by the following. In 1922 Sir L.A. Selby-Bigge, the Permanent Secretary, questioned whether too much emphasis was being put on full inspections in secondary schools and made a number of suggestions for improving the way in which inspection was carried out. For example, he wanted more inspection of below-average schools, more subject inspection as opposed to inspection of individual schools, less elaborate but more critical reports and more reliance on sampling the work of schools. The criticisms drew a spirited reply from the chief inspector of secondary schools, Mr W.C. Fletcher, which is interesting not only for the different view expressed (he was, for example, clearly sceptical about the value of subject inspection), but for its different philosophical attitude to inspection. To the charge, for example, that there were large gaps in the department's knowledge he replied

> I think that reliance can very safely be placed on the general knowledge of their schools now possessed by the district inspector,

and if the Board wanted information on the teaching of particular subjects staff inspectors could give it, though they were hardly ever asked for such information.[20]

However, it was not so much formal interventions of this kind by the Permanent Secretary as the growing need of 'the Office'.[21] for information on educational matters which brought about increased contact between the administrative side of the department and the inspectorate, with consequences for the work of the inspectors. Already in the 1920s it was noted that the administrative duties of inspectors were increasing, that they were from time to time asked to use their personal influence to deal with difficulties which had arisen in dealings with LEAs, and that responsibility had been devolved on them for settling matters which could be better dealt with locally and personally than by correspondence.[22] By 1950 the inspector continually receives references from the Ministry on all sorts of topics. It may be some question of the adaptation of buildings or some problem arising from re-organisation or some general inquiry about the incidence of homework or teaching about UNESCO,

and in all these cases not only facts but judgments were being sought.[23]

Yet if the liaison, information and expert adviser sides of the inspector's role were tending to increase in the first half of this century, it was nevertheless true that for most inspectors their work in the schools and in particular the advice and help which they could offer remained for them the dominant part of the work. It is significant that an inspector who began work in 1933 and retired in 1966 has argued that an inspector of his generation and one starting in 1966 would agree

that their first task was to visit schools, and that what they did when they got there must be for each individual to decide. Their first aim would be to look into what was happening, the work being done, the human relationships, the appropriateness and use of the building and equipment, everything in fact with the further aims of helping the teachers in any way in which they needed help and of satisfying themselves that the children were receiving as good an education as possible. They would not separate in their minds the functions of inspection and advice, consultation and discussion, and would feel that to advise without first of all having inspected, or set up as consultants without free discussion first, would be intolerably arrogant.[24]

Such a view of the inspector's role put a great deal of weight on his personal qualities. Since he was not applying fixed standards or using specific powers of enforcement, and had no direct sanctions which he could apply to a particular school or teacher, his influence depended on an unwritten authority and powers of persuasion rather than on the kind of legal backing which in the last resort other inspectors, like those of factories, could call on. Although it is hardly possible to measure such qualities, there was a general assumption until at least the 1950s that the contribution of HMIs in education was a valuable one. There might from time to time be questions about the methods they used or the way in which they were recruited,[25] but hardly anyone queried the need for inspectors or doubted that they were a valuable if not an essential part of the educational scene. Very largely this view rested on their role in inspecting schools and the contribution they made to improving standards rather than on their other functions.

INSPECTION SINCE 1944: INCREASED IMPORTANCE OF NATIONAL ISSUES

The role of the inspectorate in the post-war years, and in particular in the last ten years, needs to be seen in the context of general educational development and its consequences for the central department. The Education Act 1944 was for twenty years the accepted basis for educational policy-making, and this was a period of practically uninterrupted growth in education. The last fifteen years have seen much more controversy about education policy. A more explicitly egalitarian approach, exemplified in the drive towards comprehensive secondary education and in the establishment of Educational Priority Areas, was marked by the election of a Labour Government in 1964. This in turn provoked much debate over the quality of educational standards, of which the 'great debate' of 1976–77 was in some sense a culmination; it also led to a breakdown in the consensus approach to educational problems which had been a characteristic feature of the years 1944–64. The favourable conditions for the expansion of education in that period might well have been slowed by these more explicit and public controversies over the direction in which education should be going.[26] But in any case a critical look was made more certain by the deepening economic crisis of the 1970s, even before the election of a Conservative Government in 1979 committed to a sharp reduction in public expenditure.

Against this general background needs to be set the part played by the central department in the development of educational policies. The department has played a very active role, but largely on the basis of co-operation with LEAs rather than rigid central control, promoting rather than imposing its views.[27] At the same time, it has also been pointed out that 'the objectives and values underlying policies' were not explicitly stated.[28] The breakdown of consensus over educational policies coincided with attempts at a more systematic approach to the determination of objectives and policies, as, for example, in the establishment of a planning branch in DES in 1966.

The formal position of inspectors was scarcely more explicit after 1944 than it had been before. The Minister (now Secretary of State) is required under section 77 of the 1944 Act to 'cause inspections to be made' of educational premises, but no indication is given of the purpose of such inspections. Once more, therefore, everything turns on how this obligation is interpreted in practice. In the light of what has been said above it is possible to identify two possible sets of influence on the work of the inspectorate, especially in the last ten years or so: (1) external pressures, deriving particularly from the concern with standards of education; (2) internal pressures connected with their part in the policy-making process within DES. In 1968 the House of Commons Select Committee on Education and Science carried out an inquiry into the inspectorate. At that date there was little indication of the influence of either of the two factors on the work of the inspectorate. Yet there had been some changes since the war: for example, a decline in the use of regular, formal inspections, and especially full inspections; an extension of activities other than inspection, such as the publication programme and provision of courses for teachers; and a decline in the numbers of inspectors since a peak reached in the 1950s. Perhaps of more significance was the fact that a variety of views was expressed to the Select Committee on the role of inspectors.

Much of this discussion centred on a contrast between inspection and advice and on the question whether the title 'inspector' was a misnomer. The National Union of Teachers, for example, quoted a 1961 resolution of their annual conference calling on the Ministry of Education to replace the inspectorate by an advisory service for schools.[29] More explicitly, the National Association of Schoolmasters wanted inspection abandoned, but saw no objection to having a group of advisers with the right to visit schools who could make known worthwhile new developments, advise schools on difficulties and give professional advice to the Secretary of State.[30]

It is quite clear from the evidence and from the report of the committee itself that the word inspection is used in the sense of a critical examination in detail of a particular school. In considering for example, the role of local authority inspectors (or advisers as most of them were called), the possibility was raised that they might gradually take over the work of inspection from HMIs. At the same time it was not disputed that the Secretary of State needed to have the right to go into schools.[31] The committee were much impressed by the fact that there were about four times as many LEA inspectors/advisers as there were HMIs[32] and this was one reason why they saw an increased role for the former in inspection since HMIs were too few in number to carry out detailed inspections regularly. At the same time the DES also encouraged the idea that eventually, perhaps in fifty years' time, all inspection might be carried out by local authorities.[33]

What was only indirectly brought out by the 1968 report and was to some extent disguised by the contrast drawn between inspection and advice was the familiar problem of priorities. The main tasks of inspectors might remain much the same but priorities and methods might change. The fact that formal inspections were declining meant that more emphasis was being put on general surveys or surveys of particular aspects of education. This could be seen either as a move away from the function of assisting the individual school and in the direction of providing more information to the Secretary of State, or as simply a different means of providing information, as the DES hinted.[34] The reasons for the change were not made explicit, and the antithesis between inspection and advice disguised the fact that inspection could serve more than one purpose and might be conducted in an advisory or a regulatory mode.

In fact, in 1968 the reasons for the changes in the activities of inspectors were somewhat complex. Externally, the increased professionalism of teachers since the war, and the strengthened position of many LEAs, made it less easy and less necessary to carry out as much formal inspection. At the same time, the change in the nature of the information provided by HMIs was perhaps the beginning of a recognition that changing conditions might require the DES to have a firmer basis of knowledge, with possible implications, as the Select Committee hinted,[35] for a closer involvement of the inspectorate in policy-making. Certainly the 1970s have seen a strengthening of the emphasis on the national and informational role of the inspectorate rather than its role in relation to individual schools, and have also brought to the fore the problems of involving it more in departmental policy-making. The national emphasis is evident in a speech to the Council of Local Education Authorities in July 1977 by the Senior Chief Inspector, Miss Sheila Browne. She suggested that the characteristics of the service provided by HMIs were: that it was an information service for the Secretary of State and the DES concerned with establishing generalisations 'which may be of use to those who take decisions or make policy at national level'; that it was professionally independent; and that it encouraged good education both nationally and in individual schools.[36]

Outward evidence of the inspectorate's increasing concern with national issues can also be found in its recent publications. There was, for example, the Education Survey series in which particular subjects were examined on the basis of surveys carried out by HMIs.[37] More recently there has been the series of papers called 'Matters for Discussion',[38] and such ad hoc discussion papers as 'Curriculum 11–16' which is referred to later. In the late 1970s, even more general surveys of primary and secondary education were launched.[39]

There were specific reasons for this increasing emphasis on a national approach. For example, the process of strengthening the local authority advisory services, which had been going on for some time, received impetus from local government reform in 1974 since that offered both the occasion and the opportunity for the new authorities to review their policy in this area. Local authority advisers have significantly different functions from HMIs but in terms of providing support and advice to individual schools and teachers they are in one sense better placed than HMIs – there are more of them and they can be more often in the schools than HMIs could hope to be. Again, teachers, with their increased professional status, had other sources of advice than HMIs. The Schools Council, for example, set up in 1964 as an advisory body for the curriculum questions.[40] Its governing body was dominated by representatives of teachers' organisations.[41]

Of greater importance, however, were the political pressures resulting from the breakdown of the consensus on educational policies. These were most obviously seen at the time of the Yellow Book and the great debate on education. The Yellow Book itself was produced by DES in response to a request from the Prime Minister, which itself resulted from the increased public concern over educational standards.[42] Two major questions dealt with were whether the criticisms of the educational system were justified, and to the extent that they were what could or should be done about them. On both scores there was implicitly a key role for the inspectorate, described in the Yellow Book as

> without doubt the most powerful single agency to influence what goes on in schools, both in kind and standard.

For although it stopped short of endorsing the most fundamental criticisms, the Yellow Book did implicitly recognise that there was substance in them by proposing in effect that there should be a greater central involvement in questions of the curriculum and methods of teaching, and this would inevitably mean a stronger role for the inspectorate, for example,

> to try to establish generally accepted principles for the composition of the secondary curriculum for all pupils.

For this purpose it would not need additional powers but should, in relation to LEAs, 'use a more direct style, particularly on specialist matters'. This aspect of the Yellow Book has been seen as almost amounting to the inspectorate casting doubt on the methods which it had been using for forty years or more,[43] but in the subsequent public debate, in which the curriculum figured prominently, the inspectorate deprecated any idea that it wanted to impose its ideas on others. The foreword to a volume of papers on the curriculum published subsequently was disarmingly modest:

> They take their place along with all the other writings about the curriculum and with them may contribute to discussion about how schools implement their purposes. They are not meant to be read at a sitting; they are intended to be thought and argued about, dipped into and tried out. The single framework they present is compatible with many interpretations . . . the debate about the curriculum will go on and we hope these papers will still be of interest in the continuing discussion.[44]

Furthermore, it is explicitly stated that the papers in the volume, which deal with the case for a common curriculum for children 11–16, represent only the views of the anonymous group of inspectors who wrote them.

THE INSPECTORATE AND EDUCATIONAL POLICY-MAKING

Inevitably, the much sharper political divisions over educational policies of which the Yellow Book and the great debate are reflections, have affected the work of the inspectorate. Not only are Ministers likely to have more direct concern with its work, but its role in departmental policy-making has become important. It is in this context that the question of the degree of independence of the inspectorate needs to be considered. Formally, inspectors are civil servants, just as are other 'Her Majesty's Inspectors', such as those of constabulary. However, in the case of education inspectors alone, there seems to have been some tendency, particularly in the post-war period, for inspectors and to some extent teachers and administrators as well to regard the fact of being 'HM' as conferring some special kind of independence and not just as being a historical survival. This, as a former chief inspector has pointed out, is a myth.[45] Nevertheless, given that the inspectorate has no specific statutory function other than the tautological one of carrying out inspections, the question of what inspectors should be doing takes on greater significance in the case of schools inspectors as compared with other inspectors. And it is not only the content of inspectors' work which is important but the manner in which decisions are made about that content.

At first sight, the inspectorate seems to enjoy a degree of practical autonomy greater than one would expect from what has been said above. A DES publication of 1970 acknowledged that inspectors were ultimately answerable to the Secretary of State, but nevertheless there were

> things which the Secretary of State would not wish, in the course of their duties, to instruct them to do.[46]

But, as the Permanent Secretary, Sir Herbert Andrew, made clear to the Select Committee in 1968,[47] inspectors in this did not differ from other departmental professional advisers. There was no question of instructing them on matters within their professional competence. Clearly this kind of professional independence is important; it is, as the present Senior Chief Inspector has suggested, the basis of the inspectorate's usefulness, 'which, at all levels within the system, has from the beginning protected its acceptability'.[48] What distinguishes the inspectorate from other specialist advisers – the lawyers, architects, economists and statisticians who also proffer their professional skills in the complex business of administering the education service at national level – is the fact that its professionalism and expertise depend to a large extent on its knowledge of and contacts with the other elements which go to make up the education service, especially the schools and the local education authorities.

However, professional independence of this kind requires as a corollary that there should be some means of ensuring that the expert professional advice is effectively used. Here, recent developments within the department are very relevant.

Formally, the head of the inspectorate (the Senior Chief Inspector) ranks as a Deputy Secretary and is answerable to the Secretary of State through the Permanent Secretary. But this statement of the position needs to be set against the fact that a marked feature of the last ten years has been the development of formal machinery for policy planning in the DES, and the involvement of the inspectorate in that machinery. So far as the early 1960s are concerned, we have the evidence of the then Minister that the inspectorate played less part in policy-making than he would have liked to see, for reasons connected both with the administrative structure of the department and the personalities involved.[49] By the early 1970s a Policy Steering Group had been set up in the department, served by two Policy Groups concerned with developments and future policy in schools education and higher and further education respectively. The Senior Chief Inspector was a member of the Policy Steering Group under the chairmanship of the Permanent Secretary, and HMIs served on the Policy Groups.[50] By 1974 the then SCI could point to this development as indicating the closer involvement of the inspectorate in policy-making which had taken place since the Select Committee's report in 1968.[51]

The preoccupation with formal machinery has continued. The House of Commons Expenditure Committee in 1976 expressed some doubt about the role of HMIs in policy-making, despite the assertions of both the Permanent Secretary and the Senior Chief Inspector that the new system was working successfully.[52] The DES did however seem tacitly to be acknowledging that there were limitations in the system when, in response to the committee's recommendations, they announced changes in the planning organisation, including the establishment of a new unit under a chief inspector to be responsible for the department's involvement in educational research which would

serve to involve the Inspectorate more directly than hitherto in the planning process.[53]

Even so, when in 1977–78 a management review of DES was carried out jointly by the department and the CSD the linked questions of the effective contribution of the inspectorate to departmental policy-making and 'the need for improving mutual understanding between Office and Inspectorate about policy for inspection' were seen as requiring attention.[54] Not only was another Policy Group – for inspection – recommended, but it was suggested that the Policy Steering Group should be explicitly concerned with major questions of inspection policy, and that there should be a review of the inspectorate's work to ensure that it was more systematically related to the work of the remainder of the department.[55]

These various strands – the inspectorate's increasing concentration on national questions, the concern with making an effective contribution to departmental policy-making, the closer look at the nature of inspection policy – can be related to the greater need for a more explicit statement of policies in a period of heightened political controversy about education. But before attempting to explore the implications for the role of the inspectorate it is necessary to look at that other distinguishing feature of the inspectorate, its relationship with LEAs and the schools. This too bears on its professional independence and therefore on the question of accountability. Of the state of education, whether in a particular area or a particular sector of the educational system, the inspectorate can judge without being required to conform to some external standard or norm. This is not to say that the judgment is exercised arbitrarily or that it cannot be challenged. Inspectors are influenced by what they hear and see, they have their prejudices and limits to understanding. Yet having said this one has really said nothing that would not equally apply to any other professional person, a doctor for example. If we feel bound to look beyond this to ask to whom is the inspector accountable it is precisely because the inspecting role distinguishes him from other professional people. Since he goes into schools on behalf of the central authority his relationship both with that authority and with the schools and LEAs requires more definition than that of other professional advisers if we are to understand what it is he is trying to do.

THE INSPECTORATE AND THE LOCAL SCENE

The relationship of the inspectorate to the rest of the central department may be complex. The relationship to the schools and the local authorities with which it spends so much of its time is also complex – but for different reasons. The possibility of overlap, for example, with the work of local authority inspectors and advisers, which has long been debated, has become more prominent with the more recent attempt on the part of many LEAs to provide a range of subject and specialist advice corresponding to the range of the authority's responsibilities, instead of the rather restricted subject specialisms, notably physical education and domestic subjects, which were the original basis of most local advisory services and indeed remained so for a long time.

The development of local advisory services suggests that they stand in somewhat the same relation to the LEAs as HMIs do to the DES. That is to say, the authority needs to know what is going on in its schools for all kinds of planning and administrative purposes, just as the DES needs to know the national state of education. But apart from anything else, there is a major difference in that the authority has the direct responsibility of seeing that the schools are properly run. If supplies or equipment are deficient in a particular school, or equally if there are not enough teachers of the right kind, it is the authority's job to try to do something about it. So the adviser is both an administrative officer and more directly involved with the individual school than the HMI, and has tasks to perform which spring from the fact that he is responsible to the LEA.

At the same time there is an area where overlap is possible. Both HMIs and local advisers visit the schools, and both see at least part of their function as being to give help and advice where needed. For both inspectors (HMIs) and advisers there is a problem of trying not to get in each other's way, but from some teachers' points of view the two sources of advice arouse very different attitudes. HMIs are quite clearly independent of LEAs and, because they are a relatively much smaller body, are not so frequently seen in the schools as the local advisers; their advice is seen as being objective, whereas there may be suspicion that the teacher's response to the advice offered by the local adviser may affect his promotion prospects. This at least is the view put forward by the National Association of Schoolmasters/Union of Women Teachers, which sees the real difficulty of the local adviser's position as being the conflicting tasks put on him by the authority.[56]

In this situation the HMI's relationship to the individual school and local authority is likely to vary a good deal according to the strength of the LEA advisory service. Where such a service is well developed, one of its main tasks is likely to be dealing with problems, perhaps immediate problems arising from parents' complaints or poor staff relations or the rather longer-term problems of trying to find solutions where there is, for example, an inadequate head teacher in a school. In such cases, and especially the more difficult ones, the LEA is likely to find the HMI's view useful as a second opinion. Where the local services are less well developed LEAs may still rely, as they used to, on HMIs' advice to a greater extent.

The change in the relationship between HMIs and local advisers is part of the wider changes which have been noted as taking place in recent years. At one time, with the exception of a few of the big city local inspectorates, especially London, local advisers and inspectors lacked the experience and ability to undertake the full range of inspection and advisory work which HMIs did. The development of local advisory services and their improved status was taking place at the same time as the need for more and different kinds of information about the national state of education was becoming evident. There was an interaction between a number of different factors, which has led to the present situation where HMIs are much more likely than they ever were in the past to be visiting a school as part of a general survey, whether of the use of library facilities in certain kinds of school, or the teaching of mathematics, or the range of curricular work; and less likely to be going to assess the work of that particular school or because it has specific problems to be resolved.

Nevertheless, just because the HMI is still the only official of central government with the right to go into individual schools and examine what is going on there he can hardly help being drawn also into giving what help he can when he is there. It is true that he has no power to get things done; he can only advise and persuade with no certainty that anybody will take any notice of what he says; so that his influence is a highly personal one, backed by whatever prestige and authority the inspectorate generally possesses. To the individual teacher, who now has many other sources of advice – local advisers, Schools Council publications, teachers' centres, for example – an HMI whom he probably sees very rarely, if at all, must seem increasingly remote. Even head teachers may hardly be aware of HMIs for much of the time.[57]

The relationship of HMI with LEAs has changed less than it has with individual schools simply because, although the number of authorities diminished in 1974, there was no change in the relationship between DES and the local authorities and hence no change in the role of HMIs as the chief interpreter of the local situation to DES and vice versa. The district inspector needs to have the confidence of the local authority and in particular of the Chief Education Officer if he is to be in a position to influence him, and there are occasions when a CEO may welcome an HMI's view to reinforce his own when trying to persuade his elected members. At the same time the inspector must not be too closely identified with the particular authority if he is to give information and advice to DES which is useful to them. To that extent the HMI may be said to occupy a middle, independent position. But once again the independence relates only to his professional judgment and advice. He must be able to give as unbiased a view as possible whether he is talking to the CEO or to the administrator in DES. But this does not alter the fact that he is a civil servant accountable to the central authority.

THE ROLE OF HMI

The inspectorate, then, retains independence of judgment on matters within its professional competence, but is accountable to the Secretary of State. It must, therefore, work within the framework of departmental policy, and also contribute to that policy. Nevertheless, in reviewing its long history and its current role there are puzzles about its position which never seem quite to be resolved. Significantly it was perhaps during the period of 'payment by results' that there was least ambiguity about the inspector's role. He was quite clearly then an instrument of central government control, and primarily of control over the way in which government money was spent. Of course, even then this was not the whole story. Government would not have been involved at all if it had not been for the fact that without government money the standard of education would have remained unacceptably low. Even with payment by results the overriding concern with standards remained. There was this difference, however, between the payment-by-results period and the periods both before and after. In the former the task given to the inspector was much more precise and specific than before and since. At these other periods, although the ultimate objectives might remain the same, the relative importance of different functions and of different ways of carrying them out could vary quite considerably under the influence of many factors, including changes both within and outside the educational world. There is in this sense no one function which has consistently remained the central or most important thing that inspectors have been trying to do. In recent years, the political pressures which have made more urgent the need for a comprehensive and coherent account of the state of education nationally have contributed to the feeling of a change of direction in the work of inspectors. But this in turn seems to have made more explicit the differing views of those outside the inspectorate of what its function should be. The NUT, in its evidence for the DES management review, still saw advising individual teachers as an important element in the role of inspectors: others have stressed the importance of inspectors seeing how effectively local authorities carry out their responsibilities as a means of raising standards, rather than through their activities in relation to individual schools and teachers.[58]

This continuing debate springs essentially from the fact that, unlike enforcement inspectors, there is no core function which schools inspectors have to perform. Enforcement inspectors have certain statutory regulations to administer and have powers and sanctions correspondingly. They have at least this specific duty to carry out. Schools inspectors do not. It is to that extent a more open question how political and administrative considerations operate to determine the scope of the inspectorate's work. Within the inspectorate and in the relations between it and Ministers and the rest of the department there is no set pattern but rather a continuously evolving approach to questions of functions and priorities.

Not only that: the question of standards inevitably remains at the heart of any debate about the role of the inspectorate. The thread which links the national information function of inspectors, as exemplified in assessing the state of primary education, and their activities in the local context, as exemplified by the giving of advice to teachers at a particular school following an inspection visit, is the promotion of educational standards. Yet those standards are very largely unmeasurable. One of the questions, for example, which the inspectors who carried out the national primary survey were interested in was the extent to which the work in primary schools matched the abilities of the children; and one of their more interesting findings was that where there were deficiencies in this respect it was nearly always because the work was not sufficiently demanding: children were rarely asked to do work which was too difficult for them.[59] The standard which inspectors were here applying derived from their individual and collective knowledge and experience of what children of different ages were capable of learning, and of what they were learning in some schools. The validity of this process is a pragmatic one. If the standards proposed were seriously challenged – by teachers for example or others in the educational word – the effect would be to diminish the influence of the inspectorate. For if they are to have any influence at all it must be because they are accepted as having something worthwhile to say. They are not in a position to force their views either on the department or teachers or local authorities. Hence in a very real sense inspectors cannot be either too far ahead or too far behind current thinking and ideas about education.

This is particularly so because of the implicit assumption in their work that what has already been achieved by some should be urged on those who lag behind, as indeed was the premise behind the original Minute of the Committee of Council of 1840. In the last resort inspectors must rely on their knowledge and experience. Others may challenge the standards which they apply, or their assessment of the state of education, but who else is in a better position to do these things? To that extent, much rests on their professional competence.

This situation inevitably leads to a number of practical problems. How, for example, can inspectors acquire and retain sufficient knowledge of their schools? The argument about whether they are now advisers rather than inspectors scarcely seems relevant to the current situation. HMIs have no formal powers or statutory sanction so far as LEAs and their schools are concerned. They would therefore be bound in any case to act in an advisory mode. But this tendency is reinforced by the way in which the central authority operates generally within the education system. This is far less clear-cut than is implied by the statutory duty of the Secretary of State

> to secure the effective execution by local authorities under his control and direction of the national policy for providing a varied and comprehensive educational service in every area.[60]

It is indeed a matter for debate how far the DES can and should go in seeking to direct; and in practice the common description of the system as a 'partnership' indicates the limits within which the department and therefore the inspectorate operate.

At the same time inspectors cannot operate with any credibility or effectiveness at all without going into schools, observing what goes on and talking to those who are present – in fact, in basic sense, inspecting. The real questions arise in asking what inspecting is for and what use is to be made of the information gleaned from inspecting work.

ASSESSMENT AND PROBLEMS OF THE INSPECTORATE'S ROLE

How, finally, is it possible to judge the work of schools inspectors? Given the role of the inspectorate as a body which is formally required to carry out inspections but functions in effect as a body of professional advisers based mainly in the field, it is peculiarly difficult to assess its effectiveness. Even more so that in the case of other inspectorates examined in this study, inspection has to be regarded as a means to ends which it is not always easy to specify precisely. Even considering more limited questions, such as whether the inspectorate's views have been effectively brought to bear in the policy-making process, it is not easy to be precise. Clearly, as the SCI has said, the inspectorate is able to feed in information and views at many levels in the department.[61] And major pieces of work, like the national primary survey, not only arise out of current policy preoccupations but provide the material for influencing future debate.

The difficulties of assessing more positively the contribution of the inspectorate appeared at the time of the Yellow Book. Critics were quick to point out what appeared to be a contradiction at the heart of the inspectorate's work. If it was true, said one, that the inspectorate was, as the Yellow Book claimed, 'without doubt the most powerful single agency to influence what goes on in schools, both in kind and standard', what had it been doing in the last two decades when the alleged weaknesses in the educational system had been developing?[62] And the NAS/UWT commented that in spite of the high regard in which HMI were held they must share the blame in part for any decline in standards:

Ironically, the present debate over standards in schools is reputed
to have been promoted largely by the observations of Her Majesty's
Inspectors, many of whom were instrumental in bringing about the
very sort of unceasing change-cum-confusion that has characterised most schools.[63]

Whether these criticisms are fair or not they spring inevitably from
the particular mode of operation of the inspectorate. They have no
responsibility for standards but they claim to influence them. The
'great debate' of 1976–77 followed a period of unusually outspoken
criticism of what was happening in schools. The department acknowledged that some of the criticism was fair, especially to the extent that
some schools had been over-ambitious in, for example, introducing
new methods of teaching mathematics without adequate staff and
without having fully thought out the consequences.[64] Is the fault that
of the individual school, or the local education authority, or HMI, and
in any case what proportion of the whole do the failures represent?

The questions show the vulnerability of HMI to criticism but also
the extreme difficulty of assessing that criticism. The two things
indeed go together, 'Concern' and 'influence' are the most elusive of
words; yet they are the words which come most readily to mind in
considering the position of HMI. Cultured, urbane men and women,
they shrink from any suggestion that they should have power; they
positively prefer to work in an atmosphere of exhortation and advice,
trying, as they honestly believe, to win acceptance of their ideas by
their very reasonableness, prepared to have them rejected if they fail
to convince. There is no difficulty about such an approach when there
is broad agreement about standards and methods both inside and
outside the schools. When there is not, the HMI's position is liable to
become an uncomfortable one, showing both the limitations to his
influence and his vulnerability to criticism.

An illustration is provided by the question of the secondary schools
curriculum. The Yellow Book of 1976 suggested that the DES ought
to try to aim at establishing principles for a curriculum applicable for
all secondary pupils, a core curriculum for secondary schools. Such a
proposal, as the Yellow Book recognised, faced a number of practical
hazards, the main one being to gain acceptance for it from teachers
and local authorities against the suspicion that it was an attempt by
central government to gain control of the curriculum. The inspectorate itself has never committed itself to the view that there ought to be a
core curriculum. It has simply suggested that there are reasons why
this question deserves serious consideration.[65] When in December
1977 the inspectorate published some papers on the subject they were
termed 'a contribution to current debate', and it was stressed that they
did not commit the inspectorate, still less DES; they were simply

'working papers written by a group of HMI for discussion by HMI and, we hope, by advisers, schools, groups of teachers and those responsible for the education in our schools'.[66] At the same time, careful reading of the papers makes it clear that the inspectorate or at least those anonymous members of it who wrote the papers are firmly committed to the idea, but with a subtle sense of the possible opposition to it. The emphasis is on putting forward ideas which it is suggested teachers themselves have a professional interest in considering, but at the same time

some strongly held assumptions are bound to be questioned, not least those concerning the degrees of autonomy to be enjoyed by the school, the head, the head of department and the teacher in the classroom; but our experience suggests that most teachers would welcome partnership, and are not defending isolation.[67]

This example illustrates the method of working of schools inspectors and the constraints under which they operate. Believing as they do that their proposals would help to ameliorate the inconsistencies and irrationalities which at present exist the authors nevertheless can only urge others to try them, to set a debate in motion rather than decide what ought to be done.

More important is the difficulty of the dual role of professional advisers to the DES and promoters of higher educational standards. In the broadest terms the objectives of the inspectorate may not have changed fundamentally over the years; but, as has been seen, there have been considerable changes in the range of their activities and their methods of working. As professional advisers to DES they may be providing information and assessment of the work of both schools and local education authorities, taking part in the work of such bodies as the Assessment of Performance Unit, or planning the department's research programme. At the same time, as professionals concerned with the maintenance and improvement of standards in education they may be giving advice to teachers and local education authorities, taking part in short courses for teachers, or holding conferences and discussions.

The problem of relating these various activities to one another and of assessing their value centres on the role of the inspectorate in relation to the remainder of the department. The recent stress on administrative machinery for planning has brought to the fore differing perspectives of that role. If HMI now tend to put more stress on their role as a provider of information to the centre this inevitably brings into prominence questions of priorities in the work and the means by which current Ministerial and departmental needs for information are brought into relation with HMI's continuing programme. It remains to be seen whether the recent proposals of the Management Review, if they are carried out, result in a clearer definition of role and priorities. In any case, clarification is needed to provide answers to other important questions: for example, the question of what resources should be devoted to inspection. The 1968 Select Committee was surely right to argue that the number of inspectors should be related to the work to be done, whereas the department gave the impression that having got a certain number of inspectors it then gave them work to fit that number. It is not surprising that the committee found itself somewhat baffled by the view of the department and the inspectorate that 500 seemed a good number, even though this meant that they were hard pressed to do the work they thought they ought to do, and even though they could use 1,000 or manage on 250.[68] More recently, the present SCI has stated enigmatically that there are enough inspectors to do what it is proper for them to do.[69]

One may look at the position in this way. The criteria for judging the work of schools inspectors may not differ in essentials from those applying to other professional groups. We trust to their professional competence and standards, based on their individual and collective knowledge and experience, to give accurate information, valid assessment and useful advice. The trust can diminish if results do not come up to expectations, just as trust in the surgeon will diminish if all his patients die on the operating table. In spite of the dangers to the inspectorate in the 'great debate' and criticisms of declining standards in the schools their professional competence is on the whole still unchallenged and their advice still respected. But then, as has been pointed out, their responsibility is indirect, unlike the surgeon's.

But there are two difficult matters of judgment here. If we are to say that the work of the inspectorate must be judged in the end by whether the general standards and progress of education are satisfactory, this presupposes both that we have some means of measuring that progress, and that in doing so we also have some means of judging the particular contribution made by inspectors and indeed its relation to their particular methods of operation. Such questions are relatively easily disposed of when there is general agreement about the progress of education, but much less easy once doubt is raised about standards. It is likely, therefore, that there will be continuing debate about what inspectors should be doing, and questioning of their role.

What we have witnessed in recent years is what to some extent has also happened in the case of the factory and weights and measures inspectors. Public pressures for change, partly in response to what inspectors themselves have found have reinforced internal tendencies to question some aspects of the work and methods of operation. In this questioning the very distinctive nature of advising individual teachers and schools as compared with other functions has become more evident. To the extent that inspectors could provide authoritative advice on an individual basis and that advice was followed they could justifiably regard their work as contributing to the improvement of standards, as well as being satisfactory to themselves. Now the degree to which such work can be carried out may be diminishing. Furthermore, in a period when public concern over standards in education is becoming a major political factor, the inspectorate will inevitably find itself more open to challenge, more under pressure to justify the standards it implicitly advocates. Correspondingly, the more systematic relation of its views to the policy debate will grow increasingly important if it is not to risk losing that influence on the individual schools and teachers to which it has always attached so much importance. For in the end the real test of what the inspectorate does is whether not only those in the educational world but the general public feel that it is doing a good and necessary job.

NOTES: CHAPTER 5

1 *Minutes of the Committee of Council on Education, 1839–40* (HMSO, 1840), p.16.
2 ibid., p.17.
3 E.L. Edmonds, *The School Inspector* (Routledge & Kegan Paul, 1962), pp. 46–50; John S. Harris, op. cit., p. 79.
4 Minutes of the Committee of Council, 1839–40, p. viii.
5 *Report of the Commissioners appointed to inquire into the state of Popular Education in England* (PP 1861, XXI).
6 The various requirements of the Committee of Council were first brought together in a single document known as a code in 1860; the Revised Code is printed in PP 1862, XLI.
7 Sir George Kekewich, *The Education Department and After* (Constable, 1920), p. 10, quoted in Edmonds, p.81. He served in the Education Department from 1867 as an examiner, becoming Secretary in 1890.
8 *Report of the Board of Education 1922–23* (Cmd 2179, 1924), p.17.
9 ibid., p. 19.
10 *Education in 1949* (Cmd 7957, 1950), p.96.
11 Tenth Report from the Expenditure Committee, 1975–76, *Policy–making in the Department of Education and Science* (HC 621, HMSO, 1976), Questions 1454–6.
12 Elementary Education Act, 1870, s.7.
13 *Memorandum on the Employment by Local Education Authorities of Local Officers for Inspection of Schools or Work Analogous to Inspection* (Cmd 1878, 1923).
14 See Gerald Rhodes, 'Local Government Finance 1918–1966' (in *Appendix 6 to the Report of the Committee of Inquiry into Local Government Finance*, HMSO, 1976), paras 77, 89 ff.
15 Sir L.A. Selby-Bigge, *The Board of Education* (Putnam, 1927), p. 152.
16 *Board of Education Report 1913–14* (Cd 7934, 1914–16), pp. 33–4.
17 ibid., pp. 35–41.
18 *Report 1922–23* (Cmd 2179, 1924), pp. 22, 44.
19 See memorandum by Sir Aubrey Symonds, Permanent Secretary, Board of Education, and his answer to question 9630 (Minutes of Evidence, 26 March 1930).
20 See PRO Ed 12/288.
21 A term still in use to distinguish the remaining parts of the department from the inspectorate.

22 Selby-Bigge, op. cit., pp. 152–3.
23 *Education in 1949* (Cmd 7957, 1950), p.91
24 John Blackie, *Inspecting and the Inspectorate* (Routledge & Kegan Paul, 1970), p.48.
25 There was, for example, in the early years of the century much debate over the failure of the Board of Education to recruit into the inspectorate people with experience of teaching elementary education (see Edmonds, op. cit., 144–6).
26 See on the position generally Maurice Kogan, *Educational Policy-Making* (Allen & Unwin 1975), pp. 27–38; and *The Politics of Educational Change* (Fontana/Collins, 1978), p. 43.
27 cf. John A. Brand, 'Ministry control and local autonomy in education', *Political Quarterly*, 36, 1965, pp. 154–5; J.A.G. Griffith, *Central Departments and Local Authorities* (Allen & Unwin, 1966), pp. 522–3.
28 Kogan (1975), p.71.
29 *Report of Select Committee* (Session 1967–68, Part I, HC 400–1), p. 161.
30 ibid., p. 211.
31 ibid., pp. x–xii, paras. 34, 37, 38, 46.
32 ibid., para. 36. There were over 2,000 local inspectors/advisers as against about 550 HMIs.
33 ibid., questions 60, 62, 63, 70.
34 ibid., p.5, para. 14.
35 ibid., para. 42.
36 *Curriculum: an HMI View.*
37 e.g. *Open Plan Primary Schools* (ES 16, 1972); *Curricular Differences for Boys and Girls* (ES 21, 1975).
38 e.g. *Ten Good Schools* (1977); *Mixed Ability Work in Comprehensive Schools* (1978).
39 See *Primary Education in England* (HMSO, 1978).
40 e.g. 'New problems in sixth-form modern language studies' (Working Paper 26, 1970); 'Geology in the school curriculum' (WP 58, 1977).
41 The constitution was, however, modified in 1978.
42 The Yellow Book was not published. The edited extracts from which the following quotations are taken were published in the *Times Educational Supplement*, 15 October 1976; their authenticity has never been questioned.
43 Kogan, op. cit. (1978), p. 65.
44 *Curriculum 11–16*: working papers by HM Inspectorate; a contribution to current debate (DES December 1977).
45 Blackie, op. cit., p.52.
46 *HMI Today and Tomorrow* (DES, 1970), p.1.
47 HC 400–1, question 55.
48 *Curriculum: an HMI View.*
49 Sir Edward Boyle in Edward Boyle and Anthony Crosland (in conversation with Maurice Kogan), *The Politics of Education* (Penguin, 1971), pp. 130–1.
50 Expenditure Committee, *Policy-Making in the Department of Education and Science* (HC 621, 1976), p.9.
51 In a letter to the *Times Educational Supplement* (see Kogan, op. cit., 1975, p. 176).
52 HC 621, 1976, p. xviii, para. 36: questions 473–5, 1476.
53 *The Government's Reply to the Tenth Report from the Expenditure Committee Session 1975–6 HC 621* (Cmnd 6678, 1976), para. 6.
54 *Management Review of the Department of Education and Science. A Report of the Steering Committee* (DES 1979), para. 5.25.
55 ibid., paras 5.26–5.33.
56 See the report in *Education*, 8 April 1977, p. 242.
57 For example, one head of a comprehensive school said that in 11 years he was visited by an HMI on only 7 occasions, each visit averaging under 2 hours (letter from Tom Rolf, *Times Educational Supplement*, 29 October 1976, p. 17).
58 See the paper by Tyrrell Burgess, John Pratt and Tony Travers for the DES

Management Review (Centre for Institutional Studies Working Paper 43, NE London Polytechnic, May 1978).

59 *Primary Education in England* (HMSO, 1978), p. 81.
60 Education Act, 1944, s.1.
61 HC 621, 1976, question 476.
62 *Times Educational Supplement*, 29 October 1976, letter from Sir Alex Smith, then Chairman of the Schools Council.
63 *Education*, 8 April 1977, p. 242.
64 *Education in Schools* (Cmnd 6869, 1977), para. 1.3.
65 See, for example, the speech of SCI Sheila Browne to the CLEA Conference, July 1977 ('Curriculum: an HMI view'): on the other hand, the Conservative government elected in 1979 has committed itself to establishing a framework for the curriculum. (See report of speech by Lady Young, Minister of State, DES, in *The Times*, 15 November 1979.)
66 *Curriculum 11–16* (DES 1977), pp. ii, iv.
67 ibid., p.1
68 HC 400–1 (1968), p.vi and questions 16 and 54.
69 HC 621 (1976), questions 484–5.

CHAPTER 6

INSPECTION IN THE CONTROL OF POLLUTION: THE PROBLEMS OF AIR AND RIVER POLLUTION

A national evil is fast growing up which demands immediate and serious attention. (Sewage Commission, 1858)

A stronger power than has hitherto been available must be brought to bear if the present abuse and pollution of streams is to be arrested, and Government supervision and inspection must enforce and strengthen the action of local authorities. (Rivers Commission, 1867)

The scandal of river pollution is fully recognised and must be dealt with. (Parliamentary Secretary, Ministry of Agriculture and Fisheries, 1947)

The principles of pollution prevention are well known but had not been applied effectively prior to reorganisation. (Yorkshire Water Authority, 1975)

The contemptuous attitude which local authorities, private companies, nationalised industry and even government departments have held towards river pollution control is now plain for all to see. (Jon Tinker, *New Scientist*, 1975)

The inspectorate must abandon its meek conception of itself as 'a partner'. It must conceive itself as an industrial air-pollution police force: its role being to protect the public, to see that laws are enforced and miscreants duly punished. (Jeremy Bugler, *Polluting Britain*, 1972)

I think it is a measure of the relationship we hold with scheduled industry that so much as been achieved in industrial air pollution control in these critical times. (Chief Inspector, HM Alkali and Clean Air Inspectorate, 1977)

A recent government publication on the control of pollution discusses the subject under seven separate headings: air pollution; fresh water pollution; marine pollution; waste disposal; radioactivity; pesticides; and noise.[1] Of these, only the first two have a long history, and the last four, especially waste disposal and noise, have a very short history so far as statutory regulation is concerned. Yet in seeking to control pollution much use is made of inspectorates of both central and local government, and of other public-sector bodies, most notably regional water authorities. The growth of concern about pollution questions which is reflected in the recent expansion of pollution prevention measures has had repercussions on the work of the inspectorates, and this will be a prominent theme in the later part of this chapter. But later developments cannot be understood without looking first at ways in which inspectorates were established in the two areas of air and fresh water pollution, which were the first to receive attention.

SMOKE AND RIVER POLLUTION

Much the earliest and for long the most obvious form of pollution was smoke, especially after the burning of coal became common. The fourteenth-century Royal Proclamation prohibiting the use of sea-coal in furnaces is often taken as the starting-point of attempts to control smoke pollution.[2] Certainly its method, that is, simple prohibition without any specific means of enforcement, was still being advocated in the middle of the nineteenth century, even though the growth of industry and towns was creating a far bigger smoke problem than anything hitherto experienced. A select Committee in 1843, for example, concluded that it was possible to diminish very greatly the amount of industrial smoke and wanted legislation to prohibit the production of smoke from furnaces and steam engines.[3] Nothing came of this except that an Act on these lines was passed in 1853 but applied only to London. It did however provide for enforcement by the police, who had specific powers of entry and inspection for this purpose.[4]

Meanwhile, another consequence of the Industrial Revolution was a deterioration in the state of many rivers and streams, caused at first not so much by the waste products of industry draining into them as by their use practically as open sewers by the rapidly growing towns in the industrial area. The appointment of inspectors of nuisances under the Public Health Act 1848 with power to take action over certain insanitary conditions was an attempt to deal with some of the worst hazards of the growing industrial towns, but neither smoke pollution nor river pollution was at this stage singled out as a statutory nuisance.

The Sanitary Act 1866 was the first to treat industrial smoke as coming within the category of a statutory nuisance.[5] Black smoke might be emitted from a chimney in such quantities that it constituted a nuisance; a furnace too could be treated as a nuisance if it did not 'as far as practicable' consume the smoke given off.[6] But there were many obstacles in the way of the inspectors of nuisances attempting to enforce these provisions. For example, the Act itself made it clear that if a case were brought to court the magistrates could find that there was no nuisance if they were satisfied that a furnace was constructed to consume smoke as far as practicable 'having regard to the nature of the manufacture or trade' and that it had been carefully looked after.[7]

Perhaps of greater practical importance, however, was the fact that smoke was only one of many nuisances with which the inspectors were concerned, and one which might well seem less important and urgent for its effect on public health than, say, accumulations of rubbish or unwholesome food. Certainly the Royal Sanitary Commission reported in 1871 that the suppression of smoke was

> not effectually carried out in many places, and we have had witnesses who still deny its possibility in certain cases.[8]

The Public Health Act of 1875 elaborated the procedures for dealing with statutory nuisances, and formed the basis of smoke control, with certain modifications, until the Clean Air Act of 1956. The essence of the procedure was that if a local authority believed that a nuisance was being caused they had to serve notice on the owner or occupier of the premises concerned specifying what steps he must take to deal with the nuisance and within what period of time he was to do this. If the notice was not complied with the local authority was to apply to the courts for an order requiring the owner/occupier to take action. Local authority officers including especially in this context inspectors of nuisances (or sanitary inspectors as they were increasingly called) had powers of entry to premises for the purpose of examining as to the existence of any nuisance thereon and also to see that any order made had been carried out.[9]

The problem of sewage disposal and the consequent pollution of rivers was much debated in the 1850s and 1860s; and increasing attention was paid to the effects of the discharge of industrial waste into rivers. As in other spheres, the Victorians sought to find a balance between two conflicting needs; to prevent pollution, but at the same time to do so, as the terms of reference of one Commission put it, 'without . . . serious injury to industrial processes'. This Commission, appointed in 1865, and its successors of 1868, produced a series of detailed reports on major river systems as well as investigating technical questions such as standards of purity. For enforcing such standards the Commission concluded that there should be a central inspectorate so that inspectors should not be subject to local influences.[10]

It was not, however, until 1876 that comprehensive legislation on river pollution was passed.[11] The Rivers Pollution Prevention Act of that year formed the basis of river pollution control measures for over 70 years. Three main sources of pollution were dealt with in the Act: (1) there was a prohibition on the deposit of solid matter which would interfere with the flow of the river or pollute it; (2) sewage was likewise prohibited, but anyone accused of contravening would not be found guilty if he could prove to the court that he had used the 'best practicable and available means' to render the sewage harmless; (3) poisonous, noxious or polluting liquids from factories were not to be allowed into rivers, but again the defence of 'best practicable and reasonably available' means of rendering harmless was open to anyone accused. Enforcement of the Act was entrusted to local sanitary authorities, but with a considerable degree of central supervision. Proceedings could only be taken by sanitary authorities with the consent of the Local Government Board, which was not to be given unless they were satisfied that means for rendering the polluting matter harmless

> are reasonably practicable and available under all the circumstances of the case, and that no material injury will be inflicted by such proceedings.

on local industrial interests.[12] Furthermore, if an inspector 'of proper qualifications appointed for the purpose of this Act by the Local Government Board' gave a certificate that the means for rendering harmless were the best or the only practicable ones in the circumstances of a particular case, that was to be taken as conclusive evidence.[13] It was also open to the LGB by order to give the sanitary authority a specified time in which to adopt the best practicable means in relation to their treatment of sewage.[14] A further feature of the 1876 Act was that it required sanitary authorities to provide facilities to manufacturers to discharge their wastes into the sewers, but they could not be compelled to do so if this would damage the sewers or if the sewers were only sufficient for the needs of the district.[15] Hence arose the threefold division of sources of pollution which has persisted in river pollution control: sewage; industrial wastes discharged into sewers; industrial wastes discharged (with or without treatment) directly into rivers.

Part of the reason for the division of responsibility between central and local government lay in the fact that sanitary authorities were themselves potential polluters through their control of sewage disposal works. But another significant feature of the 1876 Act was that it represented a compromise with powerful manufacturing interests. Much opposition had been expressed to a strict control of pollution on the grounds that it would harm manufacturing industry.[16] An earlier attempt to bring river pollution within the statutory nuisance provisions of the Public Health Acts had been withdrawn because of this opposition,[17] and even the original proposals in the 1876 Bill were modified to make them acceptable to the manufacturers. In the end the President of the Local Government Board argued that it was better to have the Bill than nothing at all.[18]

THE ALKALI INSPECTORATE

Meanwhile, a very different form of control was being applied to industrial air pollution by the alkali inspectorate.[19] The hydrochloric acid which came out of the chimneys of alkali works caused objections not primarily because of the health hazards of this form of pollution but because it caused the blighting of vegetation and the corrosion of metal in the surrounding areas to the concern of the local landowners.[20] The remedy incorporated in the Alkali Act 1863 was to require alkali works to condense 95 per cent of the hydrochloric acid gas produced. The Board of Trade was empowered to appoint an inspector whose duty it was to see that all alkali works were operated in conformity with the Act and to enforce its provisions, with power to enter and inspect works at all times for this purpose.[21]

At first sight the 1863 Act seemed to give the inspector a right of intervening directly in the manufacturing process such as the existing factory inspectors did not possess, and to that extent to represent an extension of central government's power of intervention in private industry. But in the first place, it has been pointed out that the remedy of condensing the gases was a comparatively simple one, already used by some manufacturers, and agreed to by the majority provided that all were obliged to apply it.[22] Secondly, the Act specifically laid down that the inspector was not entitled to demand alterations in the process of manufacture or the apparatus used.

Indeed, so far from being a threat to the manufacturers, the first inspector, Augus Smith, earned their gratitude by demonstrating that the hydrochloric acid which they had previously wasted could be put to profitable use in the manufacture of bleach.[23] In addition, his method of operation was that, as he himself said later:

I therefore work simply, at present, by advice and friendly admonition, and prosecutions will come in their proper time.[24]

The alkali inspectorate was unusual in that it required a degree of technical expertise rarely found in other inspectorates at that time. As Smith pointed out, it was 'utterly useless' to suppose that his job could be done by simply 'looking in at an alkali work': it was necessary for

him to carry out chemical analyses of gases, salts and acids.[25] However, in considering the further development of the alkali inspectorate, it is important to stress how much Smith saw his role as being one
of winning the confidence of the manufacturers, and also how the
development of that role was very largely left to him. At the same
time, he was well aware how limited the 1863 Act was.

A significant development was the passing of a further Act in 1874
which provided that the owner of an alkali works

> shall use the best practicable means of preventing the discharge
> into the atmosphere of all other noxious gases arising from such
> work, or of rendering such gases harmless when discharged.[26]

Later extensions of the legislation to other works and processes continued to be based on this concept of the best practicable means.

In the latter part of the nineteenth century there were thus very
different means of control for three types of pollution specifically
identified in legislation – industrial smoke, certain industrial gases,
and river pollution. The one thing they had in common was that they
depended on inspectors for enforcement, but the type of inspector
and the means open to him varied. The closest parallels are between
the control of smoke and of river pollution in that both depended on
enforcement by local sanitary inspectors, and would indeed have been
brought under the same nuisance legislation if the 1872 proprosals
had been accepted. The final result, however, was to emphasise the
piecemeal approach so characteristic of Victorian legislation,
especially in the very distinctive statutory control of alkali works.

CHARACTERISTICS OF NINETEENTH-CENTURY INSPECTION

By the end of the nineteenth century there was general recognition
that control of smoke and river pollution had not proved successful.
Thus the Royal Commission appointed in 1898 to inquire into sewage
disposal soon came to the conclusion that the 1876 Act had not
resulted in the general purification of the rivers.[27] As regards smoke
pollution, continued agitation over a number of years, particularly by
smoke abatement bodies, led to the appointment of a departmental
committee in 1914 whose terms of reference acknowledged 'the evils
still arising' from such pollution. By contrast the control of gases from
industrial processes by the alkali inspectorate was regarded as sufficiently satisfactory to lead to successive extensions of their powers
and responsibilities.[28]

Clearly, many factors other than the competence of the different
inspectorates accounted for these differences. Adequacy of powers,
and the scope and cost of technical remedies available were important,

but there were also differences between a general inspectorate subject to local authority control and a specialised central inspectorate with a considerable degree of practical automony. Furthermore, there were particular reasons why individual local authorities might be reluctant to enforce the Acts for which they were responsible. Vested interests on the town council, for example, might inhibit action on smoke nuisances.[29] Or where local authorities were themselves polluters, as in the case of inadequate sewage works, they might postpone the necessary work because of the expense involved.[30]

The success of the alkali inspectorate was based on a number of factors, and especially important were certain distinctive characteristics which it possessed. It was, to begin with, a small specialised body of professional chemists with the single limited task of enforcing the Alkali Acts. It had relatively few works under its charge,[31] and its task in relation to the registered works was confined to controlling the escape of noxious gases. Equally important was the fact that so far from being subject to the overriding direction and control of a particular local authority's policies and priorities, the alkali inspectorate not only had a great deal of freedom to develop its own methods of dealing with the problems of emission of gases from factory chimneys, but was also able to exert considerable influence on the course of legislation particularly as it affected the extension of this means of control to further processes.

Again, although it was a feature of the nineteenth-century legislation relating to pollution control that it depended on the use of the 'best practicable means' (bpm) or some similar phrase, the provisions operated rather differently under the Alkali Acts from those applying to smoke and river pollution. In the case of the latter, bpm was in effect a defence to the charge of contravening the Acts. In the case of works coming under the Alkali Acts it was specifically an obligation on the owner to use the bpm of preventing the discharge of noxious gases. The difference can be expressed by saying that the smoke and river pollution legislation operated by means of simple prohibition which it was open to the person accused to challenge, whereas the alkali legislation in theory left the challenge to the enforcing authority to claim in effect that the owner had failed to use the bpm.

This in turn is important for the question of the standards being enforced and methods of enforcing them. The original alkali legislation was based on a fixed emission standard, but alkali inspectors themselves strongly favoured the flexibility of bpm and wanted it extended to river pollution control. Their argument was that, as one of them put it:

standards would grow up and be formed subject to the stress of conflicting interests. They would vary with the place, the volume of the stream and the service to which the water is subject, and higher standards could be applied as technical knowledge grew.[32]

The question 'who is to judge the best practicable means?' was not answered directly but it was suggested that all the inspector needed to do was to point out that someone else was using a better means in order to secure improvements.[33] In effect, great stress was being put on the professional competence and integrity of the inspector in being able not only to assess what was technically feasible but what manufacturers could reasonably be expected to do.

But the absence of precise standards and the marked leaning of the inspectorate towards a co-operative and persuasive role inevitably raised the question whether it was operating as effectively as it might. As early as the 1870s criticisms were heard that the inspectors did not enforce the law strictly enough, particularly in the matter of prosecutions. The Royal Commission on Noxious Vapours, although acknowledging the 'great amount of injury and inconvenience' which had been prevented by their efforts, thought that a stronger line should have been taken with manufacturers who did not comply with the law. However, they also acknowledged that 'premature or injudicious severity'

> might have created a sense of injustice and a spirit of opposition among the manufacturers, which would have greatly aggravated the difficulties of those charged with the administration of the Acts.[34]

Angus Smith, on the other hand, claimed 'I have done something better than mere fining' by citing examples of the considerable expense incurred by some manufacturers in installing new equipment and recruiting better qualified staff:

> I do not know a more severe mode of fining or one that can be equally advantageous to the community.[35]

The difficulty was that there was no objective way of measuring the relative effectiveness of these alternative approaches. One problem was that there was a great difference between enforcing a simple right or wrong requirement, and introducing modifications into industrial processes. In the former case, of which weights and measures provided a good example, there was no dispute that the requirement could be met; in the latter, everything turned on what could be done, complicated by the fact that this was seen in terms not only of what was technically possible but also of what could be done at reasonable expense. As Smith well knew, he was inviting criticism: 'of course, it may be asked, when all is done, is it enough?'[36]

Certainly Smith and his successors saw his method as one of

gradually increasing pressure for higher standards. They also constantly pressed for the extension of the Alkali Acts. More particularly, they wanted an extension of the means of control by more emphasis on regulating gases rather than processes. However, in spite of strong pressure from the inspectors, they were not able to persuade senior administrators and the President of the Local Government Board to change the policy. The Alkali &c Works Regulation Act 1906, the basis of the alkali inspectorate's work until it became part of the Health and Safety Executive in 1975, continued to be based on the specification of individual classes of works. The discussions which preceded the 1906 Bill illustrate the strength and the limitations of the alkali inspectorate's position. The status of the inspectorate as professional advisers to the Board on matters within their sphere of competence was not in question, but on the matters of general policy theirs was only one view, to be balanced by other practical and political considerations.[37]

Nevertheless, this whole discussion of the alkali inspectorate marks them off from other inspectors in the pollution field both in status and in the kind of work they did. In fact we know much less about inspectors in smoke and river pollution control in the late nineteenth century. To elucidate their work would require detailed study in the archives of many local authoities. Nevertheless, there are some indications of the attitudes of local authorities to such work and, as has been suggested, these attitudes largely governed the way in which inspectors operated.

The prevention of river pollution provides one illustration. Many of the nineteenth-century inquiries had advocated watershed authorities for river pollution control. The 1876 Act, as has been seen, rejected this in favour of enforcement by local sanitary authorities. Under the Local Government Act 1888 the new County Councils also had powers of enforcement under the 1876 Act. The 1888 Act also contained general provisions for joint action by groups of authorities through the formation of joint committees. Two joint committees (Ribble, and Mersey and Irwell) and one joint board under a local Act with special powers (West Riding of Yorkshire Rivers Board) were soon formed by the joint action of the county councils concerned with certain county boroughs and other authorities, for the purpose of administering the Rivers Pollution Prevention Act 1876.

These joint authorities appointed their own inspectors who gave evidence to the Royal Commissions on Sewage Disposal and Salmon Fisheries, which naturally tended to support the idea that better enforcement could be achieved by authorities responsible for a whole watershed area, not least because such an authority could justify the employment of specialised inspecting staff.[38] But whether local authorities or other bodies were to enforce the 1876 Act, it was unlikely that there could be active enforcement throughout the country without some general agreement on the standards to be applied. The Commissioners of the 1860s had proposed standards consisting of a series of tests to determine whether liquid was to be regarded as polluting.

One of the difficulties applying to pollution standards generally, and not just in relation to rivers, is what the nature of the standards should be, whether one applying to the emission or discharge, as is generally the case with the standards of the alkali inspectorate, or an environmental standard, that is, a standard specifying the quality of the air or water. A further problem is whether standards should be fixed or variable according to circumstances. The 1860 standards applied to discharges but proved controversial and were not incorporated into legislation. There was, therefore, as the chief inspector of the West Riding River Board told the Royal Commission on Salmon Fisheries, no legal standard to apply – 'only a working standard'; furthermore, it was one which varied from place to place according to circumstances; what was good sewage in one place might not be good enough in another. But he agreed that the standards applied in the West Riding were similar to those in the Mersey and Irwell area.[39]

If it was difficult for these *ad hoc* bodies to devise and apply uniform standards, small authorities who were not in any case very enthusiastic about enforcing the 1876 Act doubtless found the question of standards an added disincentive. It is not perhaps surprising therefore that the Royal Commission on Sewage Disposal devoted a great deal of attention to the standards to which sewage effluent should conform. They devised standards based on the volume of suspended solids and the biochemical oxygen demand (BOD). These too were never incorporated into legislation, but the 'Royal Commission standards' gradually became almost universally recognised in this country as the basis of river pollution control for over sixty years until in the 1970s the regional water authorities created by the Water Act 1973 took a fresh look at standards.

Apart from its relevance for the way in which authorities responded to their responsibilities for river pollution control, this discussion is also illuminating for another contrast with the alkali inspectorate. Neither the alkali inspectorate nor river pollution inspectors had specific legislative standards to enforce, but whereas the former were in effect left to develop their own standards in consultation with industry through the concept of bpm, the latter were in practice dependent very largely on standards devised by others. Nor is this surprising, given the technical knowledge required and the lack of expertise among all but the largest authorities such as the joint committees.

The position at the beginning of the century then may be summarised by saying that in its limited sphere and in its own unique way of operating the alkali inspectorate was making progress in controlling pollution by a mixture of winning the confidence of industry through its knowledge of industrial processes and using this knowledge to persuade industry to instal preventive equipment; but in smoke control and the prevention of river pollution the picture was much more patchy, with, however, a general feeling that despite a quarter of a century of control measures smoke and pollution of rivers were still present to an excessive degree. Apart from specific reasons which have been discussed for the ineffectiveness of the legislation, it must be said that pollution control did not have a high priority in many people's minds, except to the extent that it could be shown to have an adverse effect on health. And here even medical opinion was not unanimous. In evidence to the Royal Commission on Noxious Vapours, a doctor who claimed to have made a very careful examination of the influence of vapours on health said he found no evidence of 'special deterioration of health' in the districts he had visited, and even the MOH for St Helens, one of the areas worst affected by industrial gases, went no further than to say that they 'act as a depressant, keeping the people somewhat below par in health'.[40] Even as late as 1932 it was said that medical opinion was not unanimous on whether smoke was a serious danger to health, although by then the great majority of MOHs thought it detrimental – a view which led one official to argue pessimistically:

it seems unlikely that any big drive in smoke abatement work will take place until a definite relation of cause and effect has been established (it has not) between atmospheric pollution and injury to health, just as the impetus to pure water supplies came from the establishment of a relation between polluted water and outbreaks of cholera and typhoid.[41]

In the twentieth century the separate development of pollution control measures continued for a remarkably long time – it was not, for example, until the 1970s that an integrated approach to air pollution control was seriously examined, and even in 1979 we can only be said to be beginning to appreciate fully the interconnection between pollution of the air, land and water, with its implications for control measures. The alkali inspectorate continued for almost 60 years after the Act of 1906 to operate on basically unchanged lines but periodically adding further types of works and processes to be controlled. Only since the 1960s has its work come under increasing attention and criticism which have compelled a re-examination of its fundamental principles.

Smoke and river pollution have had this in common in the twentieth century as compared with the pollution under the alkali inspectorate's control: that periodically there has been pressure for more effective control. This pressure was, however, for a long time unsuccessful. For smoke control it was not until the 1950s that measures were taken which succeeded very largely in eliminating the smoke-laden atmospheres which for so long had characterised the major industrial areas. River pollution has perhaps received really serious attention only since 1961, although tighter control measures have gradually been introduced over the past thirty years. In all this pollution control, as indeed in the control of other forms of pollution now receiving attention such as noise, inspectors are the chief means by which control is exercised.

RIVER POLLUTION CONTROL IN THE TWENTIETH CENTURY

(1) Local authorities and river boards

The preoccupation of official inquiries into the state of the rivers with administrative machinery for enforcing pollution control continued in the twentieth century. Both the Royal Commission on Sewage Disposal and that on Salmon Fisheries recommended not only watershed authorities but a stronger central authority which could take action where local authorities defaulted.[42] No action was taken on these recommendations, for the same reason as had inhibited action before.

Piecemeal legislation such as the Salmon and Freshwater Fisheries Act 1923 further complicated the position, but the low priority of river pollution questions between the wars is illustrated by the fact that although the Ministry of Health's advisory committee on river pollution also recommended that there should be authorities responsible for entire river basins, the Ministry contented themselves with circularising local authorities on their powers to set up joint committees. Even this brought the comment from the Principal Assistant Secretary responsible:

> it would probably be an excess of optimism to expect much substantial result unless the Ministry are able to exercise a good deal of stimulation, which will mean an additional drain on the staff.[43]

Both machinery and powers were lacking for effective enforcement as deputations from the Ribble and from the Mersey and Irwell Joint Committees told the Ministry.[44] The power of angling clubs to bring actions against polluters for damaging private fisheries was often a more effective means of action than the use by local authorities of their powers under the 1876 Act. It was not until a wartime re-examination of water resources that government finally endorsed the view that there should be river boards to take over the responsibilities of the forty-five fishery boards, fifty-three catchment boards and 1,600 pollution authorities in England and Wales.[45] In introducing a Bill in 1947 to establish thirty-two river boards in England and Wales, the Parliamentary Secretary of the Ministry of Agriculture and Fisheries declared:

> the scandal of river pollution is fully recognised and must be dealt with.[46]

But the creation of special authorities to deal, among other things, with river pollution could not automatically solve the problems of river pollution. It was rather a recognition of the fact that the existing fragmented administrative arrangements were an obstacle to effective action. The question of what, if any, additional powers the river boards needed for this purpose proved more difficult. The government referred this question to a sub-committee of the Central Advisory Water Committee (CAWC). Echoes of the past can be found in the report of the sub-committee, particularly in its stress on the need for long-term measures such as a 'very large programme' of sewage disposal and other works, but also in its view that it was necessary in considering further measures not to neglect the 'great importance' of maintaining industrial production.[47]

Clearly the last point was, as it had always been, a stumbling-block to the strengthening of controls. Most of those giving evidence to the sub-committee thought that some additional powers were needed, but the Federation of British Industries argued that the law was adequate provided that it was applied with reasonable uniformity.[48] The sub-committee rejected this argument on the grounds that they were proposing a new procedure which should provide adequate safeguards for industry. The procedure, like the objections, mainly concerned the troublesome questions of standards. It was proposed that river boards should be able to prescribe standards in by-laws subject to the prescription of minimum standards by the Ministry of Health.[49] The procedure was incorporated in the Rivers (Prevention of Pollution) Act 1951 together with a new system of control, also recommended by the sub-committee, for new or altered discharges only. Such discharges, whether for sewage or industrial effluents, required the specific consent of the river board, which had the power either to refuse an application or to impose conditions on the quantity and quality of effluent discharged.[50]

The 1951 Act proved in practice a limited weapon for river boards in the control of pollution. In particular, the by-laws mechanism was not effective, and no by-laws were in fact confirmed. On the other hand, the consents procedure from its modest beginning in 1951 has developed into a major part of the control mechanism. It was extended to new and altered discharges to tidal waters in 1960, and, more significantly, to existing discharges (in non-tidal waters only) in 1961.[51] In 1965 river boards were replaced by a slightly fewer number of river authorities with somewhat stengthened powers in pollution control, for example for obtaining information from those discharging effluents.[52]

Before considering the background to these and further measures which have been taken since, it is also necessary to consider the practical operation of their powers by river boards and river authorities, and the factors influencing their effectiveness. An official report published in 1970 showed that nearly 60 per cent of sewage works were, on a yearly average basis, operating outside the consent conditions of the river authorities, with perhaps over 3,000 works producing effluent 'inferior to what could reasonably be expected by the use of modern treatment methods'.[53] This situation seemed to imply that the river authorities were failing to enforce the Acts on a large scale – the very reason which had led so many inquiries over such a long period to advocate the appointment of river-based authorities. It was not that the authorities were inactive. Their annual reports indeed show a great deal of activity in the way of pressing for the closure of inadequate sewage works and advising on ways of reducing pollution caused by operation deficiencies in the smaller works.[54] The real problem, however, was long-term. For local authorities in particular to meet consent conditions under the 1961 Act a large programme of works was needed. In theory the river authorities' responsibility was simply to point out to a local authority what needed to be done to meet the consent conditions and if they failed to carry out the work to institute proceedings against them. In practice, local authorities were hardly ever prosecuted and consent conditions were frequently treated more as targets to be attained eventually than as immediately applicable standards. Nor was it only the river authorities which adopted this attitude. In 1966 the Ministry of Housing and Local Government advised authorities that where existing discharges were below Royal Commission standard it might be 'appropriate' to make improvements by stages and to judge the effect at each stage before considering further improvements. More detailed advice was given for cases where a more restrictive standard was needed; this would have to be fully justified by local circumstances and after consultation with the local authority, since otherwise it 'might lead to diversion of resources from more important tasks'.[55]

This latter argument points to one dilemma for the river authorities. Essentially what they were seeking to do so far as sewage effluent was concerned was to get local authorities to spend more on sewage treatment works. Since this involved capital expenditure, a vigorous policy of enforcement could only succeed if MHLG were willing to sanction increased capital expenditure. The majority of members of river authorities were in any case appointed by county and county borough councils, and only too well aware of the difficulty of securing more resources for sewage works even if their authorities were willing to give priority to this particular form of expenditure. There were thus inhibiting factors on the river authorities' ability to put pressure on local authorities, and this reacted on the work of the inspectors, who were well aware that consent conditions were not being met but often could do little about it. Furthermore, as the Working Party on Sewage Disposal pointed out, this situation affected the attempt to control the quality of industrial effluents discharged direct to rivers, which in many cases was even less satisfactory than sewage effluent:

> It is difficult for river authorities to insist on the standards required for industrial discharges if the discharges of the local sewage authorities are not up to standard.[56]

One may sum up by saying that by the end of the 1960s progress was being made in dealing with river pollution, as indeed it had been for nearly a hundred years, but it was very much an 'essay in gradualness',[57] and certainly nothing like as rapid as the conditions of consent seemed to promise. A national river survey carried out in 1970 showed 17,000 miles of non-tidal rivers as unpolluted compared with 14,000 miles in a more limited survey in 1958. Further progress has since been made particularly in the reduction of the mileage of poor quality and grossly polluted rivers, which now account for less than 8 per cent of the total (see Figure 6.1.).[58]

(2) Regional water authorities
In the further development of river pollution control measures in the 1970s two factors have been prominent, one general and one more specific. The general factor is the increased political pressures generated by growing public concern over pollution. Already in 1960 an official report noted:

> There is developing a public sensibility to the poor state of many of our rivers, an increasing awareness of the amenity, recreational and health value of cleanliness, and a general will to secure within the bounds of what is practicable the greatest improvement in the shortest possible time.[59]

On the whole this increased concern which became more manifest in the course of the 1960s did not result, as it was to do in the case of the alkali inspectorate, in severe criticism of river authorities for short-

Figure 6.1   Chemical classification of non-tidal rivers (England and Wales), 1958, 1970, 1973, 1975

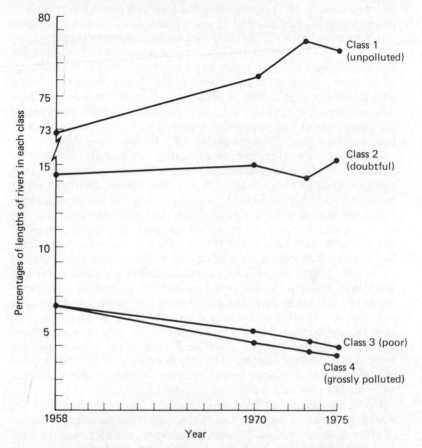

Source: Report of a River Pollution Survey of England and Wales, 1970, Vol. 1, Table 1: updated 1975.

comings in enforcing the statutory provisions. Criticism was more likely to be made of local authorities for the inadequacy of their spending on sewage works, and on industrial firms for paying too little attention to the need to avoid pollution.[60] Nevertheless, increased concern with pollution focused attention on the need for relating the standards to be enforced more closely to inspection if the obvious dangers of having standards which were largely ignored in practice were to be avoided.

The more specific factor affecting measures for controlling river pollution was the increased importance attaching to the subject of water resources. The growing demand for water during the post-war period led in the first place to the strengthening of the administrative mechanism for ensuring that there were adequate resources of water. The Water Resources Act 1963 not only established river authorities but gave them additional powers to conserve, redistribute and augment water resources. It also established a Water Resources Board which not only had the duty of advising river authorities on their new duties but more specifically of bringing to their attention cases where the proper use of water resources required an improvement of water quality by the use of powers under the 1951 and 1961 Acts.[61]

There was, however, increasing realisation that the problem of ensuring an adequate quantity of water was inseparably connected with questions of water quality. With conventional sources of water becoming both more expensive and more difficult to use (e.g. through public opposition to large reservoirs on environmental grounds) the re-use of water was seen as an increasingly important means of ensuring adequate water resources. But if water was to be re-used on a larger scale than before then it clearly became more important to ensure that pollution was reduced to a minimum since badly polluted water was either unfit for re-use or needed expensive treatment. These considerations in turn focused attention on the administrative structure for dealing with water questions, and, in particular, the division of responsibility among a large number of authorities; there were, for example, over 1,300 local authorities responsible for sewerage and sewage disposal. Thus the need for strengthened control of pollution was one factor in the complex process by which changes were made in the administrative structure.[62]

Under the Water Act 1973, ten regional water authorities (RWAs) were established in England and Wales[63] and took over the functions of river authorities, and of local authorities in water supply[64] and sewage disposal. Thus the RWAs became responsible not only for the control of pollution, but also for the management of one of the main sources of pollution. The 1973 Act was followed by the Control of Pollution Act 1974 which replaced earlier legislation on the subject and made a number of changes designed to strengthen the control of pollution and provide more information to the public; but this part of the Act has not yet come fully into force.

Some of the early reports of the new water authorities have a familiar ring in drawing attention to the failings of the operations which they inherited. Huddersfield sewage works 'had to be seen to be believed'.[65] 'Substantial young trees' were found growing on the biological filter beds at another unnamed works.[66] It is not surprising therefore that most authorities were able to report short-term improvements in pollution control simply by tackling the neglect or, as in the case of Huddersfield and similar places, by getting rid of ancient local Acts which had permitted the works to get overloaded with trade effluent.[67] In the longer term it was recognised that progress depended largely on the speed with which capital expenditure on new and improved works could be increased. This now became a difficult internal problem for RSWs. The expenditure needs of sewerage and sewage disposal now had to compete with other capital needs, especially those relating to water supply, within total annual capital budgets approved by the Secretary of State.

At the immediate practical level was the pressing problem of the standards to be applied to effluent discharges, and the principles on which consent conditions should be based. Here there was a difficulty that the power to fix conditions rested with the ten individual water authorities, whereas the expectation of national legislation was that there should be some generally accepted principles as the basis for standards. The Water Act 1973 had, however, established a National Water Council as well as the regional water authorities. This was a body without powers but with a co-ordinating role emphasised by the fact that half of its membership consisted of the 10 chairmen of the RWAs.[68] It was in this forum that at attempt was made to formulate a new approach to discharge consent conditions, largely on the basis of a two-stage approach: first, RWAs should specify river quality objectives for each of their rivers; secondly, they should review existing consent conditions in the light of these objectives.[69] As the NWC pointed out, this procedure would mean that dischargers in different areas might well have to meet different conditions; for that reason the Council were anxious that all authorities should adopt a new classification of river quality based specifically on mainly quantitative criteria.[70] Not only would a common approach of this kind be more equitable but there were cogent practical reasons for the whole attempt to make consent conditions more realistic in terms of enforcement. The Control of Pollution Act 1974 extended the information available to members of the public and their opportunities to take action on it. Registers of consents kept by river boards and river authorities under the 1951 and 1961 Acts had been open to 'interested persons'. Under the 1974 Act not only were registers to be open to inspection by the public but they were also to include additional information on, for example, samples of effluent or water taken by RWAs, information resulting from the analysis of samples, and action taken on that information.[71] At the same time the 1974 Act repealed the section of the 1961 Act under which prosecutions could in effect only be brought by the authorities responsible for pollution control. RWAs are therefore aware that the system of consents is likely to come under much closer public scrutiny. But, as the Director of Operations of the Anglian Water Authority put it, 'there is little sign of a definite improving trend' in the condition of the rivers; that still depends on increased allocation of resources to pollution prevention rather than on simply making consent conditions more realistic.[72]

The part played by the pollution prevention inspectors of the RWAs is important in all this. Not only do they perform the usual tasks of carrying out routine inspections, taking samples of effluent for analysis and investigating complaints, but it is largely on the information they provide that RWAs determine the consent conditions for individual discharges. It is their job to know what is happening in their area, and this knowledge must clearly form the basis of any attempt to draw up realistic consent conditions. At the same time, persuasion rather than prosecution has in the past been the main approach to enforcement, and this has not so far changed under the new authorities.

AIR POLLUTION CONTROL IN THE TWENTIETH CENTURY:

(1) *Local authorities*
The dominance of questions of administrative structure in the evolution of river pollution prevention measures in this century is not paralleled in the air pollution field. It is not so much who should be responsible for pollution control as what powers are needed and how they can be effectively applied that has been the main subject of debate. In the 1920s, for example, local authorities such as Leeds and Bradford which were attempting to deal vigorously with smoke pollution urged stronger legislation and wanted some stimulus to be applied to those authorities which were reluctant to act. They were supported by the Smoke Abatement Society which saw no reason why factories should smoke if furnaces, etc., were properly looked after.[73] But as with river pollution, the Ministry were reluctant to press too hard for action.

When a new Minister (Sir Edward Hilton Young), appointed in 1931, appeared to be taking smoke pollution much more seriously than his predecessors his officials seemed more positive about the way in which local authorities should go about enforcement than about any means of making enforcement more effective;

> the Ministry are constantly preaching the doctrine that prosecution is the last resort and that local authorities should co-operate with industry in a friendly manner.[74]

The situation remained practically unchanged for another twenty years. The progress which was made depended on the vigour with which individual local authorities undertook enforcement together with external factors such as the substitution of gas or electricity for coal. So far as domestic smoke was concerned some local authorities took power under local Acts to declare smokeless zones but not much use was made of these powers. As so often it was an external event, in this case the great London 'smog' of December 1952, which provided the opportunity for those who wanted stronger measures to control pollution to exert more effective pressure. In particular, the official analysis of the mortality figures seemed to demonstrate conclusively the health hazards of air pollution,[75] thus providing in a dramatic form that stimulus to public opinion which had largely been absent before. A committee on air pollution was set up and recommended more positive and immediate steps to deal with the problems.[76] Even though there still remained some opposition to the idea of stronger pollution control measures the government acted quickly, remarkably so in view of past history, and with a large measure of support from the opposition, to give effect to the committee's recommendations. The Clean Air Act 1956 gave local authorities power to declare smoke control areas in which it was an offence to allow smoke to be emitted from a chimney unless specific exemption had been given: it was also made an offence to emit dark smoke from any chimney, again with exemptions; furthermore, new furnaces were required to be smokeless 'so far as practicable', and there were certain controls over chimney heights and over the emission of grit and dust as well as smoke.[77] In effect local authorities were left to control air pollution from all works except those controlled under the Alkali Acts.

Although the 1956 Act (and a further Clean Air Act in 1968) gave local authorities greater powers to control smoke and to a lesser extent grit and dust, perhaps its chief significance was that it marked the beginning of a period of greater public and political concern which ensured a higher priority for control of air pollution, as the more active local authorities as well as outside pressures groups had been urging for years. In 1952, before the Clean Air Act, a survey showed that only 14 per cent of sanitary inspectors spent even as much as between 1 per cent and 2 per cent of their time on smoke abatement, and 5 per cent spent no time at all.[78] To a large extent such figures merely reflect the fact that sanitary inspectors spread their time over a wide variety of tasks. Nevertheless, not only does this figure compare unfavourably with such major tasks of inspectors as inspection of dwellings or of food premises, but it is also less than that for other tasks such as inspection under the Shops Act.[79]

There are no comparable figures for a more recent date, but it is significant that a 1976 investigation lists pollution control among the major functions of environment health officers, and shows that in those authorities – admittedly a small minority – which organise the work on a functional specialist basis nearly 20 per cent of EHOs are assigned to pollution work.[80] Bearing in mind that the air pollution problem varies greatly in different parts of the country, this at least suggests that a good deal more effort is now being devoted to air and other forms of pollution by local authorities than was the case before 1956.

That the problem of industrial smoke has diminished greatly in the last twenty years is obvious. Emissions of smoke from industrial processes went down by 96 per cent in the period 1956–73; whereas smoke from domestic fires accounted for 94 per cent of the reduced total of smoke emitted in 1973 as against 43 per cent in 1952.[81] Similarly, there has been some reduction, though less dramatic, in concentrations of sulphur dioxide (see Figures 6.2 & 3). How far these reductions can be attributed to the increased activities of local authority environmental health departments as compared with, for example, the tendency to use oil or gas in boilers in preference to coal, which would probably have taken place anyway, is not a question which can be answered with certainty. So far as industrial smoke is concerned, however, it is clear from the report of the committee that the remedy was simple, known and not even likely to be all that expensive given that excessive smoke nearly always indicated a waste of fuel.[82]

As so often, however, comprehensive data on the performance by local authorities of their functions is lacking. The committee on air pollution thought that smoke in heavily populated areas should be reduced by about 80 per cent in ten to fifteen years. The total amount of smoke in the air has been reduced by this amount,[83] but many areas are still a good way off the targets which they set themselves for smoke control areas, the average for the whole country being just under 60 per cent.[84] But air pollution control is in any case still the responsibility not only of local authorities but also of the alkali inspectorate. It is therefore necessary to look at their work as well as that of the environmental health officers, including relations between them and methods employed.

(2) The alkali inspectorate
In the years following the 1906 Act the alkali inspectorate continued to emphasise the advantages of its method of combining persuasion with the rare threat of or occasional prosecution. In 1909, for example, the view that proprietors were 'most anxious to do all they could to comply with any suggestions made to them' was coupled with 'serious warnings' to three works and threats of prosecution met by an undertaking to take the necessary remedial measures.[85] The view of the chief inspector, who retired in 1955 after twenty-six years in the post, did not differ:

Figure 6.2 Smoke emissions and concentrations in the United Kingdom

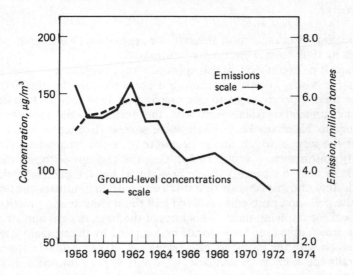

Figure 6.3 Sulphur dioxide emissions and concentrations in the United Kingdom

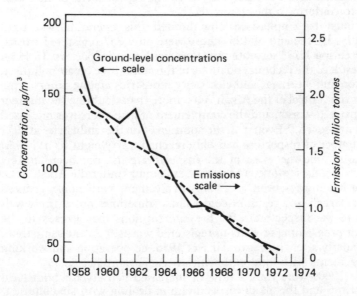

Source: Royal Commission on Environmental Pollution, 4th Report (Cmnd 5780), pp. 12–13, by permission of the Controller of Her Majesty's Stationery Office.

Experience has convinced me that a spirit of mutual confidence and goodwill between inspectors and industrialists is essential to progress.

In the year 93 infractions of the statutory provisions were reported, but as in 1909 there were no prosecutions.[86]

There is no doubt too that this approach was generally welcomed in industry: 'visits, co-operation and aid are welcomed by the firms under their supervision', said one manager in 1934, contrasting the position under the Alkali Acts with the 'unreasonable' provisions relating to black smoke.[87] There were several distinctive features about the way in which the inspectorate operated and indeed still largely continues to operate. In applying the concept of 'best practicable means' to a process newly brought within the control of the Alkali Acts, the inspectorate first discussed with the industry concerned the pollution problems involved and the technical and practical problems of resolving them. This formed the basis of emission standards drawn up by the inspectorate and applied by them, again after discussion with the industry, in carrying out inspections. However, generally speaking, such standards were only applied immediately to new plants. Existing plant was not required to conform to these standards, but allowed to continue until it became due for replacement in the normal way when the replacement plant would have to conform to the standards.

It must be emphasised how limited this operation was until recently. By the end of 1957 there were only 857 registered works, representing 1,733 separate processes, with nine inspectors. In 1958, as a result of the recommendations of the committee on air pollution, the iron and steel, gas and electricity industries among others came under the control of the Alkali Acts, more than doubling the number of registered works, and the complement of inspectors was increased to twenty-seven.[88] Even with the addition of further industries in 1971 the number of inspectors had only reached thirty-eight by 1977. At the same time the work of the inspectorate has not been entirely confined to those works and processes coming under the Alkali Acts. There has always been a certain involvement with non-registered works, largely as a result of complaints, sometimes not entirely welcome to the inspectorate for the interruptions they caused to the regular programme of visits to registered works.[89] At the same time, particularly after the Clean Air Act 1956, co-operation and working arrangements with local authorities became more necessary.

The 1960s were thus a time of increased activity for both local authorities and the alkali inspectorate in dealing with air pollution. They were also a time when increased public concern about pollution generally began to make an impact on the work of the inspectors. This was particularly true of the alkali inspectorate, which had not been in the public eye for many years and had rarely had much contact with the general public. Sanitary or public health inspectors were of course much nearer the ground in this respect, but they now had more extended contact through their work on smoke control areas and their increased responsibilities for industrial smoke.

Under a new chief inspector, Frank Ireland, the alkali inspectorate began to explain their approach and methods in the annual reports which hitherto had been largely filled with technical matters. There is little doubt that this development was in response to the new public concern with pollution. Thus in 1966 the chief inspector explained that the aim was to be fair to both industry and the general public; but 'practicable means have to be tempered to suit the times', although this did not mean that the inspectorate was 'soft' with industry: on the contrary they never lost sight of the goal, which was to have all scheduled works operating harmlessly and inoffensively as soon as possible. But because much personal judgement was involved in the inspectorate's approach there was the possibility of controversy 'with those who allow their fears and emotions, instead of facts, to rule their opinions'.[90]

In the 1967 report the chief inspector explained his policy of having good relations and co-operation with local authorities, and also went at some length into the important question of his policy on enforcement and prosecution. Because inspectors were accepted as advisers, industry was prepared to spend money on solving its pollution control problems; because district inspectors could negotiate agreements with individual works with the minimum of red tape, industry was prepared to accept tougher decisions than would otherwise be the case; because trade associations were brought fully into resolving technical problems, they could be relied upon for support in enforcing the requirements ultimately agreed upon. Prosecution would be used if necessary (but 'it cannot solve technical problems'); the usual procedure in the case of an infraction of the requirements was, however, for the inspector to write to the firm concerned; if the firm then took steps to put matters right no legal action would be taken. Not only did he believe that this policy had been 'outstandingly successful' but he ended by defending the inspectorate's attitude in the following terms:

Abating air pollution is a technological problem – a matter for scientists and engineers, operating in an atmosphere of co-operative officialdom. Great care has to be exercised by all to prevent the development of adversary attitudes.[91]

Strongly held views of this kind provoked opponents to argue that the inspectorate had indeed been too soft to industry and to criticise its

self-convinced role as an agency to help industry get on with the job, rather than an air-pollution-control agency above all.[92]

The argument which developed between the inspectorate and its critics did indeed raise fundamental questions about the role of inspectors, and centred on two particular aspects of the alkali inspectors' work, whether the standards which they applied were stringent enough, and whether in any case they were adequately enforced. The critics were in effect saying that the degree of air pollution which existed was intolerable and therefore looked to a tightening up of the inspectorate's controls as a means to achieving further reductions. The inspectorate replied that this was not necessarily the best means of making progress; at every stage the advantages of reducing pollution had to be weighed against the costs of doing so, and this was what they attempted to do both in fixing standards and in enforcing them. The two contrasting views of inspectors have rarely been so obvious; on the one side, inspectors as simple law-enforcers; on the other, inspectors as interpreters of the spirit of the law in the light of individual circumstances and the longer-term consequences of their actions.

The controversy was perhaps sharpened by the fact that the inspectorate was not used to challenge of this kind from those who claimed to speak for the general public. It was after all as recently as 1954 that an official committee had endorsed its work, which

constitutes the best means calculated to apply a continuing challenge to, and exert effective supervision and control over, those industrial processes which present special technical difficulties in the prevention of dark smoke, grit and dust,

and had recommended that many further processes should be brought under the Alkali Acts.[93] Yet in a way which is unique among inspectorates the alkali inspectorate has continued to be the target of strong criticism. Much the most sustained attack of this kind was a lengthy report produced by Social Audit in 1974. This discussed in detail the question of standards and how they were applied by the inspectorate. It also contained the comments of some local authorities, which, although not unduly critical of the inspectorate generally, saw the need for more contact between them and public health inspectors (as they then were). Furthermore, it was evident that many local authorities had a different attitude from the inspectorate to such questions as the need for prosecutions.[94] EHOs are the people most likely to get complaints whether they are on matters for which they are responsible or not, and who are liable to be criticised in the local press if things go wrong. But there has certainly been no general criticism of the way in which EHOs carry out their pollution control responsibilities in the way that the alkali inspectorate has come under fire.

POLLUTION BECOMES A POLITICAL ISSUE

The increased public concern over pollution which was one important factor in changing the scope and nature of the work of river pollution inspectors in the 1960s and 1970s had a more general application to pollution control. Discussions of pollution multiplied and made environmental pollution a political issue in a way in which it had not been since the middle years of the nineteenth century. But there was now a significant difference. In the nineteenth century the threat to health had been the main concern. That threat was still present – notably in relation to the disposal of radioactive waste – but it was overlaid by a much wider concern for the quality of the environment, for the external conditions under which people had to live. With this went a broadening of the definition of pollution, most notably by the inclusion of noise.

Two consequences in particular are important for the development of inspection work. First, new statutory provisions have added to the work of inspectors; for example, legislation relating to noise has added to the duties of environmental health officers.[95] The second consequence has been to focus more attention on the work of existing inspectors and especially on their methods of operation. As has been seen, this has particularly affected the alkali inspectorate, but it has gone beyond that in that it has raised questions about the relationship between the work of different inspectorates. Characteristically, inspectorates have been established in response to specific problems. There could hardly be a better example than the alkali inspectorate itself, but the process has continued: a separate radiochemical inspectorate was, for example, established in 1960 in the Ministry of Housing and Local Government largely to enforce the statutory provisions relating to the disposal of radioactive waste.[96] It is not surprising that greater interest in pollution matters and in methods of control should lead to questioning of whether the machinery of control was the most effective which could be devised for the purpose.

Considerations of this kind led the Secretary of State for the Environment in 1974 to ask the Royal Commission on Environmental Pollution to 'review the efficacy of the methods of control of air pollution', including the relationship between the various authorities concerned. Ironically this inquiry was complicated by the fact that in accordance with the Robens Committee's recommendations the alkali inspectorate was transferred to the Health and Safety Executive under the Health and Safety at Work [etc.] Act 1974.[97] The alkali inspectorate had always been concerned with what went on inside a factory from the point of view of its effects outside, a very different perspective from that of the factory or mines and quarries inspectorates. The Robens Committee emphasised the links between the factory inspector's concerns and those of the alkali inspector, and also wanted health and safety legislation to be more concerned with the consequences for the general public of industrial and other operations. The Royal Commission, on the other hand, regarded the alkali inspectorate's primary responsibility for environmental pollution as incompatible with its forming part of HSE; on the contrary they wanted the alkali inspectorate merged into a new pollution inspectorate with

an integrated approach to difficult industrial pollution problems at source, whether these affect air, water or land.[98]

However, in many ways a more difficult problem for the Royal Commission was the relationship between central and local inspection for the control of air pollution. Here they acknowledged the impossibility of comparing the effectiveness of the alkali inspectorate with that of environmental health officers engaged on air pollution control,[99] but in effect endorsed the present system because of the need for somebody to deal with technically difficult problems which local authorities generally were not equipped to deal with.[100] Indeed their proposals for a unified pollution inspectorate would have extended the idea of dual control, so that the new inspectorate would have stood in a similar relationship to waste disposal authorities and RWAs as the alkali inspectorate does at present to local authorities.

It is noticeable too that the Royal Commission was enthusiastic about the concept of 'best practicable means', wishing to extend it to local authority control of air pollution and to control by the proposed new inspectorate.[101] At the same time they recognised the dangers. For example, in visiting works which were the subject of local complaints they found it hard to decide whether this was because the agreed bpm were not being followed or because they had not been defined strictly enough for the particular works.[102] In either case they recognised that for bpm to work effectively there had to be not only competence and integrity on the part of the alkali inspectors, but more openness in the system; decisions should not be taken simply by the inspectorate and industry but should be open to public participation; and their sharpest criticism of the inspectorate generally was of their failure to respond adequately to the greatly increased public interest in their work.[103]

It is interesting in this connection that the Royal Commission recommended that their proposed pollution inspectorate should be answerable to a central pollution policy body within the Department of the Environment, with specialist committees providing expertise in scientific, medical and other matters including economics and accounting.[104] The effect would be to diminish the large degree of autonomy which the alkali inspectorate enjoyed at least until 1975,[105] but at the same time to reinforce its decisions on matters where it cannot claim expertise. It would also no doubt have the effect of diminishing the ability of the District Inspector to give a quick decision on the spot to which, according to a former chief inspector, industry attached so much importance.

These would be modifications of the inspectorate's traditional role rather than a complete change. They would not satisfy the more radical critics. But then as the Royal Commission also pointed out:

> One cannot have it both ways; either we have, as now, an authority which because of its close relationship with industry and consequent understanding of the problems is able to assess the technical possibilities for improvement in detail and press for their adoption; or an authority which sees its job as one of imposing demands on industry and which, because of the sense of opposition this approach would create, could not obtain the same co-operation by industry in assessing the problems and devising solutions.[106]

It is not yet known what will be the outcome of the Royal Commission's recommendations. The government issued a consultative document inviting comments particularly on the question of a unified pollution inspectorate, and has also itself undertaken an inquiry into the need for such an inspectorate.[107] But whatever the outcome it can hardly be doubted that we have not reached the end of discussion of the best means of securing a degree of control over pollution. Nevertheless, even the stage we have now reached and the long history recounted here offer some significant comments on the role of inspectors.

FACTORS IN THE DEVELOPMENT OF POLLUTION INSPECTORATES

Two themes are particularly important here. The first is the influence of external factors on both the effectiveness and the methods of operation of inspectorates concerned with pollution control. The second is the contrasting roles of specialised central government inspectorates on the one hand, and local government (and 'quango') inspectorates on the other. In some ways they seems almost to be two different types of inspectorate despite a basic similarity in the purposes for which they were established.

Lack of political will and incentive to overcome the resistance of powerful interests long characterised the approach at both central and local level to industrial smoke and river pollution. The lack of incentive was mainly the result of the fact that there were not, as there were in the case of other hazards such as impure water, strong health reasons for taking effective action. Both smoke and river pollution therefore had for many years a low priority, symbolised by the fact that even in the 1960s there was reluctance to sanction expenditure on replacement of inadequate sewage works. For most of its long history, therefore, inspection as a means of controlling smoke and river pollution was subject to severe limitations on its effectiveness. This does not mean that no progress was being made, but that it was a good deal less than the legislation seemed to promise. Whereas, for example, it has been argued, nuisance legislation had by the end of the nineteenth century led to noticeably improved conditions in the provision of water or cleanliness of food, it had made a much less noticeable impact on the smoke problem.[108] Public and political pressures have more recently created the conditions for greater effectiveness of inspection, especially in smoke control.

In looking at the alkali inspectorate the perspective is different. Not only do central government inspectorates in general have a greater freedom in their approach to their task, but the concept of bpm with its greater reliance on the expert and professional knowledge of inspectors in framing standards suggests a more complex situation, in which they were not simply enforcing an external standard but themselves to a large extent determining the standard in collaboration with industry and the speed with which it should be applied. Effectiveness therefore in their case is much more directly related to the approach they adopted and the progress made, to the extent that it can be measured. On both counts there was general acceptance and little challenge to the inspectorate until recently.

The more intense debate about pollution in recent years might be expected to have both advantages and disadvantages for inspectors, on the one hand strengthening their ability to take effective action, but on the other subjecting their activities to a more critical public examination. The changing context of the inspectors' work might thus have implications for both their objectives and their methods.

In one sense objectives have remained the same. Inspectors still have strictly limited tasks defined by statute. The alkali inspectorate may have a vastly wider range of processes to deal with than it had in 1863, but it is still basically concerned with ensuring that the bpm is used in those processes to limit the discharge of specified gases. Environmental health officers may have greater powers to deal with smoke than they had in 1866, but they are still concerned with limiting rather than eliminating smoke, except in the specially designated smokeless zones. RWAs may have the ultimate aim of restoring all rivers to an unpolluted state, but for the foreseeable future the most that pollution prevention inspectors are likely to aim at is the reduction of existing pollution.

Similarly, one might see the effect of recent changes as being simply to provide inspectors with the means to deal more effectively with what, essentially, are unchanged problems. As Lord Ashby put it in approving the fact that British legislation does not lay down rigid standards, this approach

> gives the authorities responsible for administering the legislation discretion to adjust what are really permits to pollute according to the circumstances of the place and time and industry or corporation concerned.[109]

'Permits to pollute' accurately sums up the history of the legislation over more than a century; it implies that argument should centre on the degree of pollution to be permitted and the means to be adopted to see that this level is not exceeded. It also implies that so far as industry is concerned there is a balance to be struck between the degree to which pollution should be limited and the ability of industry to operate economically.

However, it is precisely in the fact that such an approach is now being challenged that the possibility of a greater impact on the work of inspectors exists. If, for example, it were generally accepted that the quality of the environment is more important than purely economic considerations, and that

> a company should operate only if its pollution load is insignificant, irrespective of its economic importance or factors such as contribution to exports,[110]

the consequences for the work of inspectors could be very great. So far, however, the main consequences of the sharpening of the pollution debate into a political issue on a scale not experienced for a hundred years or more (and then for very different reasons) have been additional legislative provisions, such as those in the Control of Pollution Act 1974, and greater public attention to the work of inspectors, rather than any more fundamental changes.

EFFECTIVENESS AND ACCOUNTABILITY

The striking fact is, however, that although recent developments are significant for the work of all the pollution inspectorates considered here, their visible impact has been much greater in the case of the alkali inspectorate than of the others. Not only has the inspectorate been criticised in a way that the others have not, but that criticism has been directed at its basic philosophy and approach which, as has been seen, have been built up over a period of more than a hundred years. In particular, the long-held view that the determination of 'best practicable means' was a matter for the inspectorate to settle with industry has been much criticised. To the critics, it seemed to imply that the general public had no right to question the inspectorate's decisions, and this in turn aroused suspicion that the inspectorate was not enforcing a strict enough standard. Even the Royal Commission on Environmental Pollution, which was in general favourably disposed to the inspectorate, criticised a certain 'clumsiness and insensitivity' in their public pronouncements, and their 'air of irritation' with those who questioned their decisions.[111] Undoubtedly the inspectorate is responding to these criticisms and making far more effort than in the past to explain what it is doing and make information available.

It is not, however, just a question of public relations. There is an underlying problem of basic philosophies which the alkali inspectorate raises above all others because of its history and traditions, and in particular its marked degree of independence – which remained unchallenged until very recently and largely accounts for its strong reaction to public criticism. An inspectorate which interprets its role as being to judge the balance at any given moment between the technical means of controlling pollution and the cost to industry of doing so, which aims to lead industry along the road of gradual progress rather than to state absolute requirements which industry must somehow meet or face the prospect of prosecution is far removed from the simple idea of an inspector as a man who comes round with his list of requirements and is only interested in whether the person inspected does or does not conform to them. It is also extremely vulnerable to misunderstanding and suspicion of its motives. This is because there are bound to be conflicts of interest between the public desire for clean air (or water) and the industrialist's desire to keep the costs of production down. Few anti-pollution measures bring profit in the way that Angus Smith was able to demonstrate with the original method of dealing with hydrochloric acid. On the contrary, research into methods of prevention and the installation of the necessary equipment once a method has been found are often expensive. The alkali inspectorate is well aware of the conflict of interest but claims that its methods not only balance these interests against one another but are in fact the best way of achieving gradually improving standards of control.

But is it enough, and is it seen to be enough? Ever since the time of the Royal Commission on Noxious Vapours the inspectorate has been vulnerable to the charge that more could be done by the use of higher standards or stricter enforcement – or both – precisely because it has taken upon itself a responsibility which goes beyond simply seeing that the Alkali Acts are carried out. For much of the time the charge was not articulated, and there was tacit agreement that as much was being achieved as could reasonably be achieved in the view of the inspectorate. But then some people did begin seriously to question whether enough was being done. In the words of one of the protesters in the United Carbon Black incident at Swansea:

> This air pollution may be all right by the Alkali Inspector but it's no good to us.[112]

This brief statement conceals a number of difficult questions: what degree of pollution should we tolerate in our society, and how and by whom is this question to be determined? Are we prepared to see certain industries or plants closed down because the costs of introducing anti-pollution measures make continued production uneconomic? Or to argue that pollution is so intolerable an evil that we should be prepared to pay a higher price for, say, cement if that is the inescapable cost of suppressing the dust nuisance from cement works? Or do we agree rather with Frank Ireland that

> the quality of life is important to us, but it is not at the top of the list of priorities when the country is struggling to earn its bread and butter.[113]

The wide gulf between the two points of view was underlined for the alkali inspectorate by the fact that they were justifiably proud of what had been achieved by their efforts and approach, and by what was still being achieved. They could, for example, point to the way in which emission standards were constantly being revised and made more stringent as the result of technological developments. They could argue that they would not have been able to achieve these improving standards without the co-operation of industry. The arguments on the other side started from a totally different point of view, that there were numerous examples of intolerable air pollution. Since it was the job of the alkali inspectorate to deal with industrial air pollution these examples were taken as proof that the inspectorate was failing in its job.

To the inspectorate it seemed a curious paradox that they should be singled out in this way. Why, for example, should they be accused of being too soft with industry on the basis of figures of prosecutions, when local authorities, so far as could be gathered from the figures,[114] were at least as reluctant to prosecute over contraventions of the air pollution legislation?

The answer is that neither EHOs nor for that matter river pollution inspectors were such an easy target. The information which the alkali inspectorate provided in the chief inspector's annual reports about such things as its methods and its records of prosecutions could easily be seized on. Although information about individual local authorities or river or regional water authorities might be easily obtainable, it was, and still is, difficult to put together a reliable picture of what is happening throughout the country in those areas of pollution control for which local authorities or RWAs are responsible. Furthermore, whereas EHOs in particular are enforcing requirements laid down in Acts or regulations, the alkali inspectorate seemed to be making its own rules and the main constraint on its operations appeared to be what it could get industry to accept. Again therefore the alkali inspectorate presented a more obvious target than the local authorities or the authorities concerned with river pollution.

The difficulty and vulnerability to criticism of the alkali inspectorate's position amount to this. The logic of its interpretation of what was intended by bpm has drawn it into considering, and answering – by default as much as anything else – questions which are essentially political in character. Questions like 'How much can this industry – or this plant – afford to spend on anti-pollution measures?' or 'If we insist on this particular measure will it force certain firms out of business and how therefore can we measure the resulting unemployment against the benefits of reducing pollution?' followed naturally from the inspectorate's co-operative approach to industry. In finding answers it has implicitly been deciding not only what degree of pollution is tolerable but at how fast a rate pollution should be diminished. As soon as the consequences of these answers began to be challenged publicly the inspectorate was vulnerable not only to the charge that it was not solely for it to provide them, but that it was not equipped with some of the expertise needed; in particular that it lacked economic expertise and in consequence was liable to attach too much importance to economic considerations.[115]

In the case of smoke control and river pollution the answers to similar questions seemed to lie less with the inspectors than in external factors over which they had less influence; and this applied not only to standards but to remedies, as in the case of inadequate sewage works. Correspondingly, successes which have been achieved in recent years may be attributable less to the activities of inspectors than to external factors. The continuing improvement in the quality of river water, for example, depends to a large extent on an increase in capital expenditure on sewage treatment works together with improved management of such works, both of which were assisted by the administrative reorganisation which took place under the Water Act 1973. The activities of river pollution inspectors, as also of EHOs in smoke pollution control, are clearly important; but questions of their effectiveness and accountability have to be related to this wider context. The existence of explicit policies on the degree of pollution control to be aimed at and of appropriate administrative arrangements to achieve them, and the influence of technological developments, are among the most important of the factors which are relevant. But even though much has been achieved, there still remain considerable areas of doubt about future pollution control. The spectacular figures for the reduction of industrial smoke need to be set against the fact that pollution from grit and dust is still prevalent and the subject of many complaints.[116] Undoubted progress in reducing river pollution nevertheless raises doubts, in view of past events, whether the river quality objectives now being set will be attained.

Some problems for the future are technical, and the means to control certain kinds of pollution may depend on the ability and will to devote sufficient resources to the necessary research. Some problems may be complicated by differences of approach: the EEC, for example, appear to favour the use of discharge standards in river pollution control, whereas British experience has been based on water quality standards, which are claimed to be more flexible and effective. Some problems may arise from the present administrative arrangements: the fact, for example, that RWAs are bodies which both control pollution and are themselves polluters may reduce the effectiveness of pollution control measures.

The overriding factor in the control of pollution is, however, economic. A great deal of existing pollution could be eliminated at a price. In this wider context the accountability and effectiveness of inspectors depends on there being general agreement on what are realistic targets for pollution control. Here one effect of the recent upsurge of interest in pollution seems to have been to produce a degree of confusion. Perhaps not surprisingly, people want something done especially about such obvious unpleasantnesses as the dust afflicting those living near cement works, but may not welcome the consequences in, for example, higher prices for cement or less employment in cement works. Decisions of this kind are likely to become much more difficult at a time, like the present, of severe economic problems. The ability of RWAs, for example, to achieve reasonable progress in reducing pollution, already made difficult by the necessity for determining priorities between competing demands for capital expenditure, is likely to be put under further strain by increased financial restrictions.

It must be said, however, that the determination of pollution control policies is itself made more difficult by the lack of information on the effectiveness of past methods used to control pollution. Most discussion is either in terms of general trends – measurements of smoke concentrations or river quality, for example – or specific instances of pollution. Neither can be very directly related to the effectiveness of control measures, and thus cannot resolve questions such as whether stringent standards rigidly enforced would achieve better results, a question which has been with us for a hundred years or more. One consequence of the current debate should be that more attention is paid to evaluating the methods used. For there is a need to demonstrate that confidence in the methods employed is justified if inspectors are to be truly accountable, and be seen to be reducing pollution to an extent and at a rate which is acceptable. If the history of pollution inspectorates illustrates the difficulty of their making much impact without the political impetus deriving from perceptions of the importance of reducing pollution, it also illustrates the difficulty of demonstrating that inspection works.

NOTES: CHAPTER 6

1 *Pollution Control in Great Britain: How It Works* (DOE Pollution Paper No. 9, HMSO, 1976; rev. edn 1978).
2 See, for example, Royal Commission on Environmental Pollution (RCEP) 5th Report, *Air Pollution Control: An Integrated Approach* (Cmnd 6371, HMSO 1976), para. 42.
3 PP 1843 (583), VII.
4 16 and 17 Vict., cap. 128.
5 Domestic smoke was not brought under legislative control at this stage.
6 Sanitary Act, 1866, s.19.
7 ibid.
8 *Second Report* (PP 1871, C 281, vol. XXXV), p. 45.
9 Public Health Act, 1875, ss. 91–6, 102; cf. Public Health Act 1936, ss. 93–4.
10 *Fifth Report (Second Commission)*, PP 1874, C 951, vol. XXXIII, p. 50.
11 Other legislation, e.g. the Salmon Acts, dealt incidentally with pollution. See Roy M. Macleod, 'Government and resource conservation: the Salmon Acts administration, 1860–1866', *J. British Studies*, vol. VII, no. 2, May 1968, pp. 114–50.
12 Rivers Pollution Prevention Act 1876, s.3.
13 ibid., s.12.
14 ibid., s.3.
15 ibid., s.7.
16 For example, speech of J. Fielden, HC Deb, 3rd series, 210, 5 April 1872, col. 852.
17 Public Health Bill 1872, cl. 32, 33 (PP 1872, vol. IV); HC Deb 210, col. 883.
18 HC Deb 230, 24 July 1876, col. 1879.
19 For convenience, the terms alkali inspector or inspectorate will be used, although since 1971 the official title has been 'Her Majesty's Alkali and Clean Air Inspectorate'.
20 See R.M. Macleod, 'The Alkali Acts administration 1863–84', *Victorian Studies*, vol. IX, 1963, p. 88.
21 Alkali Act 1863, ss. 4,7,9.

22 Eric Ashby, 'The politics of noxious vapours', *Glass Technology*, vol. 16, no.3, June 1975, p.62.
23 Macleod, op. cit., p.92.
24 *Report of Royal Commission on Noxious Vapours* (PP 1878, C 2159, vol. XLIV), question 152.
25 *Alkali Act 1863. First Annual Report by the Inspector of his Proceedings during the year 1864* (PP 1865, vol. XX), p.7.
26 Alkali Act 1874, s.5. The Act also provided for the registration of works with the inspectorate.
27 *Interim Report*, Cd 685 (PP 1901, vol. XXXIV), p. xi.
28 For example, under Acts of 1881 and 1892.
29 See evidence of J. Ponsonby, Town Clerk, Oldham, in *First Report of Royal Sanitary Commission* (PP 1868–9, vol. XXXII), questions 2233–7 and 4049–51.
30 *Report of Royal Commission on Salmon Fisheries*, Cd 1188 (PP 1902, vol. XIII), p.45.
31 The 84 works recorded in the first year had grown to over 1,200 by 1905, only 73 of which were alkali works (*First Annual Report*, pp. 26–7; *42nd AR*, HC 289, 1906, p.5).
32 *Report to Her Majesty's Secretary for Scotland by Alfred E. Fletcher, Inspector for Scotland under the Rivers Pollution Prevention Act, 1876* (C. 5346, PP 1888, vol. LIX), p.5. He was also Chief Alkali Inspector in succession to Angus Smith, who had himself been the first central inspector for England under the 1876 Act.
33 ibid., p.6.
34 C 2159 (PP 1878, vol. XLIV), p.16.
35 *Intermediate Report on proceedings under the Alkali Acts 1863/1874* (PP 1876, vol. XVI), p.1.
36 ibid., p.5.
37 For the attempt to influence the form of the 1906 Bill, see PRO HLG 29/87.
38 Cd 1188 (1902), questions 19,965–19,972 and 20,123–8.
39 ibid., questions 20,129–30.
40 C 2159, 1878, questions 1647, 2852–3.
41 Memo by J.C. Dawes, 9 August 1932, and minute, W.A. Ross to I.G. Gibbon, 7 November 1932 on PRO HLG 55/8.
42 Cd 685, 1901, paras 30–1; Cd 1188, 1902, p.46.
43 I.G. Gibbon to Sir Arthur Robinson (Permanent Secretary), 17 July 1928 on PRO HLG 50/26; see also HLG 50/113.
44 PRO HLG 50/22.
45 See *Third Report of the Central Advisory Water Committee: River Boards* (Cmd 6465, 1943); *A National Water Policy* (Cmd 6515, 1944), p.22.
46 Earl of Huntingdon (HL Deb 152, 18 November 1947, col. 716): river purification boards were established in Scotland under the Rivers (Prevention of Pollution) (Scotland) Act 1951 on a broadly similar basis to river boards in England and Wales.
47 *Prevention of River Pollution* (Report of the River Pollution Prevention Sub-Committee of the CAWC, HMSO, 1949), paras 39, 42.
48 ibid., paras 46, 74.
49 ibid., para. 92.
50 s.7.
51 Clean Rivers (Estuaries and Tidal Waters) Act 1960: Rivers (Prevention of Pollution) Act, 1961, s.1; for Scotland, Rivers (Preventions of Pollution) (Scotland) Acts 1951 and 1965.
52 Water Resources Act 1963, s.114.
53 *Taken for Granted*, Report of the Working Party on Sewage Disposal (HMSO, 1970), para. 50.

54 See, for example, Mersey and Weaver River Authority, annual report 1965–6, p.6; 1969, p.42.
55 MHLG Circular 37/66: Sewage Effluents, paras 2, 4–5.
56 *Taken for Granted*, para. 152.
57 John Temple, moving the Second Reading of the Rivers (Prevention of Pollution) Bill (HC Deb 637, 24 March 1961, col. 839).
58 *Report of a River Pollution Survey of England and Wales 1970*, Vol.1 (HMSO, 1971), Table 1, p.1; updated 1975 (HMSO, 1978). Similar surveys were carried out in Scotland.
59 *Final Report of Trade Effluents Sub-Committee of CWAC* (HMSO, 1960), para. 20.
60 Jeremy Bugler, for example (*Polluting Britain*, Penguin, 1972) is noticeably more sympathetic to the problems of river authorities than to those of the alkali inspectorate; but for an example of a more critical attitude see Jon Tinker, 'River pollution: the Midlands dirty dozen', *New Scientist*, 6 March 1975, pp. 551–4.
61 s. 12(3)
62 For a discussion of the background to these changes, see A.G. Jordan, J.J. Richardson, R.H. Kimber, 'The origins of the Water Act of 1973', *Public Administration*, vol. 55, Autumn 1977, pp. 317–33.
63 The position is somewhat different in Scotland (see Appendix 2, p. 248–9).
64 But not the private water companies which were not absorbed into the RWAs.
65 Yorkshire Water Authority, AR 1974–5, para. 3.4.
66 Anglian Water Authority, AR 1974–5, p.26.
67 See, for example, Wessex WA, AR 1974–5, p.24; Welsh National Water Development Authority, AR 1974–5, para. 10.2.1.4–6.
68 Water Act, 1973, s.4; the chairman of the NWC is appointed by the Secretary of State for the Environment; and up to ten other members may be appointed by ministers.
69 *National Water Council: Review of Discharge Consent Conditions, Consultation Paper* (January 1977), para. 10.
70 *NWC: River water quality, the next stage* (July 1977), paras 22, 28.
71 Control of Pollution Act 1974, s.41.
72 *Third Report from Select Committee on Nationalised Industries, 1977—78* (HC 128, 1977), question 173.
73 PRO HLG 55/17, minute H.R. Hooper to H. Fawcett, 18 March 1922: deputation SAS to Minister, 24 March 1922.
74 PRO HLG 55/8, memo by I.G. Gibbon, 15 January 1932.
75 It was estimated that 4,000 additional deaths had occurred in London as a result of the smog: see *Interim Report of Committee on Air Pollution* (Cmd 9011, 1953), pp. 15–17.
76 *Report of Committee on Air Pollution* (Cmd 9322, 1954).
77 Clean Air Act, 1956, ss. 1,3,5,6,10,11.
78 *Report of Working Party on Recruitment, Training and Qualifications of Sanitary Inspectors* (HMSO, 1953), para. 58.
79 ibid., paras 37, 41, 50.
80 *Staffing in Environmental Health* (Assoc. Dist. Cos., etc., 1978), para. 2.1 and Table II (EL), p.89.
81 *RC Environmental Pollution, Fifth Report* (Cmnd 6371, 1976), paras 53, 142.
82 *Report of Committee on Air Pollution* (Cmd 9322, 1954), paras 24, 28.
83 Cmnd 6371 (1976), para. 53.
84 ibid., para. 56.
85 46th AR Alkali Inspectorate for 1909 (HC 191, 1910), pp. 7, 79.
86 91st AR Alkali Inspectorate for 1954 (HMSO, 1955), pp. 3,6.
87 R.H. Clayton, Managing Director, Manchester Oxide Company in *Journal of the National Smoke Abatement Society*, Summer 1934.
88 95th AR for 1958 (HMSO, 1959), p.5.

89 88th AR for 1951 (HMSO, 1952), p.1; visits to unregistered works were time-consuming and had led to the annual average of visits to registered works falling from four to three.
90 103rd AR for 1966 (HMSO, 1967), pp. 2–4.
91 104th AR for 1967 (HMSO, 1968), pp. 9–13.
92 Jeremy Bugler, *Polluting Britain* (Penguin, 1972), p.17.
93 *Committee on Air Pollution* (Cmd 9322, 1954), para. 45.
94 Maurice Frankel, *The Alkali Inspectorate* (Social Audit, 1974), pp. 39–44.
95 Noise Abatement Act, 1960; Control of Pollution Act, 1974, Part III.
96 Radioactive Substances Act, 1960.
97 In Scotland the industrial pollution inspectorate, which has responsibilities in connection with water pollution and waste disposal as well as air pollution has not been transferred to HSE but remains part of the Scottish Development Department.
98 *RCEP, 5th Report, Air Pollution Control: an integrated approach* (Cmnd 6371, 1976), paras 255, 271.
99 ibid., para. 145.
100 ibid., para. 160.
101 ibid., paras 166, 198–200, 267–70.
102 ibid., paras 220–2.
103 ibid., paras 123–4, 201–3.
104 ibid., para. 293.
105 The position since 1975 has been confused; pending the outcome of the RC's report the Alkali Inspectorate has not been fully integrated into HSE, but has nevertheless been brought into closer co-operation with other HSE inspectorates.
106 Cmnd 6371, para. 120.
107 *Health and Safety: Industrial Air Pollution 1976* (HMSO, 1978), para. 10.
108 W.M. Frazer, *History of English Public Health 1834—1939* (Bailliere Tindall & Cox, 1950), pp. 222–3.
109 HL Deb 347, 27 November 1973, col. 35; as Sir Eric Ashby he was the first chairman of the Royal Commission on Environmental Pollution from 1970 to 1973.
110 Bugler, op. cit., p.20.
111 Cmnd 6371, para. 124.
112 Quoted in Bugler, op. cit., p.8.
113 *Health and Safety: Industrial Air Pollution 1975* (HMSO, 1977), p.1.
114 The Royal Commission on Environmental Pollution found difficulty in obtaining comparative data and in interpreting it; see Cmnd 6371, paras 230–2.
115 A particularly severe criticism on these lines is in Frankel, op. cit., pp. 12–13.
116 See *RC Environmental Pollution 4th Report* (Cmnd 5780), para. 42.

CHAPTER 7

INSPECTION: AIMS AND METHODS

———————◆———————

Two of the key questions identified in Chapter 1 as important for determining the role of inspectorates were the aims of inspection and the means employed for achieving those aims. These questions will be explored in this chapter, drawing both on the information provided by the detailed studies of individual inspectorates and more widely on the experience of other inspectorates.

THE AIMS OF INSPECTION: SIMPLE OR MULTIPLE

The aims of inspection seem at first sight to be straightforward both in theory and practice. The early inspectorates were established to ensure that certain obligations imposed on others were in fact carried out. These obligations were generally set out in specific statutory requirements, and the aim of inspection was first to find out whether these requirements were being met, and, secondly, to take appropriate action if they were not. Inspectors of weights and measures, of factories and of nuisances, among others, had these tasks laid on them. Even schools inspectors who were not originally appointed by statute, had to see that the specific requirements laid down by the Committee of Council for the payment of grants were observed.

It is however also necessary to consider whether this was the sole aim of inspection even when the early inspectorates were established; and equally important is the question whether it has remained as the sole aim. The Mines Act 1850 was the first under which inspectors were appointed not to see that specific statutory requirements were being met, but in effect to look into the safety arrangements in mines and take action on anything they found seriously wrong, although in fact the Act did not give them very effective powers of action. Schools inspectors from the start were concerned with the more general promotion of educational standards, in addition to inspecting for the observance of specific grant requirements. And factory inspectors, who began simply with the task of seeing that quite specific statutory requirements were being observed, developed over the years a much broader concern with the promotion of health, safety and welfare in factories.

The latter in many ways provides one of the most significant examples of development in the aims of inspection. It can best be appreciated by considering how the HSW Act 1974 now defines the task of the factory and other inspectors brought within the scope of this legislation. The effect of the 1974 Act is to put on the six inspectorates of central government forming part of HSE and on local authority inspectors (primarily EHOs) with duties in this field a range of duties from the very specific to the very general. Some of these duties are precisely formulated in measurable terms. For example, some of the regulations made under the Factories Act 1961, such as the Asbestos or Woodworking Machines Regulations, contain such requirements.[1]

At the same time there are other less specific requirements, phrased in such terms as 'securely fenced' or 'best practicable means', which in their turn may be in part interpreted in terms of specific requirements. However, alongside these requirements inspectors are also concerned with carrying into effect Part 1 of the 1974 Act. This means in the first place that inspectors have a responsibility for seeing that employers, manufacturers, employees and others with duties under this part of the Act do in fact carry out those duties. Secondly, since Section 1 of the Act states that its aim is to secure the health, safety and welfare of persons at work, the implication is that inspectors should have regard to this underlying purpose in carrying out their work.[2]

The aims of inspection under the 1974 Act can thus be stated at various levels of generality: to promote health, safety and welfare at work; to secure observance of the provisions of the Act relating to the general duties of employers and others; to enforce specific requirements in existing Acts and Regulations. Not every inspectorate has multiple and complex aims of this kind. Some, such as the wages inspectorates of the Department of Employment and the Ministry of Agriculture, Fisheries and Food, or the horticultural marketing inspectorate of the latter department, still have aims which can be expressed largely in terms of the enforcement of specific statutory requirements. Nevertheless, as a generalisation one may say that there has been a certain tendency for inspectorates to develop broader and more complex aims. The consequences of this tendency for the role of inspectorates are best considered in terms of the limits of responsibility of inspectors.

LIMITS OF RESPONSIBILITY

Where, as in the weights and measures legislation, precise and specific requirements are laid down, there is no doubt of the respective responsibilities of inspectors and traders: the latter must operate in conformity with the Acts and regulations, the former must ensure that they do. Difficulties arise where inspectors, in addition to trying to ensure that specific requirements are met, are also in effect aiming to promote the underlying purposes of the legislation in a broader way –

as factory inspectors, for example, have increasingly become concerned with the promotion of health and safety in working conditions and not simply with the enforcement of particular regulations.

Theoretically there should be no difficulty; and the responsibilities of inspectors and those whom they inspect remain quite distinct. Acts regulating conditions in factories and mines for example have never given inspectors responsibility for providing safe and healthy working conditions: there has never been any doubt that the responsibility lay with employers, and that has been made quite specific in the 1974 Act. The task of inspectors was limited to trying to ensure that employers carried out those responsibilities, and this again has been made clear in the 1974 Act. Nevertheless, in practice this division may not appear quite so clear cut. Suppose for example, that a factory inspector, either unprompted or at the request of a manager, makes a suggestion for improvement of safety in a situation not precisely covered by the regulations. That suggestion can only, strictly speaking, be advice. It is not for him but for the courts to determine whether the law has been complied with, and the fact that the inspector has suggested ways in which in his opinion the owner *might* meet his obligations cannot be a conclusive defence for an owner who has followed the suggestion, if he should find himself prosecuted. At the same time, since it is the inspector who effectively decides in the great majority of cases whether a prosecution is to be instituted it is hardly surprising if, in spite of these theoretical niceties, it becomes accepted practice to treat the suggestions and advice of the inspector as being equivalent to the necessary requirements to comply with the terms of the statute. Indeed, it is hardly surprising that, as the chief inspectors of factories complained over the years in their annual reports, many employers treated specific requirements together with suggestions made by the inspector on his periodical visits as together constituting all that was needed to meet their general obligation for securing the health and safety of their employees. To satisfy the inspector when he came was, on this view, the equivalent of being absolved from further responsibility, in spite of the fact that from 1833 onwards legislation had been framed on quite a different principle.

The reason why it is not surprising that this should happen is that there is bound to be uncertainty about the limits of the inspector's responsibility once he goes beyond simply checking on specific and measurable requirements. The central government inspector, in particular, who is in this position is or soon becomes an expert in this field of work. It is not only the mines or the alkali inspectors, or in our own day the nuclear installations and radiochemical inspectors with their obvious scientific and technical knowledge who come into this category; it is the combination of that knowledge with the particular area of application which marks out the inspector's expertise. Mines did not have safety officers, alkali works did not have chemists, factories did not have people specifically concerned with the health and safety of those working there when inspectors were developing expertise in these areas. And even though this is no longer true to the same extent, the accumulated knowledge and experience of the inspectorates is in general much more broadly based than that of those working in particular industries. Furthermore, this knowledge is being exercised by people from outside industry with considerable authority derived from their statutory powers.

But once this wider role is acknowledged and accepted, at what point does the inspector cease to be an inspector and become the man who *de facto* if not *de jure* is assuming some responsibility for the standard of safety? In other words, is there not inevitably a grey area between the strict interpretation of what the inspector is expected to do and the strict interpretation of what the employer is expected to do? Who is responsible for safety becomes a question which in practice is not quite so simple to answer as theory – or for that matter the Health and Safety at Work [etc] Act 1974 – makes it appear. Theoretically, in his wider role the inspector is only an adviser; he cannot enforce something which by definition is not expressed in enforceable terms. Advice does not have to be accepted; but if it is accepted, and especially if it is accepted after being asked for in the first place by a manager anxious to do 'the right thing', it may seem difficult if as a result of something going wrong (e.g. an accident) he is then told that doing everything the inspector suggested is still not enough.

The mines inspectorate provides another example on this theme. Granted that there was a great deal of special pleading in the mine-owners' argument that inspection would weaken their responsibility for safety, the argument cannot be disposed of too lightly. Of course the implied antithesis in the 1878 instructions to mines inspectors between the main object of inspection ('promote and enforce the uniform observance of the legal obligation . . . ') and the 'plainly impracticable' idea that they should personally regulate 'or even superintend' the operation of mines was a false one.[3] The real antithesis was between the inspector as enforcer of specific statutory requirements and the inspector as the man who was there to use all the means in his power to promote greater safety in mines. He did after all have the power under the 1872 Act to require owners to remedy 'any matter, thing or practice' which he found dangerous and likely to lead to bodily injury, even though it was not specifically referred to in the Act.[4] It is true that this wide-ranging power was subject to various safeguards, but this did not alter the fact that the inspector was expected to concern himself with safety matters generally, and that there could therefore be doubt about the limits of the owner's and the inspector's responsibility so far as the aim of securing safety of working conditions in mines was concerned.

Nor was it only a question of the terms in which Acts of Parliament were drawn up. The way in which inspectors, under the Railway Regulation Act 1840, were drawn into considering safety questions[5] shows how the underlying principles of legislation rather than the strict terms of the Act could determine what inspectors did. Theoretically, their aim was confined to enforcement of the Act; in practice they assumed responsibility for the promotion of safety, although the safeguarding of the travelling public was – and still remains – legally the responsibility of the railway companies and their successors.

But perhaps the most interesting examples of the general as opposed to the specific responsibilites of inspectors are those in which they are concerned not with enforcement of the law but with the efficient performance of duties by others. Inspectors of constabulary, for example, were originally required simply 'to visit and inquire into the state and efficiency of the police' with a hint that numbers and discipline were the main ingredients to be considered.[6] They still have the duty of inspecting and reporting on efficiency, and now the added duty of carrying out other duties, under the direction of the Home Secretary, which are aimed at furthering police efficiency.[7] Inspectors of reformatory or industrial schools were to 'examine into the condition and regulations of the school and its fitness for the reception of youthful offenders or children'.[8] And inspectors of schools today, whatever was expected of them from the Committee of Council and under the revised Code, have the most indefinite aim of all, since the Education Acts require nothing of them at all beyond carrying out inspections, except in limited circumstances such as the registration of independent schools.

What these various inspectorates have in common is the relatively small part which precise requirements play in their work.[9] Correspondingly, their aims are more closely linked to the underlying purpose of the Acts under which they are appointed, and again this raises questions about the limits of their responsibility. An illustration is provided by the debates on the Police Bill in 1964. The Royal Commission on the Police had recommended that the Home Secretary should have responsibility for the efficiency of the police. In rejecting this, the Home Secretary, Henry Brooke, suggested that a statutory responsibility of this kind might require powers for the Home Secretary which would result in his having direct responsibility for the police generally such as he already possessed in the case of the Metropolitan Police. Instead of having a regulatory function and aiming to correct inefficiency he would, if the Royal Commission's views were accepted, have a much more positive duty to ensure efficiency.[10] The police authority, then, and not the Home Secretary acting through the inspector of constabulary remains responsible for seeing that the force is run efficiently. Yet the aim of the inspector, although strictly limited to ensuring that police authorities fulfil their obligations, almost inevitably goes beyond this, since he is in a position both to interpret what constitutes efficiency and to set in motion the machinery of sanctions if in his view a police force is not efficient. Furthermore, he has at least by implication the more positive task of aiming to increase the efficiency of the police in furtherance of the Home Secretary's duty to exercise his powers 'in such manner and to such extent as appears to him to be best calculated to promote the efficiency of the police.[11] The inspector's powers fall short of accepting responsibility for efficiency, but he is at least as closely involved in efficiency questions as the factory inspector is with safety in the factory.

Schools inspectors differ only in the fact that their aims are not expressed in terms of a specific concept like efficiency. Rather those aims are implied and subject to interpretation and different emphasis at different times, as was seen in Chapter 5. To say that inspectors aim to maintain and if possible improve standards of education is to say no more – and no less – than that they are concerned with the underlying purposes of the Education Acts. But once more the question is how far the responsibility of inspectors extends for the maintenance and improvement of standards of education. Certainly the Secretary of State has under the terms of the 1944 Act a duty to see that a varied and comprehensive educational service is provided in every area, and such a duty implies that he has a broad concern with the creation and maintenance of standards. School inspectors are a principal means by which attempts to promote this concern are carried on.

DIFFERING VIEWS OF THE INSPECTOR'S ROLE

Different perspectives of the inspector's role, deriving from a complexity of aims and revolving around questions such as the limits of responsibility, have become more prominent where the work of inspectors has come in for public comment and criticism. For a long time, going back certainly to the 1920s[12] there had been debate over the need to stimulate employers' efforts in the matter of safety and especially safety organisation. But in the 1960s increased concern about health and safety questions in factories brought into greater prominence the question of the extent to which inspectors could or should be held responsible for safety in factories. Those who felt that not enough was being done in the health and safety field criticised both employers and inspectors. The theoretical distinction between the employers' direct responsibility for taking action to secure health and safety, and inspectors' responsibility for ensuring that they carried out their responsibilities, tended to get blurred. At the same time the inspectorate could not argue that they were there simply to see that employers followed the specific requirements laid down in the Acts and regulations. They saw themselves, and others saw them, as having a function to promote health and safety practices in factories in a way which was not precisely laid down in the Factories Acts. Because of this, a failure to improve health and safety standards to the extent that the critics wanted made inspectors vulnerable to the charge that they were not effectively carrying out their aims. As some inspectors saw, this inevitably led to inspectors being criticised for matters which were not strictly speaking, their responsibility. And this was a factor as was shown, in the attempt in the 1974 Act to make more precise the boundaries between the responsibilities of employers and those of the factory and other inspectors brought within the Health and Safety Executive.

Nevertheless, the problem still remains but in a slightly different form. Inspectors may now be primarily concerned with examining not whether a particular safety measure has been adopted but with whether employers' organisation and procedures for safety purposes are adequate. It is thus, strictly speaking, no part of their task to tell employers to adopt a particular organisation or particular procedures. Indeed a major part of the thinking behind the new Act is to get employers away from the idea that all they have to do is to conform to some set formula devised or at least approved by the inspector. That many employers find difficulty in the new concept of self-regulation is a major theme of the chief factory inspector's 1976 report: the fact that some local authorities, for example, have simply adopted as their safety policy the document drafted by the Local Authority Joint Negotiating Committee received criticism from the chief inspector.[13] It seems that there may well still be a grey area between the inspector as the man who monitors the employer's safety arrangements, and the inspector as the man who is seen as in some measure setting the requirements for safety policy.

But doubt or misunderstanding about the inspector's role can take many forms. For example, the view that river pollution inspectors should not only investigate incidents such as oil spillages but act as 'official salvage operators' was complained of by one river authority.[14] But a more serious and difficult example in the pollution field is that of the alkali inspectorate. Here, in the view of the critics, the existing degree of pollution is not acceptable, and both industry and the inspectorate have been criticised for the situation. As with other inspectorates, there is a clear theoretical distinction between the responsibility of employers to use the best practicable means to prevent or limit the emission of gases and the responsibility of inspectors to ensure that employers do in fact carry out this duty. But, as the Royal Commission on Environmental Pollution pointed out, the alkali inspectorate operate not by standing back from industry but by closely collaborating with it to work out a best practicable means in each case; and through the provisions of the Act which require the inspectorate's approval for the use of new plant, they are also involved in the incorporation of pollution requirements in the design of new plants.[15]

Whatever the practical merits of such a method of operation – and the Royal Commission saw it as providing tougher and more practicable solutions to bpm than the alternative of adopting a detached attitude – it is liable to lead at least to misunderstanding about the inspectorate's role, if not to blur the respective responsibilities of industry and the inspectorate. For what to the inspectorate is simply a question of means – how best to secure the adoption of bpm – can easily appear as acceptance of a joint responsibility for securing a reduction in polluting emissions. The aims of the inspectorate could be expressed as the reduction of certain forms of pollution to the extent and at the speed that it and industry jointly think practicable. Thus the chief inspector could refer to research and investigation carried out by industry coming within the scope of the Alkali Acts as spent by scheduled industry on behalf of the inspectorate.[16]

FACTORS IN THE DEVELOPMENT OF THE AIMS OF INSPECTION

Given the fact that a multiplicity of aims can give rise to differing views of the inspector's role, it is important to examine the circumstances in which general as well as specific aims are found. One factor which distinguishes inspectorates with general or multiple aims from those with relatively limited and specific aims is the degree of professional expertise or technical knowledge required.

Inspectorates with more specific and limited aims generally are those where the degree of specialised knowledge required is much less. Wages inspectors, inspectors of ship's provisions and horticultural marketing inspectors are examples of central government inspectors who clearly need specialised or technical knowledge of their particular spheres of investigation; but it is of a relatively limited nature. Similarly, in local government, environmental health officers have a very wide range of duties from inspection of meat and unfit dwellings to pollution control and health and safety in shops and offices. Each of these requires its own specialised knowledge; but again this is not of the same order as that of the alkali or nuclear installations inspectors.

The inspectorates with the more general aims also appear to be associated with central rather than local government. Inspecting for specific requirements forms a major part of the work of all local government inspectorates, especially the more specialised ones, such as building control officers and fire prevention officers. EHOs and TSOs with their somewhat broader aims nevertheless spend the bulk of their time on inspecting for specific requirements. The extent to which, for example, TSOs can promote consumer protection generally is limited, and certainly legislation such as the Trade Descriptions Act or the Fair Trading Act does not require local authorities to promote better trading standards in the general way that HSE inspectors are concerned in promoting health and safety at work.

To some extent these factors reinforce one another: central inspectorates tend to be smaller and more specialised than local inspectorates. But even where this does not apply, central inspectorates tend to have a different character from local inspectorates, and this is reflected in the aims they pursue. A particularly important example is the factory inspectorate. The nature of the work under the original 1833 Act did not require specialised knowledge. From that point of view it could have been a local inspectorate. And that there was no inherent reason why local authorities should not be responsible for enforcing legislation relating to hours of work or health and safety at work was demonstrated both by their involvement in the regulation of workshops in the nineteenth century and, more particularly, by the provisions of the later Shops Acts and the Offices, Shops and Railway Premises Act 1963; and indeed by the fact that under the HSW Act 1974 enforcement is shared between HSE and local authorities. Moreover, at a more general political level, there was a strong current in mid-nineteenth-century Britain in favour of local self-government and against the extension of the powers of central government. The explanation of why the factory inspectorate nevertheless was made the responsibility of central and not local government lies in the nature of government intervention in factory matters as well as in the particular political and social circumstances of the time. The argument in favour of local rather than central government was strong in matters of social policy, as exemplified in the series of public health measures which were passed in the middle years of the nineteenth century. Intervention in the economic sphere was a different matter. That government should seek to regulate manufacturing industry at all was bitterly resisted, and only proved acceptable through the argument that the 1833 Act was a limited measure of protection for those who could not protect themselves.

Nevertheless, the factory owners were a powerful class of men who could appeal to economic arguments to support their view that government regulation would be ruinous for manufacturing industry. For inspection to be successful in such circumstances required that the inspectors should be a strong body of men with standing in the community and able to deal with the manufacturers on equal terms. This could only be done by bringing them under central rather than local control.

However, the fact that they were established in this way as a central inspectorate was important in contributing to their further development along lines which they would have been much less likely to follow if they had been a local inspectorate. In particular, inspectors themselves through their reports both provided information on conditions in factories and suggested the possibility of further regulation of manufacturing industry in the interests of the health and safety of those who worked in it. Thus began a complex process of interaction between the views of the inspectors and public opinion which was a major factor in the broadening of their aims to bring in the more general underlying purposes of legislation, as well as contributing to a more general acceptance of their role.

One may contrast the position of the factory inspectorate with that of the weights and measures inspectorate. The scope for the latter to press for a wider role in consumer protection was limited; it lacked the independence and authority of a central inspectorate. The developments in public opinion which ultimately were to broaden its role somewhat were ones to which the inspectorate reacted but which it did not initiate. And incidentally its broadened role led to discussion of whether inspection should be national rather than local, in a way which had hardly arisen when it was simply concerned with specific weights and measures regulations.

That the distinction between small centralised inspectorates with multiple aims and less specialised local inspectorates with more specific aims is by no means entirely fixed and clear-cut may be seen by considering two examples. When in 1877 the ravages of the Colorado beetle first compelled action to control insects and diseases which adversely affected farm crops, the method was for the Privy Council (and later the Board of Agriculture) to publish orders specifying the particular disease or pest to be controlled and the steps to be taken, such as destruction of affected crops; but local authorities were to administer the orders.[17] Later Acts (as in 1907) extended the procedure, but in 1914 the Board of Agriculture took over administration from the local authorities, and ever since inspectors of the department (now MAFF) have continued to enforce the Acts.[18] What is surprising is not that the central department should have taken this step but that it was ever made a local authority responsibility in the first place. A large number of local authorities – over 250 in England and Wales – had powers of enforcement and even where they appointed inspectors there was not enough work for them to do. Even in today's changed conditions, with far more work checking on imports and exports and far more regulations to enforce, the MAFF only employs seventy-five inspectors for the whole country in its plant health and seeds inspectorate. The original decision seems to have derived from earlier measures to stem cattle plague, where enforcement was a local authority responsibility – as indeed it still is under the Diseases of Animals Acts.

The other example is that of the wages inspectorates of both DE and MAFF. Here one would at first sight have expected local enforcement. This is a straightforward regulatory function, not requiring a great deal of specialist knowledge and with the establishments to be inspected found throughout the country. Yet the idea of local inspection seems never to have been considered. The explanation is mainly to be found in the circumstances which led to the appointment of the original wages inspectorate in 1909. The factory inspectorate was active in providing the information on which the proposals were founded for the establishment of trade boards to regulate conditions in certain trades. Enforcement of the minimum wages provisions of the Trade Boards Act 1909 was still seen as relying partly on information reported by factory inspectors on their routine inspections but with 'special peripatetic inspectors' appointed under the Act as the main means of enforcement.[19] To this extent the wages inspectorate may be seen as an offshoot of the factory inspectorate and hence a central government inspectorate, although from the point of view of the work carried out this could equally well have been a local inspectorate.

Despite this lack of a rigid dividing line between what was appropriate to a central inspectorate and what was appropriate to a local authority inspectorate, the contrasting characteristic of the two kinds of inspector were important for their future development. The professionalism and relative freedom of central inspectors not only gave them a higher status but made it more likely that they would seek positively to develop the work, and would be in a position to have their views taken seriously. By contrast, local authority inspectors were men of humbler status who had a struggle in the first place to establish their separate indentity, let alone the status deriving from technical competence that they have since achieved. They were therefore in a very weak position to press for and develop aims, at least until collectively they had the organisations which could speak effectively for them on such issues; and in some cases this did not really happen until well on into the twentieth century, as was the case with the weights and measures inspectors. The contrast is between people like the early factory inspectors – lawyers, merchants, scientists – or the early schools inspectors, who were mainly clergymen, and the early weights and measures and nuisances inspectors, who, if they were not policemen, often combined the work of inspecting with another occupation such as relieving officer.

A complicating factor in tracing the development of the aims of inspection is that many inspectorates carry out other functions in addition to inspecting. In some cases this has been a later development in inspectorates which originally only had the job of inspecting, whereas in others there was a range of functions from the start. A particular example of the former is the development of inspectors of central government into professional advisers of ministers and departments. Railway inspectors advise the Department of Transport on railway investment plans, drugs inspectors advise the Home Office on the extent and nature of drug abuse and the Department of the Environment look to the ancient monuments and historic buildings inspectorate for archaeological advice. For the most part this kind of advisory function is closely connected with the provision of information which is an essential part of the inspecting function. The inspector becomes an expert in factory conditions or the conditions of laboratories in which animal experiments are conducted, both because he is in most cases the only government official who regularly visits such places and because of his special knowledge which, as in the case of the alkali inspectorate, may well be a major reason for his appointment as an inspector in the first place.

The role of professional adviser is also common for those inspectors who originally had functions additional to that of simply inspecting. Schools inspectors provide an obvious example here. But schools inspectors also provide an example of an inspectorate which at different times has acquired a whole range of functions, some closely allied to inspection work and others which seem much more remote. To throw more light on this phenomenon it is worth looking at two very different modern inspectorates, sea fisheries and nuclear installations.

The sea fisheries inspectorates of MAFF and DAFS seem to have had their origin in certain agreements between the British and French governments in the nineteenth century about fishing rights for the two countries within certain limits, the job of the inspectors being solely enforcement of the provisions of the agreements.[20] The inspectorates still have an enforcement role but with more emphasis now on conservation measures and matters such as the minimum size of fish and of nets. However, a great deal of their work is not now concerned with inspecting. Besides being the departments' technical advisers on fisheries matters they fulfil the dual role of providing general information and intelligence about the fishing industry to the departments and of acting as the means of liaison between the departments and the industry. None of these functions derives from the inspecting function: they could be carried out quite separately. Indeed, because of the preponderance of non-inspecting functions the sea fisheries inspectorates are a borderline case (see Appendix 2).

The nuclear installations inspectorate was established with a dual function. It was the body which was to provide the Minister with the necessary scientific and technical appraisal of proposals to instal and operate nuclear plant from the safety aspect as a preliminary to the granting of a licence; and it was subsequently to inspect installations, specifically to ensure that they complied with the conditions on which licences had been granted. That these two specific functions are really part of a wider role, essentially that of taking care of the central government's concern with the safety of nuclear installations, has been clear from the beginning, and is evidenced by, for example, the inspectorate's appraisal of the safety issues of various types of reactor as part of the government's need to decide which type of reactor to build in the next phase of the nuclear power programme.[21]

In drawing attention to this phenomenon of inspectors who do more than inspection we are in effect going beyond the aims of inspection. Those aims relate to a particular administrative process whose characteristic is that it depends on assigning to certain designated officials the right to go into certain premises and observe, ask questions, examine records and sometimes much more besides. In asking what are the aims of inspection we are asking what intention lies behind this particular approach, and why it is thought necessary to arm officials with powers of this kind. The distinction which has been made, in examining this question, between inspecting for specific statutory requirements and inspecting directed more generally to the underlying purpose of the legislation is also relevant to discussion of other functions which inspectors may perform. For it is in concerning himself with the underlying aims of legislation that the inspector may cease to be simply an inspector, and may pursue other activities which promote those aims – even though they may be activities which have little connection with inspecting and do not need to be performed by officials possessing the special powers which are the mark of an inspector.

When factory inspectors offer advice to employers or employees about safety at work, or nuclear installations inspectors act as professional advisers to government on nuclear safety, or schools inspectors run in-service training courses for teachers, this may seem no more than a logical extension of their activities. But in considering aims we are now concerned more with the aims of inspectors than with the aims of inspection. Inspection now becomes only one of the means which the inspector uses to achieve ends which inevitably must be viewed in broader terms than the specific requirements which still need to form at least part of the aim of his inspecting work.

It is again not easy to generalise about the ways in which inspectors are drawn into other activities, and particularly how far it arises from their own initiative and how far from external factors. There are, for example, obvious needs of central departments for information and advice on specialised matters which inspectors are uniquely placed to provide. At the same time inspectors may well be eager to enhance their professional status by becoming the accepted, and sometimes the indispensable, authority on matters within their sphere. One may simply note here that in pursuing a variety of activities, even though they may all be directed to the same broad end, inspectors are vulnerable to criticism about the relative priority of different aims. In particular, if inspection is to be regarded as only one means open to inspectors in achieving their aims, what is the relative importance of inspection and by what criterion is the relative effort devoted to it to be determined? These are questions which will need to be borne in mind in considering how inspection operates in practice.

The discussion so far has been concerned mainly with two phenomena: that the aims of inspection cannot always be seen as being simply to ensure the observance of specific requirements; and that to the extent that inspectors may be concerned with broader aims and may engage in activities other than inspection there may be significant disagreement about their role. It must be emphasised, however, that in terms of aims inspectors cover a wide range. For most inspectorates the specific requirements aim still plays a large part. This is true of the local government inspectorates and of some central government inspectorates. At the same time few of them are concerned exclusively with this aim. Similarly, in looking at the extent to which they have additional functions there is a wide range – from those which do little more than inspect, like the wages and horticultural marketing inspectorates, to those with many functions like the sea fisheries inspectorate or the Social Work Service, whose wide range of functions brings them into a borderline category.

One group of inspectorates which has both general aims and a tendency to acquire additional functions is that of the efficiency inspectorates. Again, they are not a uniform group. Inspectors of constabulary and fire services have a more restricted role than schools inspectors, but this is a group which by its nature cannot simply be confined to inspection for specific requirements.

The idea of the inspector as the man who is appointed to see that certain specified requirements are met is therefore still very much alive. And the importance of this fact is that it governs a great deal of public expectation about the work of inspectors. The original conception and ideal model of inspection was that of a means of checking that what Parliament intended should happen was in fact happening. It still has validity. This role, symbolised by the traditional weights and measures inspector, is in essentials a very narrow one. That alongside it there can exist a wider conception of the aim of inspection, one which seeks to relate inspection not simply to specified requirements but to the underlying purpose for which legislation was evolved, has been the major theme of the preceding pages. But to explore this phenomenon further and to examine its consequences requires an investigation of the methods used by inspectors to achieve their aims. Far more criticism has been directed at inspectors for the approach they have adopted to the work of inspection than to their aims, but it may well be that an elucidation of these criticisms requires a closer look at the connection between them.

METHODS USED BY ENFORCEMENT INSPECTORATES

In examining the ways in which inspectors attempt to achieve their aims the most prominent theme to be examined in the case of enforcement inspectors is the contrast between the theory, as expressed particularly in their formal powers of action, and the practice, the way in which those powers are used. Since this is a key issue in any discussion of enforcement inspectorates it will be considered first, the factors contributing to the present position examined and the consequences explored. Efficiency inspectorates raise somewhat different considerations, which will be examined later.

Enforcement carries with it the idea of compulsion, the sense that people are unwilling to carry out their obligations unless pressure of some kind is put on them. Inspectors were and still are people appointed to exert that pressure. Many of the statutes establishing inspectorates specifically provide for a duty of enforcement, notably the HSW Act 1974, or for some similar duty.[22] Clearly the action powers of inspectors are connected with this duty, but we need to know both how it was intended that inspectors should use their powers, and how they have in fact used them.

At first sight there seems to be a simple connection between the aims of inspection and the powers of action given to enforcement inspectors. Specific requirements to be enforced are laid down by statute; the powers are the means by which they are to be enforced. Yet from the beginning theory and practice diverged; the first factory inspectors were instructed in dealing with mill-owners

to endeavour to reconcile them in any way that was practicable and reasonable to the restrictions and regulations.[23]

And even when, after the government had failed in 1836 to get the Factory Act strengthened, new instructions were issued to enforce the law to its fullest extent, this did not necessarily mean using the weapon of prosecution for every breach of the Act. On the contrary, Leonard Horner, one of the original inspectors, told his superintendents (assistants) that they were to try to secure compliance 'by explanation, respectful admonition, and warning'; to make clear that it was with regret that they found things wrong, and that prosecution would only be employed against 'wilful and obstinate offenders'.[24] The emphasis in the early factory inspectorate is thus on attempting to secure a certain standard of compliance with the legal requirements by persuasion, in the main, rather than on enforcing the law with the powers available to inspectors.

In this connection it is striking to note the language which Alexander Redgrave used, little more than forty years after the factory inspectorate was established, to describe the way in which an inspector should behave on discovering a breach of the law.[25] It was not simply that prosecution was a last resort; it was the stress he laid on the inspector as a friendly adviser which seemed to go far beyond anything which Leonard Horner had said, and indeed to rival Angus Smith, the first alkali inspector, in its reliance on co-operation and persuasion rather than strict enforcement.

Other inspectorates in the nineteenth century did not necessarily go as far as the factory and alkali inspectorates in the stress laid on the friendly adviser aspect. Many, and in particular the local authority inspectors, saw their task largely in terms of strict enforcement of regulations. Nevertheless, the tendency over the years has been in the direction indicated by Alexander Redgrave, and in the 1970s the emphasis is strongly on friendly relations between inspectors and those whom they inspect. When weights and measures inspectors took on new responsibilities for trade descriptions, the Board of Trade Minister saw them as establishing friendly relations – at least with reputable traders – just as a former chief inspector of weights and measures had stressed the need for a good understanding and rapport with responsible traders.[26] And even twenty-five years ago an official report on sanitary inspectors saw them as

> able to work much more by way of explanation and persuasion and less by threats and legal action.[27]

This does not mean that all enforcement inspectorates are now like the alkali inspectorate, seeking to achieve the law's ends through co-operation, to the virtual exclusion of the use of prosecution. There is significance in the use of the words 'reputable' and 'responsible' in reference to the weights and measures inspectors. Most inspectorates would probably see themselves as working mainly by persuasion; but with the reservation that there would always be a minority of those unwilling to comply, for whom prosecution was the answer; friendly relations are appropriate for the majority who are co-operative and ready to comply but clearly ineffective for the minority.

Moreover, many inspectorates would argue that there was a need from time to time for exemplary prosecutions as a deterrent to undesirable practices. As a former chief inspector of factories put it:

> One well merited case may encourage management to review its organisation for compliance and bring about improvements in areas other than those for which the information is laid.[28]

In spite of this, however, it is characteristic of enforcement inspectorates to stress the aim of prevention rather than detection in their work. An illustration is provided by the cruelty to animals inspectorate. On the face of it this has a straightforward task of enforcement. The Act of 1876, which still governs its operations, requires anyone wishing to carry out experiments on living animals to apply to the Home Secretary for a licence, which may be granted with conditions; inspectors appointed by the Home Secretary are to visit all places registered under the Act for the performance of such experiments in order to secure compliance with the terms of the licence.[29] The Home Office interpretation of this duty is that inspectors are mainly

> to keep in touch as closely as they can with licensees in their districts, to know what they are doing, and to be ready to guide and advise them so as to remove any risk of contraventions of the Act or the conditions imposed in licences.[30]

Thus although the inspectors carry out inspections and do, as the chief inspector's annual reports show, occasionally find things wrong, they are not there in the Home Office view, just to carry out inspections, still less to supervise the actual experiments, as some people mistakenly believe. The important task was 'to ensure that licensees understand and fulfil their responsibilities under the Act'.[31]

Prevention rather than detection, persuasion rather than coercion, friendly advice rather than the heavy hand of the law – these are the characteristic ways in which enforcement inspectors behave. Differing, it must be stressed, in the extent to which they see themselves as following the first rather than the second of these alternatives, nevertheless enforcement inspectorates do have this tendency towards the first set of alternatives; and moreover this tendency has on the whole grown in the course of the long history of such inspectorates. How has this come about?

FACTORS INFLUENCING CHOICE OF METHODS

The fundamental reason lies in the nature of the offences created by the legislation which inspectors are appointed to enforce. Those offences are from the legal point of view treated as criminal matters, but for the most part are not generally regarded as crimes by inspectors, by those found guilty of the offences or by the general public. Criminal sanctions, and especially the use of prosecution, are thus not seen as appropriate weapons to use simply because a breach of the regulations has taken place, but rather require some additional factor to bring them into operation, such as persistent failure to take action in conformity with the regulations, or positive refusal to do so.

That this was not simply a view taken by inspectors but corresponded to a general feeling that there was a distinction, however difficult to formulate precisely, between 'real' crimes, which were a matter for the police, and breaches of statutory requirements, to be dealt with by inspectors, can be seen in the fact that Parliament in certain cases provided specifically for administrative action to be taken as an alternative or preliminary to prosecution when breaches were discovered. The procedure laid down for dealing with statutory nuisances provides an obvious illustration.[32] More recently, the procedures for the use of improvement and prohibition notices under the HSW Act 1974 similarly provide a formal means for inspectors to seek to achieve conformity with the law without recourse to the courts. It is, however, undoubtedly true that this attitude was reinforced, particularly in the case of central government inspectors, by the outlook of inspectors themselves. The early central government inspectors were educated, professional men, sometimes expert in their field of inspection (railways, mines and alkali), and sometimes not (factory). Such men did not see their task as the detection of crime, but rather as one of making use of their education and professional skills to achieve the purposes of the various statutes with which they were concerned. Persuasion was a more natural way of operating to men who had or soon acquired expert knowledge not of how to detect crime but of how to protect workers from dangerous machinery, how to run trains on single-track lines safely, or how to reduce the amount of sulphuric acid gas being emitted from the chimneys of chemical factories.

The early local government inspectors were not men of the same status and on the whole took a more limited view of their functions, and were in any case constrained by the attitudes of the local authorities which employed them. Nevertheless, the increasing professionalism which has marked the development of local government inspectorates in the twentieth century has been one factor in their tendency also to move towards a more persuasive mode of operation. But many would also see grounds for this change in a generally more co-operative attitude by those inspected.

More specific reasons have also contributed to the general tendency. There is, first, the attitude of the courts. As the early factory inspectors soon discovered, even where they used their powers against offenders, magistrates frequently imposed inadequate penalities; mill-owners who defied the law knew that even if they were prosecuted and fined it still paid them not to comply.[33] The problem has continued to haunt the factory inspectorate and others ever since.[34] Moreover, the work of preparing a case for prosecution is inevitably time-consuming, so that an active policy of frequent prosecution may require the committal of resources which in the view of many inspectors would be better spent on trying to secure compliance in other ways.

The latter argument involves wider considerations. Most inspectorates are relatively small in relation, for example, to the number of premises to be visited. The view of many inspectors is that it is impossible to inspect frequently enough to ensure that statutory requirements are being observed by that means alone, and that there is therefore a strong practical argument for seeking the co-operation of those inspected in securing compliance, and this is reinforced by the view that most people are willing to comply.

Implicit in these arguments is the positive justification by inspectors for the methods they employ – that they achieve better results. The case was put forcefully in the 1926 instructions to mines inspectors. The inspector, it was said, could be of great service to managers of mines

> by tactfully conveying to them the knowledge and experience which he has acquired of methods and precautions promoting safety and health. In this way much can be done which cannot be achieved by enforcement of Statutes and Regulations only. It is important that managers should regard the Inspectors as friendly advisers rather than as policemen, so far as this relationship can be achieved consistently with an Inspector's conscientious discharge of his duties.[35]

In other words, the argument is not only that by persuading people of the necessity for legislative requirements they will be more ready to comply than if they are simply told to comply or face prosecution, but that through adopting this persuasive approach even higher standards are possible than simply the minimum laid down by statutes and regulations.

There are large implications in such arguments for the future of inspection which will need to be examined later. But they also help to account for a further characteristic of enforcement inspectorates, that they not only seek to achieve compliance by persuasion but find themselves also giving advice on and explaining what the law's requirements are. Here a twentieth-century development has reinforced earlier tendencies. As the volume of legislative requirements has grown, it becomes harder for the law-abiding citizen to know what he is expected to do. Inspectors are not legal experts, but they are experts in interpreting those requirements in their practical application. Hence, as the 1953 Working Party on sanitary inspectors put it,

> traders and property owners do not find it a simple matter to ascertain and comply with the law. They have come to look to sanitary inspectors for help in solving their problems.[36]

Central government inspectorates with limited aims rely on this argument. The Department of Employment wages inspectorate, for example, has an essentially limited and specific enforcement task. When a special drive in a number of towns disclosed that more than one quarter of employers visited were underpaying their employees the remedy was not sought in wholesale prosecutions. Rather, it was explained that prosecution was only undertaken after a second visit by an inspector and where 'serious irregularities' were found. The reasons suggested for taking this course were, first, that most underpayments arose from ignorance and misunderstanding, and it would therefore be counter productive for inspectors simply to prosecute at a first visit instead of explaining the position to the employer; secondly, the courts would be critical if inspectors prosecuted 'just to ensure bare compliance'.[37]

It is, however, in those inspectorates which have the longest tradition of operating by persuasion, and which have relied on giving advice not just as a means of securing compliance but as a means of promoting the underlying purposes of legislation that the full consequences of this approach become evident. As long ago as 1956 it could be said of the factory inspectorate:

> There is no clear distinction between the inspectorial and the advisory functions of the Inspector . . . the giving of advice to individual employers is an integral part of inspection.[38]

Sixteen years later the Robens Committee identified 'the provision of advice and assistance towards progressively better standards' as the 'basic function' of inspection services.[39]

METHODS USED BY EFFICIENCY INSPECTORS AND CONTRAST WITH ENFORCEMENT INSPECTORS

This discussion has been concerned with the enforcement inspectorates of both central and local government, both because they are the more numerous group and because they raise most sharply the apparent sharp contradiction between the existence of strong penal powers and the practical preference for the use of persuasion and advice in the achievement of aims. Efficiency inspectorates also raise the question of the relation between aims and methods but in a somewhat different way.

In considering the duties and powers of efficiency inspectors scrutiny of statutes and regulations is rarely of much help. Inspectors of constabulary illustrate some of the problems. Nothing is said in the Police Act 1964, even by implication, about the powers of inspectors. But the chief inspector's annual report has in recent years generally included a formula which is significant both for the powers of inspectors and their methods of operation:

No adverse report was made that prejudiced the claims of the police authority to receive exchequer grant on approved expenditure and those measures which were necessary to rectify any shortcomings revealed in the course of inspection were brought about through suggestion and persuasion during discussion with chief officers in the course of inspection visits.[40]

What is implied here is a certain relationship between the activities of the inspectorate and the powers, formal and informal, of the Secretary of State. As the Royal Commission pointed out, the operation of the central departments in relation to the police was 'governed by influence rather than command'.[41] The formal controls have been somewhat strengthened since[42] but neverthelesss the power of the inspector is essentially limited to his ability in the first instance to exercise persuasion on the police authority or chief constable, with the Secretary of State's authority behind him. The extent, however, to which, if persuasion does not have the desired result from the inspector's point of view, he can get the department to act and exert pressure is itself very largely a function of the relationship at any particular time between the inspectorate and the administrative divisions of the Home Office concerned with police affairs. An inspector's report is thus only one element, whose strength may vary with a number of factors, in a process which may lead ultimately to the withdrawal of exchequer grant, although this sanction is now very rarely used.[43]

What is true of inspectors of constabulary is true to a greater or lesser extent of other efficiency inspectors. However, the important point is that because of this less specific nature of both aims and powers, as compared with those of enforcement inspectors, efficiency inspectors have always tended to operate by persuasion and to acquire additional functions, often of an advisory or promotional nature. The former is as clear in the early instructions to schools inspectors and inspectors of constabulary[44] as it is in the report of the chief inspector of constabulary in 1976 and in recent pronouncements by the DES.

The contrast between enforcement and efficiency inspectors may be summed up in the following way. The former have in principle a choice of means in carrying out inspecting work: they may rely on a strict use of enforcement powers to ensure compliance, or they may seek this end mainly through persuasion. Efficiency inspectors, lacking in general the direct connection between specific requirements and enforcement powers, must almost inevitably rely on persuasion as their principal means. One consequence is that inspection as supervision, in their case, is very often allied with more generally promotional aims. The blend of supervisory and promotional activities is best exemplified by the Social Work Service of DHSS. It has a wide range of functions: eleven are listed in a recent circular.[45] Most of them are of a generally promotional nature, or concerned with the promotion of professional standards, or concerned with giving professional advice to the department; but one is to exercise the Secretary of State's statutory powers in relation to the inspection of residential homes. It is clear that, as with schools inspectors, the Social Work Service in most of its dealings with local authorities is providing information, advice and encouragement. Indeed, its main function is explicitly said to be 'to advise and support' the Social Services Departments of local authorities.[46] But unlike schools inspectors SWS does still have a specific supervisory element.

The development of efficiency inspectorates to some extent parallels that of enforcement inspectorates, and for some of the same reasons. The professionalism of enforcement inspectors, which is a prominent factor in their inclination to persuasive methods and the provision of advice is equally characteristic of efficiency inspectors. Inspectors of schools, for example, have a professional commitment to the improvement of standards of education, which they may see in terms of trying to persuade teachers to adopt different methods or techniques.

Above all, however, the nature of efficiency compared with enforcement inspection makes easier the twofold development noted earlier from the use of persuasion to achieve the aims of inspection to a more advisory role; and from inspection as the sole or major function to inspection as only one of a number of functions carried out by inspectors.

CONSEQUENCES OF ENFORCEMENT INSPECTORS' METHODS

In considering the consequences of the ways in which inspectors, and particularly enforcement inspectors, seek to achieve their aims, it is important first to examine the underlying assumptions of much of their work.

It is central to the arguments for inspection by persuasion, for establishing good relations with those inspected – or at least the great majority of them – and for the usefulness of offering advice, that most of those subject to inspection accept the need for regulation or supervision, and, further, are prepared to carry out the suggestions made by inspectors to this end.

To some extent the mere existence of legislation, and of inspectors' powers to enforce it, can be expected to have an effect on people's behaviour. And it may be that, as the instructions to mines inspectors in 1878 claimed, the liability to inspection without warning is 'a most effective guarantee against abuse'. However, the argument on which inspectors rely in practice seems to go beyond this, and to assume that there is a readiness to co-operate with the inspector which is not simply due to the latent threat of penal powers.

One consequence of this assumption is that inspectors not only act by persuasion but are on the whole inclined to patience and sympathetic consideration of the difficulties of those inspected, with sanctions remaining very much in the background. In the Acre Mill case[47] one reason why the factory inspectorate was unwilling to move more quickly and decisively was because the company had appeared ready to co-operate. More generally the attitude can be seen in other studies of the factory inspectorate[48] and in the way in which the alkali inspectorate operates.

The consequences of reliance on advice, persuasion and mutual confidence, and on the assumption of a general atmosphere of co-operation, are important for any assessment of the effectiveness of the work of enforcement inspectors. They must be seen against the fact that there is a conflict of interests inherent in what the inspector is trying to do. As the 1833 Factory Commissioners pointed out in advocating a special agency for enforcement of their proposals, those proposals

> are not directly conducive to the immediate interests either of the master manufacturers, or of the operatives, or of any powerful class, and are not likely therefore to receive continuous voluntary support.[49]

The justification for having enforcement inspectors at all still remains that their concern is to press for things to be done which otherwise would not be done or certainly not to the same extent, because those whom they inspect do not have an immediate interest in pursuing these other activities. One reason is that the inspector's requirements mean additional expense, most obviously so in such traditional areas as guarding factory machines, installing proper drains or providing a good standard of accommodation for the crews of merchant ships. In other cases, such as weights and measures, it is rather that there is a positive financial incentive not to comply fully with the requirements;

and it is this which the inspector is seeking to overcome. In the case of efficiency inspectorates the conflict of interest may be rather more subtle but can still involve financial considerations; for example, an inspector of constabulary may press for a certain standard of accommodation or equipment which a police authority may be unwilling to meet because of the cost.

That there have been often quite striking changes of attitudes to these questions since inspectorates were first established need not to be doubted. Employers do accept the need for safety measures, houses would be unlikely to be built without sanitation even without the existence of inspectors, owners of merchant ships would no longer provide the cramped and insanitary conditions which prevailed in the early nineteenth century. But this does not mean that conflicts of interest have disappeared. Indeed in some ways they may be more acute. Because standards have improved, further progress may be much more costly. It was comparatively easy for Angus Smith, the first alkali inspector, to get his 5 per cent target for the emission of hydrochloric acid achieved; it needed a relatively cheap piece of apparatus, and moreover the hydrochloric acid which had been previously wasted could be put to profitable use. In the 1970s the virtual elimination of dust from cement works which has long been a source of complaint is technically feasible, but the cost is large. There is a very obvious conflict of interest here between the desire to eliminate air pollution from cement works, and the desire of the cement companies to produce cement as cheaply as possible. As a former chief alkali inspector put it, 'Problems of air pollution control are mainly economic.'[50] It is equally obvious in the case of the alkali inspectorate how the conflict of interests has been resolved. Since the inspectorate has always conceived its role as being to co-operate with industry, to lead and not drive, progress can only be through compromise, through attempting to balance the desire for improvement against its feasibility and cost.

Other inspectorates may not have gone as far in this direction, but in general the more they combine specific with general aims and persuasion with the offering of advice the more they are likely to be drawn into compromise over conflicts of interest. Factory, mines and nuclear installations inspectors pay more attention to the cost of their proposals than do wages inspectors, environmental health officers or trading standards officers; but there is an element of compromise in the activities of the latter group nevertheless. It is this element of compromise over conflicting interests which has most attracted criticism to the work of enforcement inspectors. Since the view that compliance with the law is more likely if persuasion is used depends for its justification on the results achieved, it is precisely where there is dissatisfaction with the results of inspection work that the methods of inspectors and their reliance on the assumption of co-operation are subject to the most critical challenge.

There seems to be an obvious paradox between the powers given to inspectors by statute and the use made of those powers. Parliament has given inspectors powerful weapons to make sure that the law is complied with, but what inspectors seem to be saying is that it is neither desirable nor practicable to use those powers except as a last resort. Surely, the critics argue, the discrepancy does not make sense. Powers were given to be used: if they are not used and results are unsatisfactory, this shows that they ought to be used, and this will produce better results.

Certain inspectorates in particular, and notably the factory and alkali inspectorates, have been criticised on these grounds. The criticism of methods in particular implies a different view of how divergent interests should be treated. For the critics in effect take a much less optimistic view of the efficacy of persuasion, and of the possibilities of compromise in reconciling conflicting interests. Correspondingly, they suggest that greater use of enforcement powers will induce a more positive desire to comply, or even to seek the advice of inspectors.[51]

Criticism of methods of inspection in this way has only seriously affected a few inspectorates, notably the factory and alkali and to some extent the nuclear installations inspectorates; but it is at least implied in more recent studies of trading standards officers and wages inspectors,[52] and there is certainly no guarantee that other inspectorates will not find themselves open to challenge. Until twenty years ago the alkali inspectorate was a very obscure body whose activities were of interest and indeed only known to those most directly involved. Now its activities are closely watched and criticised by environmentalists and others. As changing circumstances bring other issues into public and political prominence other inspectorates may well similarly find themselves under critical scrutiny. A particularly damaging criticism which may increasingly be heard is that because of the assumptions and methods which they employ inspectors are too closely identified with the interests they are employed to regulate.

CONSEQUENCES FOR ASSESSING THE EFFECTIVENESS OF INSPECTORATES

Inspectors ought in principle to have no difficulty in meeting such criticisms. Their appeal to and justification of the persuasive approach is entirely pragmatic. They use their method because they claim it produces better results.

Their answer to the critics should therefore be to demonstrate what has been achieved and show that these results are better than would be likely by the methods advocated by the critics. Clearly this is what they attempt to do, but in practice they have relied more on assertion than demonstration. It is one of the notable features of the public debate which has developed over the methods of certain inspectorates that inspectors have found it difficult to meet the criticisms. Yet it is crucial to any assessment of the value of the work of inspectors to have criteria against which to measure the methods employed by them against possible alternative approaches.

Critically, the arguments depend on where the balance should lie. No enforcement inspectorate denies the need to use compulsion in certain circumstances: no critic expects every breach of the regulations to be met with a prosecution. But there is a need to know whether the critics are right in supposing that more prosecutions would lead to a greater degree of compliance, or whether on the contrary inspectors are right in thinking that higher standards of compliance are achieved by persuasion. The question is complicated by the fact that it does not necessarily receive the same answer for every inspectorate.

The criteria for assessing whether inspection of weights and measures or of ships' provisions is effective are of quite a different kind from those applying to inspection to promote greater health and safety in mines or factories, or more efficient police forces. In the former group it is possible to show that there is a correlation between the intensity of inspection and the frequency with which infringements of the law are found at random inspection visits.[53] More inspection does in these cases bring higher standards of compliance, and conversely low standards of compliance may be corrected by inspecting more intensively. This is, however, only part of the story. More inspection may bring down the rate of infringements, but it does not answer the question of what level of infringements is acceptable nor of what is the best method of achieving that level. For, although the theoretical aim of inspection for specific requirements may be complete compliance all the time, no method of inspection, indeed no other administrative procedure, is likely to achieve that. Some standard of effective inspection is needed; and having established the standard some means of assessing different methods of achieving it is also needed. This is not simply a question of the balance between persuasion and compulsion. There are also practical questions, such as the balance between responsive and preventive work. How far should inspectors rely on investigation of complaints to achieve the acceptable standard of compliance, and how much on detection by routine inspection, or through provision of information and advice on the prevention of infringements? Or again one might use the volume of complaints as a measure of effectiveness; if they exceeded a certain level one could argue that this indicates that more effort needed to be put into routine inspection.

But even granted these complications, there are nevertheless considerable differences between inspectorates which make it harder to judge the methods employed. The almost universal argument of enforcement inspectors, deriving largely from their own experience, is that too much reliance on prosecution and its threat would only antagonise those whom they inspect and would as a consequence make it harder to achieve desirable standards of compliance. They cannot in the nature of the argument demonstrate this, but the argument would carry more weight if there was less divergence between inspectorates in the way they interpret it. If TSOs each on average find it necessary to prosecute three times a year, whereas most wages inspectors never handle a prosecution, this at least suggests that the relation between use of prosecutions and the success of inspection needs investigation. The difference may be due entirely to the differing nature of the requirements in the two cases; but it is by no means obviously so.

The criteria are even harder to formulate where the object of inspection is not simply conformity with specific statutory requirements but broader aims whose measurement is inevitably more difficult. By what criteria does one judge whether the factory or mines inspectorate has contributed to securing the health, safety and welfare of those working in factories and mines; or whether the horticultural marketing inspectorate has contributed to the competitiveness of the horticultural industry; or whether inspectors of constabulary have improved the efficiency of police forces? And even if one could answer these questions, how can one compare the methods they have used with what might have been achieved by other methods – by, for example, relying less on advice and by using enforcement powers more strictly?

Statistics may provide a starting-point, but they cannot give the whole answer. Death-rates in mines and factories have declined greatly since the 1850s; smoke pollution from factories has fallen remarkably since 1950; railways have for many years had a good record of passenger safety. In itself such information, although useful, does not go very far in determining what contribution inspections have made. For one thing it needs to be set against other basic information: for example, have accident rates in factories declined as much as death rates? Is pollution from other causes than smoke declining? But above all what is needed is an analysis of the factors contributing to changes. To some extent this is already being done. But it is clear that a great deal more is needed as an essential preliminary to trying to assess the part played by inspectors. The work of the Accident Prevention Advisory Unit of the factory inspectorate provides an example.[54] Its more sophisticated approach to the analysis of accidents as compared with what the factory inspectorate had done previously had a specific purpose in attempting to establish where the inspectorate could direct its activities (and which activities) most effectively. But a more systematic analysis of accidents, particularly directed towards understanding of their causes, is also essential for assessing not only the part played by inspectors in the past but even more what they might achieve in the future.

It is obvious enough that if an inspectorate is pursuing broad aims, and correspondingly employs various means other than the enforcement of statutory requirements by inspection to achieve them, it needs to be clear both about objectives and the effectiveness of the different means. It is certainly the case with inspectorates that they find it hard to answer either question with precision. The Robens Committee commented on the lack of clarity in the role of the various inspectorates whose activities they examined.[55] But did their report and the HSW Act 1974 succeed in making clear what were the limits of action by the inspectorates in the promotion of safe and healthy working conditions? The difficulty lies in the open-endedness of the ultimate goal. Since no reasonable person expects the elimination of accidents and risks to health in working conditions, one can always ask, whatever improvements the statistics show, whether more could not be done, and the 'more' can be applied to inspectors just as much as it can be applied to employers. The inspectors' involvement with general and promotional aims inevitably makes them the target of such questions.

The same is true in attempting to assess the relative value of the various means used by inspectors. Once attention is focused on them it has proved difficult for inspectors to provide precise answers. The alkali inspectorate is an example. Once public attention was directed towards its activities it tended to fasten on to a number of difficult questions: are the standards embodied in the inspectorates 'notes on best practicable means' too low; does reliance on industry to monitor emissions lead to deception; is the standard of compliance too low between the visits of inspectors, or at times when they rarely visit (as at night)? The Royal Commission on Environmental Pollution, which took a generally favourable view of the inspectorate, tacitly acknowledged that no very precise answers could be given to these questions. There was 'no reason to suppose' that standards were too lax; and as for monitoring by industry, the inspector's knowledge together with reliance on complaints 'should enable him to detect inconsistencies'.[56]

As HSE's Director General has acknowledged, in the absence of more precise techniques for evaluating their work inspectors rely on their own subjective judgements for determining the best use of resources.[57] It is surely revealing that this should remain the position in 1978, when the factory inspectorate alone in over 140 years of existence had had its methods constantly under scrutiny, and when questions like how often factories should be inspected, how many inspectors were needed and in what circumstances prosecutions should be brought had had much thought and ink devoted to them. The reason is that reliance on subjective judgement seemed adequate enough until both inspectors themselves began to doubt whether they were acting as effectively as they might and others began to query whether the wider aims which they pursued were being achieved to the extent which was desirable.

NEED FOR CRITERIA OF EFFECTIVENESS

This chapter has tried to relate the development of the aims and methods of inspection to the various factors bearing on the work of inspectors. But there is also significance in the general climate of opinion within which the use of inspection has grown. After the initial resistance to the use of inspectors in certain cases had diminished, inspection developed in a favourable and on the whole uncritical climate. Inspectorates which have come under public scrutiny – and most of them for most of the time have not – have generally been commended for their general but unspecified contribution to desirable improvements, as the Factory and Workshops Act Commission commended the factory inspectorate in 1876.[58] Demands for more inspectors have frequently been voiced. It is not therefore surprising that for the most part inspectors have evolved their own approaches to their tasks and methods of work – sometimes, as in the case of the alkali inspectorate, a highly individual approach. Nobody has drawn up manuals dealing with the techniques of inspection for the benefit of all inspectors, or called conferences of different inspectors to discuss the effectiveness of a strict enforcement policy or the extent to which advice and persuasion can achieve a high degree of compliance. Professionalism has lain not in being an inspector but in being a factory inspector or an environmental health officer or a schools inspector. Different inspectorates working in the same field of control may disagree strongly over methods and their effectiveness. Some EHOs, for example, have seen the alkali inspectorate as being too considerate to industry, and of being unable or reluctant to exercise control.[59]

One result has been the lack of any sustained pressure to analyse the relation between the results of inspection and the methods used to achieve them, with the consequent difficulties for assessing the work of inspectors which have been noted. But a further danger is that it creates uncertainty about what inspection can reasonably be expected to achieve. There is undoubtedly much faith in the use of inspection. New inspectorates are from time to time created, and more inspectors are constantly being called for and appointed to existing inspector-ates. But what others expect of inspectors is not always what inspec-tors see themselves as doing. An academic critic has claimed that for many inspectorates

the provision of advice is a major function and inspection has become, or is becoming, a purely formal activity,

whereas

if inspection is not employed, then the government is not fulfilling its role in relation to the governed, that is, of ensuring that activities are done in accordance with the wishes of both govern-ment and governed . . . strict inspection is one of the hallmarks of a truly democratic regime.[60]

This discrepancy between what is seen as the primary object of inspection and the way in which many inspectors operate in practice could clearly be overcome more easily if there were less divergence between inspectorates on these very questions and more agreement on the criteria of effectiveness of inspection work. The criticisms point to one defect in the present system, that is, the lack of any means of determining the need for inspection in a particular situation, or of evaluating how inspection should be carried out or related to other means of achieving the objects in view. It is only as particular inspec-torates have come under public scrutiny that there has arisen some awareness of the difficulties of answering these questions. For other inspectorates, the great majority, which have received little or no public scrutiny, these questions have scarcely arisen in any overt way. For the most part answers have been evolved in the course of the diverse development of different inspectorates. Inspectors as practical men responded to practical needs without on the whole looking too closely at underlying implications. The justification of their work was closely related to these practical needs – so many carcases of unfit meat found and destroyed, so many unsatisfactory sewage works closed down or improved, so many workers paid the minimum wages to which they were entitled. The results of inspection in such cases were plain to see. They showed what inspection could achieve.

It is precisely because inspection has evolved in this way and has rarely been the subject of much public scrutiny that one needs to ask the underlying questions. It is not simply a question of whether inspectors ought to inspect more and act less as advisers. That is clearly important, but in a sense a subsidiary question. It presupposes that we know the circumstances in which inspection can be effectively used, and that the achievements of inspection are only or best obtained by that means. The fact that inspection has come to be associated with certain kinds of governmental activity, notably in relation to health and safety protection and as part of central government's relationship with local government, may have a wider significance for the future development of inspection – or it may simply be a historical accident. The fact that for some inspectorates inspection now plays a relatively small part in their total activities may mean that they are failing to carry out the purposes for which they were appointed, or that there is less need for inspections or simply that the nature of inspection work has changed. Certainly we need to be clearer about the value of inspection and whether there is any alternative way of achieving the same ends before we can properly assess the charge that inspectors do not inspect enough.

NOTES: CHAPTER 7

1 SI 1969, no. 690, and 1974, no.903.
2 And equally to other matters specified in s. 1, including the protection of the general public against risks arising from work activity.
3 C 1987, para. 2.
4 Coal Mines Regulation Act 1872, s.46.
5 See Chapter 1, p.8.
6 County and Borough Police Act, 1856, ss. XV, XVI.
7 Police Act 1964, s.38.
8 Children Act, 1908, s.45.
9 This is not to deny that such inspectors may in assessing efficiency make use of specific standards, but these standards are not to the same extent the basis of their work; for example, they are rarely expressed in regulations.
10 Standing Committee D, Police Bill, 23 January 1964, cols 391–3.
11 Police Act 1964, s.28.
12 See Chapter 4, p.69.
13 *Health and Safety: Manufacturing and Service Industries 1976* (HMSO, 1978), pp. 3–4.
14 Yorkshire Ouse and Hull River Authority, 4th AR, 1968–9, p.40.
15 Cmd 6371, 1976, para. 85.
16 F.E. Ireland, 'Control of special industrial emissions in Britain', paper to 2nd International Clean Air Conference, Washington, 1970. Quoted in Frankel (Social Audit), op. cit., p.11.
17 Destructive Insects Act 1877.
18 See the evidence of Sir Francis Floud to the Onslow Royal Commission on Local Government, 21 June 1923.
19 See the speech of the President of the Board of Trade (Winston Churchill) on Second Reading of the Bill (HC Deb vol. IV, 28 April 1909, col. 392).
20 Sea Fisheries Acts 1843 and 1868.
21 See *Health and Safety: Nuclear Establishments 1975—76* (HMSO, 1978), p.v.
22 For example, 'securing the proper observance of this Act' (Agricultural Wages Act 1948); 'seeing that the provisions of the Merchant Shipping Acts and regulations and rules . . . are duly complied with' (Merchant Shipping Act 1970).
23 Quoted in Thomas, op. cit., p.75.
24 ibid., pp. 364–5; the instructions were issued in 1837.
25 Chapter 4, p. 63.
26 Chapter 3, p. 53.

27 *Report of Working Party on Recruitment* [etc.] *of Sanitary Inspectors* (HMSO, 1953), para. 17.
28 *Annual Report 1969* (Cmnd 4461, 1970), p. xiii.
29 Cruelty to Animals Act 1876, ss. 3, 8, 10.
30 *Report of Departmental Committee on Experiments on Animals* (Cmnd 2641, 1965), para. 129.
31 ibid., para. 416.
32 See above Chapter 6, p. 124.
33 Thomas, op. cit., pp. 115–21.
34 cf. 'Strict liability and the enforcement of the Factories Act 1961' (Law Commission, 1970), para. 58; Ross Cranston, *Regulating Business* (Macmillan, 1979), pp. 105–9.
35 General Instructions of the Secretary for Mines to HM Inspectors of Mines and Quarries, 4th edn, 1926, pt I, para. 1 (iii).
36 *Report of Working Party on Recruitment* [etc.] *of Sanitary Inspectors* (HMSO, 1953), para. 17.
37 'The Wages Inspector cometh', *Department of Employment Gazette*, February 1977, pp. 107–9.
38 *Staffing and Organisation of the Factory Inspectorate* (Cmd 9879, 1956), para. 18.
39 Cmnd 5034, 1972, para. 254.
40 *Report of Her Majesty's Chief Inspector of Constabulary 1976* (HC 414, HMSO, 1977), p.5; 1977 (HC 545, 1978), p.4.
41 *Report of RC on Police* (Cmnd 1728, 1962), para. 114.
42 For example, the Secretary of State can call on a police authority to retire a chief constable in certain circumstances (Police Act 1964, s.29).
43 There has been no case of withholding police grant since 1961 and less than fifty occasions since 1920 when it has been threatened (*Sixth Report from Committee of Public Accounts*, 1977–78, HC 574, question 1654, 20 March 1978).
44 Chapter 5, p.96. Inspectors of constabulary were instructed 'to secure the goodwill and the co-operation of local authorities' (T.A. Critchley, *A History of Police in England and Wales* (Constable, 2nd edn, 1978), p. 118.
45 Circular DSWS (79) 1 January 1979.
46 ibid., Annex 1, para. 3.
47 Chapter 4, p.76.
48 Chapter 4, p.75.
49 Report, p.68.
50 Alkali Inspectorate, 106th AR, 1969 (HMSO, 1970), p.5.
51 Chapter 4, p.87.
52 Ross Cranston, op. cit.; P.B. Beaumont, 'The limits of inspection: a study of the workings of the Government Wages Inspectorate', *Public Administration*, vol. 57, Summer 1979, pp. 203–17.
53 Chapter 3, p.56.
54 Chapter 4, p.73.
55 Cmnd 5034, paras 206–10.
56 Cmnd 6371, paras 90, 95.
57 See Chapter 4, p.91.
58 See Chapter 4, p.65.
59 Frankel (Social Audit), op. cit., p.42.
60 Owen A. Hartley, 'Inspectorates in British central government', *Public Administration*, vol. 50, Winter 1972, pp. 462–3.

CHAPTER 8

THE FUTURE OF INSPECTION

———————◆———————

CONTRASTING THEMES: ENFORCEMENT AND EFFICIENCY INSPECTION

The primary purpose of this chapter is to consider the future role of inspectorates in the light of their long historical development. Whether inspectorates are still needed and, if so, for what purposes and under what circumstances, are questions which underlie the discussion. Some preliminary points must be made.

A striking feature of the account of inspectorates which has been presented in this study and particularly in the previous chapter is the recurrence of certain themes. There is first the basic distinction between enforcement and efficiency inspectorates, a distinction which has grown more marked over the years. At the same time there are a number of themes which relate to both types of inspectorate: examples are professionalism as a major factor in the development of inspectorates, and the relation between specific and more general aims in their developing role.

Of greater significance, however, is the fact that a number of themes apply particularly or exclusively to enforcement inspectorates. The emphasis on prevention rather than detection, on persuasion rather than strict use of enforcement powers, and on the provision of advice as a desirable if not essential part of the work of an inspector – all these have particular relevance to enforcement inspectorates. They could be summed up by saying that whereas the rationale for the existence of enforcement inspectorates lies in the conflict of interests between the aims of legislation and the interests of those subject to inspection, their practical operation is characterised by compromise, by an insistence in most cases on minimising conflict and on achieving results through good relations between inspectors and the majority at least of those inspected.

The fact that none of this applies or at least applies to a much lesser extent, to efficiency inspectorates is due not so much to any great difference in the original concept of inspection in the two cases as to the differing circumstances in which it was applied and to a differing historical development subsequently. In the nineteenth-century theory of inspection the predominant idea was that of supervision. Parliament would entrust responsibilities to certain bodies or individuals; inspectors would go round the country to see that those responsibilities were being carried out. This is clearly so in Jeremy Bentham's elaborate constitutional code. He proposed a scheme whereby central government would oversee the activities of elected local authorities. There were to be thirteen Ministers under a Prime Minister who would be responsible not only for traditional areas of government activity such as finance and foreign relations, but also for such matters as health, education and interior communications. Once a year, or oftener if required, the Minister or someone deputed by him was to visit 'the several offices, and such other places as lie within his charge' to see that the work was being carried on efficiently, to deal with complaints, and so on.[1]

Such a theory might seem reasonably applicable to the use of inspectors of prisons to supervise the activities of magistrates in their responsibility for running prisons; or of Poor Law inspectors to supervising Boards of Guardians. It had a more limited application to the use of inspectors in factories or mines or on merchant ships. Here government had neither the inclination nor the means to supervise the activities of owners of mills, mines or merchant ships in general, but only sought to ensure that they carried out certain limited responsibilities affecting the safety and health of those whom they employed.

For present purposes, however, it is not so much the initial distinction as subsequent developments which are important. If supervision of local authorities in the carrying out of their responsibilities characterised the early efficiency inspectorates, their subsequent development can only be understood in the context of the changing relations between central and local government. Any discussion of the future of efficiency inspection must be set firmly in that context as it now exists or is likely to develop. By contrast, the development of enforcement inspectorates has to be seen in the context of the much extended relations of government with private individuals and institutions. Coming into contact with an inspector in the course of normal day-to-day activities is now liable to happen to a wide range of people and bodies – from large industrial enterprises to second-hand car dealers, from builders of nuclear power stations to owners of pet shops, from wholesale fruit and vegetable merchants to owners of slum houses. Because of the quite different contexts within which the two types of inspectorate operate, the problems they raise differ both in nature and scale.

In considering the future of inspection the contrasts may best be seen in relation to public awareness of and reaction to the work of inspectorates. The need for and effectiveness of efficiency inspectorates has rarely aroused much public concern: it is indeed doubtful whether the role of these inspectorates is well understood. Public concern over broader issues such as the alleged inefficiency of local government is not clearly linked with the activities of existing efficiency inspectorates, still less with demands for more inspectorates, since this would require more civil servants, a development which the critics would regard as undesirable.

Enforcement inspectorates, because they are involved in many concerns of daily life – safety in factories, the quality of goods and food bought in shops, the hazards of poorly maintained lorries or of dust and fumes from factory chimneys – are likely to be the focus of a more direct public concern, of demands to know what they are doing to deal with immediate and specific problems, and of a critical examination of alleged failures to act.

USE OF INSPECTING POWERS BY EFFICIENCY INSPECTORS

For these reasons the future role of the two types of inspectorate will be examined separately, beginning first with efficiency inspectorates. A number of preliminary points may be made. The first is definitional. By efficiency inspectorates is intended specially con-stituted bodies of men and women with the right to inspect, that is, to visit premises, see documents and ask questions. It is the existence of inspecting powers which is the distinguishing mark of an inspectorate in this context. A central department may have officers in the field whose duty it is to maintain contact with local authorities, but if those contacts are a matter of administrative arrangement only they do not constitute an inspectorate. The formal difference is this: a local authority which refused to let inspectors of DES enter its schools would be in breach of the Education Act 1944; a local authority which refused to let an official of DOE inspect its housing estates would be acting entirely within its rights. In other words the critical question to be examined here is what part officials armed with inspecting powers can or should play in relations between central government and local authorities.

The importance of the question derives largely from the fact that, in the first place, for many services provided by local authorities there are no inspecting powers possessed by central government officials; and, secondly, even in the services where inspecting powers do exist they are generally of a restricted nature. For housing, highways or planning central government has no inspecting powers. For education it has inspecting powers but only of schools and other educational institutions; for social services it has, similarly, inspecting powers only for institutions such as children's and old people's homes. The only service for which there is a general inspecting power specifically for efficiency purposes is the police.

These preliminary points need to be set in the context of a more general view of relations between central and local government. Much discussion of such relations is concerned with policies and their implementation, with the means by which central government seeks to ensure that national policies are carried out by the local authorities entrusted with their execution. The discussion has to be seen in relation to a major reason for having elected local authorities at all, that they can interpret national policies in terms of local needs and priorities. But although the motive of seeing that central policies were carried out was evident in the establishment of the early supervisory inspectorates and in, for example, the complaint of the General Board of Health that although it had inspectors they did not have the power to see that local boards carried out their duties satisfactorily,[2] this was inseparably connected with an examination not only of what the local authorities did but of how they did it. And it is this element with its emphasis on efficiency rather than supervision which has come to predominate.

One could therefore see in theory a distinct role for efficiency inspectors as men and women concerned primarily with means and not ends, with improving the capacity of local authorities to carry out their responsibilities rather than with ensuring that they carry out particular responsibilities in a way acceptable to central government. Although in practice such a distinction is not easy to maintain, it does offer at least a starting-point for placing inspectors in the whole spectrum of controls and influences which serve central government in its relations with local government.

Examination of existing inspectorates does not, however, suggest that this is necessarily the object for which inspecting powers are needed. The clearest example is the schools inspectorate. The original use of powers of inspection to ensure the observance of the conditions on which grants were paid established a direct connection between inspection and the efficient running of individual schools. Schools inspectors today do not use their inspecting powers primarily to ensure that schools are run efficiently. And even if they did there would be no direct relationship between inspection and attaining efficiency. If the schools in a particular area are run inefficiently this must reflect on such things as the organisation and calibre of staff of the LEA on whom rests the responsibility for providing and running schools. But inspectors of schools have no more right to inspect the LEA's internal organisation and management than Regional Controllers of the Department of Transport have to inspect those of highway authorities. In much the same way the Social Work Service of DHSS have power to inspect children's and old people's homes but no power to inspect either the organisation or other aspects of the work of local authority social services departments.

By contrast inspectors of constabulary are concerned with the whole range of questions affecting the efficiency of police forces; so too are inspectors of fire services, although with somewhat more limited powers of inspection. It must be said, however, that the police service in particular stands somewhat apart from other local government services, as is evident from the distinctive constitution of police authorities and the special status of chief constables. There are both practical and political reasons why there should be a strong national concern with standards of efficiency. As an essential protective service concerned with law and order and with such practical arguments for high standards of efficiency as the increasing need under modern conditions for co-operation between forces, there are inevitably pressures on government to demonstrate a concern with promoting efficiency. This was evident in the report of the 1960 Royal Commission and the subsequent debates on the Police Bill. The existence of an inspectorate which carries out annual inspection visits to every police force outside London, and frequently visits forces and has informal contacts with chief constables at other times, is the most visible indication that the concern for efficiency is being met. To a lesser extent similar considerations apply to the fire service. Inspection as part of the arrangement for the return of the service to local authorities after the war is also closely related to a strong concern for ensuring reasonable national standards in a basic protective service, but one without the distinctive characteristics of the police.

Before considering the implications of the present position three other inspectorates need to be briefly mentioned. The probation inspectors of the Home Office[3] are, like the SWS, statutorily limited to the inspection of institutions: their powers of entry are for the purpose of inspecting approved bail hostels, probation hostels, and probation homes and similar places.[4] This is, however, an unusual service since it is locally provided but not a local government service in the strict sense, and this is reflected in the fact that 80 per cent of the cost is met by the Exchequer. Another unusual service is the registration of births, marriages and deaths. Registration officers are appointed and paid by local authorities but are subject to detailed instruction by the Registrars General, and there are central inspectors (England and Wales) or examiners (Scotland) to see that they carry out their duties satisfactorily. Neither of these two inspectorates is significant in the general context of central/local relations.

District auditors, on the other hand, are very much part of that relationship but their position is unique. The main question which arises in the present discussion is how far their work can be regarded as being inspecting for efficiency. They have to begin with wider statutory powers than either schools inspectors or the SWS, and are not confined to a right of entry to specified institutions. They have a general power to examine documents and question officials of local authorities. This power is, however, granted for the specific purpose of enabling them to carry out a proper audit of an authority's accounts.

In practice, the district auditor's work may be regarded as falling into two parts. One part is the independent auditing of the accounts of certain public authorities. This is not inspecting work in the sense in which inspection has been considered in this study; it can be, and in certain cases is, carried out by commercial firms of auditors approved for the purpose, and its main purpose is to ensure that the accounts are in order according to 'proper accounting practices', that the special provisions relating to the accounts of public authorities are observed,[5] and that there has been no fraud or other financial malpractice. This is essentially work which the audit of any organisation's accounts requires, with some special features arising from the fact that local authorities are public bodies; in particular, auditors have to be satisfied that any expenditure incurred is authorised by law.[6]

The second part of their work goes beyond this auditing function, and may be called the value-for-money function. The very fact that auditors of local government accounts have access to a wide range of documents and officials, and are not limited to one particular service makes them, potentially at least, a most formidable efficiency inspectorate. The DOE Code of Practice for local government auditors requires them to check that there is nothing in the accounts to indicate significant loss from waste, extravagence, inefficient financial administration or poor value for money. Clearly this could involve auditors in far more searching inquiries than merely auditing the accounts: waste and extravagance in particular can hardly be fully assessed without examining the effectiveness as well as the administration of the policies followed by local authorities. For that very reason local authorities are likely to resist too rapid a development of the district audit service in this direction, and at the moment it can be said that the service is moving cautiously towards greater emphasis on the value-for-money side of the work. To that extent district auditors function only in part as efficiency inspectors at present.

NEED FOR EFFICIENCY INSPECTING POWERS

On the whole, then, formal inspecting powers seem to play a limited part in the promotion of efficiency by central government. The present position suggests two further questions, however: whether there is any significance in the fact that inspecting powers are largely confined to specialised institutions; and whether the existence of inspectors with only limited formal inspecting powers nevertheless has wider consequences.

Historically, the provision of institutions figured prominently in the work of local authorities in the nineteenth century. Prisons and workhouses were among the earliest and most important of these institutions. As also with schools, the inspection of such institutions in itself constituted the major part of assessing whether the work of the authorities responsible for a particular service was being carried out efficiently. This is no longer true. Providing homes for children and old people, for example, is far from constituting the whole work of local authorities' social services departments. And yet the inspection of such homes remains as the one formal power of DHSS in relation to the efficient performance of social services functions by local authorities.

This suggests that inspecting powers are simply a historical survival. Because originally it was necessary to inspect police forces, schools, workhouses and reformatories to ensure that they were properly run, the powers have been continued even though the nature of the authorities, the relations between them and the nature of the institutions may all have changed greatly – simply because nobody has been willing to question seriously whether the powers are still needed. This explanation ignores the fact that the need for and use of inspecting powers has been much debated, particularly in relation to the SWS.[7]

However, the fact that such debate relates particularly to arguments for a more positively interventionist role by the central department, not simply to promote efficiency but to seek the application of national standards of provision to services provided by local authorities, suggests that it is necessary to look more closely at the consequences of the existence of inspecting powers.

A preliminary argument is that such powers act as a safeguard. They may rarely need to be exercised in a formal way but the fact that they exist can be important in an extreme case. This clearly applies to inspectors of constabulary. The threat to use the sanction of withdrawal of Exchequer grant from the police authority, although rare, is not unknown, and has in the past been carried into effect on occasions. The Home Office would be in a much weaker position to use this sanction if it did not have the right to send inspectors to inquire into the efficiency of policing arrangements. With other inspectorates this argument is less strong, since there is rarely any question of applying a sanction related to the inspection of particular institutions. On the other hand, it could be argued that it was politically desirable for central government to retain some oversight of the administration of specialised institutions, especially those catering for vulnerable groups of the population such as children and old people. This particularly applies to the institutions with which the SWS is concerned, since they are residential. There is much public interest and concern over professional competence and the possibility of administrative inefficiency or error particularly as they affect children and particularly when they result in tragic consequences, as recent cases (Maria Colwell, Stephen Menhenniott)[8] have shown. In education, it is not so much administrative mishaps as general standards which arouse public concern, and again some recent cases (William Tyndale, Sutton Centre Community School)[9] have focused some of this concern. However, the fact that these cases did not come to light as a result of the activities of inspectors somewhat weakens this particular argument, although there are occasions when the central departments may need to insist on exercising their inspecting powers because of a suspicion that things have gone seriously wrong, as in a particular school.

A further argument for inspecting powers is less the direct need for them than their indirect consequences. In part the argument is that their possession of inspecting powers enables inspectors to achieve more, that because inspectors of constabulary or inspectors of schools have the right to inspect, their suggestions and advice even on matters not directly related to the inspection work are more likely to be heeded. A reinforcing argument is that the fact that inspectors have the right to visit certain places makes it easier for them to gather systematic information about the way in which central government policies are being carried out, or, in the case of schools inspectors, to assess the state of education both generally and in particular aspects.

This latter point is the key to the question how far existing inspection powers are still needed. Looked at from the formal position, and especially taking into account the limitations of those powers, there does not seem to be a strong case for retaining them, except where there is a strong and direct central government involvement. This applies particularly to the police. Central government still provides a specific grant in general support of the police service, as opposed to the more limited role now of other specific grants (as in the urban aid field). It also provides some common services. The latter is also true of the fire service (the provision of a national fire service college), although there is no longer a specific grant for this service. In both the police and fire services there is a close link between inspecting powers, and hence employment of an inspectorate, and the particular nature of central government involvement in the services.

There may nevertheless be other reasons why the existence of inspecting powers may prove useful to central government departments. In the first place, although the tasks carried out by inspectors may be for the most part just as effectively carried out by other officials acting without formal powers, the existence of inspecting powers may make it easier to establish such a body of officials by giving it a formal justification. Secondly, because an inspectorate has an unquestioned right to go into institutions, see what is going on and ask questions, it may be in a better position to provide information and advice to the central department than a body of officials which has to rely purely on establishing a relationship of goodwill with the local authorities. From the point of view of the central department the existence of an inspectorate can ease the task of effective liaison outside the strict area for which inspecting powers exist. This increased usefulness of inspectors has been commented on by a former Permanent Secretary of the Ministry of Housing and Local Government. After pointing out that general inspectors under the Poor Law were a valuable means of close liaison between the pre-war Ministry of Health and local authorities, she says that they were missed when the Poor Law was abolished in 1948 because there were then no central officials left, apart from district auditors, whose duties took them regularly into the offices of local authorities.[10]

Nevertheless, it seems somewhat paradoxical to argue for the retention of existing inspection powers not so much for their necessity for the purpose for which they were designed but rather for the indirect advantages which they bring to the central departments which have inspectorates to call on. Nor does the argument establish just how useful in practice inspectorates are in comparison with other means of achieving the same ends. This point is particularly important in view of the fact that inspectorates do not exist in many services for which local authorities have responsibility. Would there be advantages in having inspectorates for these services, and if so on what basis should they be established? For quite apart from the fact that most of these other services do not have the institutional basis which forms the *raison d'être* of inspecting powers in education and social services, could one justify the extension of such powers purely for their value in assisting the provision of information rather than for any direct relation with the promotion of efficiency?

INSPECTION IN RELATIONS BETWEEN CENTRAL GOVERN-MENT AND LOCAL AUTHORITIES

The question would be difficult to answer even if it were confined simply to the efficient performance of functions. It would require a comparative analysis of different functions performed by local authorities, and of the means employed by central departments in each to promote efficiency. It would, for example, have to examine whether the Department of Transport, with a strong regional organisation of professional officers but no formal inspecting powers, is more or less able to promote higher standards in local highway departments than are SWS officers in social services departments. Clearly the existence of inspecting powers is only one element in the complex relationship between central departments and local authorities for this purpose. The strength and influence of other factors would need to be assessed. For example, services may differ in the extent to which professional, financial or other reasons provide an incentive for central and local officials to co-operate in improving efficiency; more broadly, they may differ in the attitudes or styles which central departments or even sections of departments adopt in their relations with local authorities.[11]

However, the argument for extension of inspection powers is bound up with wider questions of central/local relations, in particular the argument for a more positive and interventionist role by central departments not simply to ensure that standards of administrative and professional competence are maintained but that the standard of provision of a service is at a level thought desirable by central government, and in particular to ensure that standards of provision are more nearly comparable from one part of the country to another.

In the case of existing inspectorates it is not possible to draw a sharp dividing line between the two concepts. This is most obviously so in the case of the inspectors of constabulary. In examining and commenting on such matters as the development of a force or the extent of provision of specialised equipment, they are implicitly drawn into questions of policy which go beyond simply an assessment of the professional and administrative competence of the force to perform the task of policing. SWS and the schools inspectorate, on the other hand, largely because of the limited nature of what they inspect, have less scope for this wider use of inspecting powers. Nevertheless, there can be no rigid line between means and ends, between the way in which an authority carries out its task and its policy for performing it. The standard of a particular service provided by an authority may fall below what the central department regards as desirable, not just because the authority's organisation or methods are inadequate but because it attaches lower priority to the provision of that service.

Because these wider considerations are involved in examination of the use of inspecting powers it is not easy to answer the question whether existing powers are necessary or whether they should be extended without examining more fully than is possible within the scope of the present project the relation between such powers and other powers which are available to central government to control or influence the activities of local authorities. These range widely from the formal controls over finance to guidance issued in the form of circulars or memoranda and to the informal advice which forms a notable part of the work of schools inspectors and the SWS, but is only indirectly dependent on the existence of inspecting powers.

The debate over the extent to which central controls over local authorities are still necessary is, and is bound to be, a continuing one. As Griffith has pointed out, each central department which looks to local authorities to carry out services for which it is responsible is faced with an inescapable dilemma between local democracy and efficiency, and must make a choice between trying to insist on authorities making adequate and efficient provision, or leaving it to the local authority, in effect, to apply a lower standard.[12] To extend greatly the use of inspecting powers, whether in services where they already exist or to other services, would alter the balance between efficiency and local democracy quite drastically in view of the limited nature of existing powers. This might be justifiable if it could be shown both that there was an intolerable degree of inefficiency in local government, and that a more interventionist role by central departments based on formal inspecting powers was likely to prove the most effective means of combating that inefficiency.

The first proposition depends to a large extent on the political stance adopted. Much criticism of the alleged inefficiency of local authorities derives, as has been suggested, from wider views about the need for greater standardisation of services. But even in the narrower context of efficient performance of services it is by no means clear that inspecting powers are or could be used more effectively to that end in comparison with other means, except in some rather special cases such as the police. In any case the extension of inspecting powers would have to encounter formidable practical obstacles.

To begin with, except for the police and fire services, existing inspecting powers, as has been pointed out, depend for their rationale on the need to maintain some kind of supervision over the running of specialised institutions. An extension of such powers would need to find some other justification. Such a justification would be particularly hard to find when over the past thirty years the climate in which central/local relations have developed has been strongly coloured by pressures from local government and commitments from central government to diminish, not increase, the formal controls over local authorities. From the time of the Local Government Manpower Committee[13] onwards, much argument and effort has ostensibly been directed towards relaxing formal central controls. Part of the argument for the introduction of the general grant in 1958 was that it would enable controls to be relaxed. The abolition of many small local authorities by the Local Government Act 1972 was justified on the grounds that larger authorities would be able to perform their tasks more efficiently without the need for detailed central control. Proposals by the Conservative government elected in 1979 to abolish over 300 controls[14] were presented as a means of eliminating duplication and reducing unnecessary government expenditure.

Many might question how far in practice there has been any real diminution in the capacity of central departments to supervise and control the activities of local authorities. Over a long period, however, there has been a marked change in the style and manner of central oversight. Inspection, from being a major means, has become of minor importance except for one or two services. Advisory and promotional activities, on the other hand, including those provided by inspectors, have become more important ways of trying to secure improvements in professional and administrative standards. To reverse that trend by increasing the formal inspecting powers available to central departments would not only make nonsense of many of the arguments of the past thirty years but would be seen as a deliberate move to reduce the importance of local authorities and make them simply agents of central governments.

The trend towards advice and promotion and away from the use of inspecting powers does however raise problems, and particularly the problem of assessing how effective such methods are in promoting efficiency as compared not only with inspection but with other methods available to central departments. The underlying question of how to achieve efficiency and of the extent to which this should be left to local authorities acting individually or collectively or how much central government should intervene requires that there should be some criteria of assessment of the methods now used, as at any rate a first step in trying to answer the question. Inspection linked to specific regulations can be assessed relatively easily. How successful schools inspectors were in seeing that the Revised Code was observed, or the SWS in seeing that children's homes keep proper records are easily ascertainable matters. But inspection linked not to specific regulations but to a more general promotion of standards, as is the case with most school inspection today, or inspection forming a small part of a wider advisory role, as is the case with the SWS, is not so susceptible to accurate assessment. Success depends on a variety of factors, as Chapter 5 showed, including the professional calibre of the advisers and the political and administrative context within which they operate. The judgement of what constitutes success is perhaps even more difficult to determine.

This suggests that one element which is missing in the present situation is a more precise and systematic attempt to evaluate the work of inspection and promotion. The case for inspecting powers, or for the use of promotion and advice by inspectors and others must ultimately rest on a demonstration of their achievements. Granted that one must rely to a large extent on the professional competence of inspectors who consciously set out to improve the performance of others, there is nevertheless an essential public interest to be met by demonstrating that standards are being maintained and improved. There is, for example, clearly value in disseminating information about good practices and procedures where a service is provided by a number of separate authorities. But is this better done by voluntary action among the authorities themselves or by some central authority; and if by the latter, are inspecting powers needed or can less formal means achieve results?

This question has been considered here in relation to local government but it has a wider importance applicable to other public services organised on a local or regional basis. The National Health Service and Regional Water Authorities are examples. It has been argued that the NHS needs a central body performing something of the function of the SWS in relation to social services departments, but without inspecting powers.[15] The case would be strengthened if the contribution of inspectors to promoting efficiency in local government could be demonstrated, and the extent to which this had been achieved without the use of inspecting powers.

The future of efficiency inspection is thus not an entirely clear one. On the one hand existing inspecting powers appear mostly as historical survivals with little strong positive argument for their continued existence, except in special circumstances such as the police. On the other hand, the fact that inspectorates do exist may bring indirect advantages to central departments which they would not or could not so easily obtain without inspecting powers. However, these considerations have to be set in a wider political and administrative context where the use of direct controls such as inspecting powers by central departments is becoming less common. The arguments for seeking to improve efficiency remain strong, but there is little to demonstrate that this requires an extension of inspecting powers as long as the present balance between central control and local autonomy is maintained in the provision of services by local authorities, and as long as there is lacking any conclusive demonstration of the value of existing inspecting powers.

TWO VIEWS OF ENFORCEMENT INSPECTION

Consideration of the future role of enforcement inspection raises, as was suggested earlier, very different and on the whole even more difficult questions. These questions are related to different views of the role of enforcement inspection, deriving in large part from certain characteristics of inspection as it exists at present.

One set of characteristics which was sketched in earlier may be summed up as a reliance on persuasion rather than legal sanctions, and on prevention of breaches of the law rather than their detection. Such generalisations conceal very wide differences among inspectorates in the degree to which they conform to these characteristics. However, there is no doubt that the generalisations point to tendencies which are evident in the way in which enforcement inspection operates in practice. Their importance here is that the consequence of such tendencies is to suggest two broadly differing views of enforcement inspection and its future development.

One view is that inspectors are failing to do the job for which they were appointed in the first place. Reliance on persuasion and reluctance to use prosecution are taken as indications that inspectors are failing to enforce the law and are resorting to compromise to resolve conflicting interests. This failure might in turn be attributed to the fact that in the absence of an effective and critical public opinion goals and objectives had been largely set by inspectors themselves; and that as a result inspectors were pursuing their own interests in reaching an accommodation with those they were set up to regulate, rather than acting in the public interest. Hence criticisms have been made that factory inspectors are too close to management and pay too little attention to the views of workers, and that TSOs who claim a neutral stance in fact neglect the interest of consumers in favour of maintaining good relations with traders. On this view, then, all that is needed is a reform of inspectorates to ensure that they actually carry out the task for which they were established.

An opposing view would argue that the criticisms misunderstand the nature of enforcement inspection in a democratic society; that it is not and never was intended that inspection should operate purely as a coercive force; and that the only way that inspectors can be reasonably expected to operate and provide an acceptable method of making progress is through compromise. There are definite limits therefore to what can be expected from inspection. On this view, then, if the results of inspection are judged to be unsatisfactory the remedy may have to be sought in some other means of achieving the end in view.

Quite different sets of values are embodied in these two points of view, not only about the use of inspection, but more broadly about what can and ought to be achieved by government action. These essentially political questions cannot be resolved within the scope of this project, but some relevant considerations need to be examined in any attempt to draw conclusions about the future of enforcement inspection. These considerations relate to two areas in particular:

(1) inspection in relation to other methods of enforcement;
(2) factors bearing on the use of compromise to overcome conflicts of interest and their relevance to discussion of the limits of inspection.

ENFORCEMENT BY INSPECTORS AND BY THE POLICE

Enforcement may be seen as one means by which government seeks to implement policies. Those policies are however of a special kind which gives enforcement its distinctive character. They are not policies by which government either itself or acting through other public-sector bodies seeks some positive achievement, such as building roads, providing social security benefits or raising taxes. Rather government is seeking to influence modes of behaviour either of the population generally or of specified sections such as owners of houses or shopkeepers. The first characteristic, therefore, of government activity for which enforcement is appropriate is that the obligations or responsibilities which are to be followed should be specified by law. Law and enforcement go together. The object of enforcement is to see that what the law says should (or should not) happen actually happens (or does not).

Not every law which is passed and which is designed to influence modes of behaviour provides for enforcement by people assigned a specific enforcement task. When, for example, a law was passed making it an offence to discriminate on grounds of sex in employment matters, no specific provision was made for enforcement; but it was provided that a person who believed that he or she had been discriminated against could apply to an industrial tribunal which could make a ruling and in effect penalise the firm or person complained of if they found the case proved.[16] Rather than a positive duty of enforcement there is here a mechanism which depends on the activation of the machinery of law by an aggrieved person.

However, a great many laws of this kind affect not so much individual rights, where it is assumed that those adversely affected will have a positive incentive to take action, but activities or practices where there is less incentive for individuals to take action or less scope, as with serious crime, or specialised knowledge or techniques are involved, as with much legislation on health and safety in factories. It is in circumstances such as these that there is generally a specific obligation on certain public servants to enforce the law, and that means in practice either the police or a specialised inspectorate.

Law enforcement might indeed be thought of as being primarily a matter for the police. The prime function of police forces is the preservation of law and order, and enforcement of the criminal law is among the more important tasks comprised in this function. This suggests that a comparison of enforcement by the police and enforcement by inspectors may provide some revealing clues to the future role of the latter. In particular, it would be useful to try to distinguish areas in which enforcement by inspection is more appropriate than, or has advantages over, enforcement by the police.

In looking first at the division of enforcement powers which exists at present, some practical reasons have been noted earlier in this study why certain matters have been found to be more appropriate to inspectors than to the police. The history of weights and measures inspection is particularly revealing in this respect. A major factor in the decline of enforcement by the police of weights and measures legislation was the growing need for specialised technical knowledge which the police found increasingly difficult to acquire. And there are clearly many areas of enforcement which have always depended on the use of specialised knowledge and techniques which the police could not be expected to acquire. The control of industrial air pollution through the imposition of standards linked to the concept of 'best practicable means' provides an obvious example.

Practical arguments of this kind do not however entirely explain the division of powers between the police and inspectors. There are many examples of enforcement by inspectors where a high degree of specialised knowledge is not required, such as enforcement by the wages inspectorates of wages councils orders. Equally the police enforce some laws where specialised knowledge and techniques are called for, notably the road traffic laws. Some further explanation is required.

In seeking an explanation in the previous chapter of the way in which enforcement inspectorates operated in practice it was suggested that for the most part the offences created by the legislation which inspectors enforce were not regarded as crimes in the same way as, say, theft or violent assault are so regarded. This seems to point to a distinction between true crimes and regulatory or administrative offences, the former being a matter for the police, and the latter for inspectors.

This is clearly a distinction of great importance. Many of the laws enforced by the police relate to activities which are generally regarded as abhorrent; serious crime in particular is in the eyes of the general public something abnormal which it is the job of the police in the first place to try to prevent; and where, if it does occur, they should be active in pursuing the offenders. But to fail to meet the requirements of MAFF for grading apples, or of the Department of Trade for the accommodation of merchant seamen may be thought reprehensible but hardly a criminal act like stealing someone's wallet. The distinction goes some way towards providing an explanation of matters which are appropriate to the police to enforce and matters appropriate to inspectors; but it does not provide a complete explanation.

In the first place, it does not entirely account for the present position. Some measures enforced by inspectors are among those which would be generally regarded as criminal. Again a notable example comes from weights and measures legislation: to use false weights and measures would generally be regarded as dishonest and a crime, although not falling in the serious category. On the other hand, by no means all police activity is directed towards the prevention and detection of what would be generally agreed to be criminal activity. Some at least of the road traffic laws fall into this category, and illustrate at least the possibility of overlap between the work of the police and the work of inspectors.

There are many parallels between enforcement of the road traffic laws and enforcement carried out by inspectors. There are specific requirements to be met such as the prohibition on driving at more than 30 mph in specified areas; or more complex requirements such as those relating to the maximum weight of vehicles and its distribution via the wheels to the road surface.[17] There are also more general requirements – driving with due care and attention, having the steering gear in good and efficient working order or not driving a vehicle so as to cause excessive noise.

There are also some parallels in the way in which the police and inspectors seek to enforce requirements. Regular police traffic patrols on major roads serve both a preventive and a detection purpose, much as do, say, the visits of factory inspectors to high-risk factories. Investigation of accidents is often in both cases the means of discovering contraventions of the statutory requirements leading to subsequent prosecution. It is noticeable, however, that although the police have the primary responsibility for enforcement of the road traffic laws, an important part is also played by inspectors, the vehicle examiners of the Department of Transport. They have a variety of tasks, including the regular inspection of the condition of public service and heavy goods vehicles. They need, however, to work in collaboration with the police in carrying out spot checks on vehicles on the road.

Again a parallel can be drawn between the general contexts in which enforcement of the traffic laws and enforcement of the laws relating to safe working conditions in factories operate. Many of the requirements being enforced in both cases would be acknowledged to be sensible – in the abstract at least – but apt to be disregarded in the individual case. There can be few drivers who have not at some time exceeded the speed limit in a built-up area. If challenged they would no doubt argue that in their view it was perfectly safe to do so. Equally, there must be many occasions when a 'short cut' is taken in a factory to avoid production delays even though this means breaching the safety rules.[18]

The parallels are close but they are not exact. The police have wide responsibilities with powers related to them, such as the power to arrest people suspected of committing a serious offence which differs from the more specific powers of an inspector to enter a factory, which is linked to his restricted and specific function under the Act giving him this power. And the more technical and specialised work in the enforcement of the road traffic laws is mostly carried out by inspectors and not by the police, although certain work, such as checking on licences or on defective tyres of lorries stopped at roadside checks is sometimes done by the police.[19]

This discussion of the road traffic laws shows that there is no rigid dividing line between work appropriate to enforcement by the police and work appropriate to enforcement by inspectors. The point was emphasised in 1936. At a time when the problems of motor traffic on the roads were increasingly becoming the subject of debate the Minister of Transport considered the possibility of having in effect a central inspectorate for enforcing traffic laws. The idea was not pursued, but the fact that the police remain responsible for enforcing traffic laws means that a great deal of their manpower is concerned with this rather than with dealing with crime.[20]

The fact that there is no rigid dividing line does not, however, mean that it is entirely a matter of administrative convenience whether the work of enforcement is given to the police or to inspectors. To a large extent the position reflects the fact that it is impossible to provide a hard-and-fast way of distinguishing 'real' crimes from administrative misdemeanours.[21] The police, with their primary responsibility for the preservation of law and order and the protection of life and property, have a much more general duty for the enforcement of the law than inspectors. That duty is very much related to public expectations that the police should accept the overriding responsibility for the prevention and detection of crime. Inspectors by contrast enforce specific rules in specific areas; they have limited powers for limited purposes; they often require specialised knowledge; and their work is frequently in places, such as factories, where the police would not normally go. In spite of some overlap, of which the road traffic laws provide the most conspicuous example, one can distinguish separate spheres of operation of the police on the one hand and inspectors on the other.

It is also characteristic of enforcement inspectorates that there has been a marked tendency in the course of their long history to emphasise their distinctiveness from the police. This is particularly so in the history of a number of central government inspectorates, such as those for factories, mines and alkali works; but it is increasingly evident in most if not all inspectorates of both central and local government. The essence of this distinctiveness is the assertion that the job of the inspector is not simply the enforcement of statutory requirements attracting criminal penalties. Crime is a matter for the police; inspectors have a wider promotional and advisory role in seeking compliance and furthering the underlying purposes of the legislation.

As against this, criticisms of inspectorates are frequently directed at this emphasis on the promotional role. The demand of the critics is that they should operate more like policemen. It is in effect an assertion of the view that administrative misdemeanours should be treated more nearly like 'real' crimes, as against the whole tendency in the history of inspectorates to emphasise the difference between them. An important question which has a bearing on this argument is the extent to which inspectors may be subject to constraints which would in any case make it difficult for them to move far in the direction of treating offences as 'real' crimes. Comparison with the police is also relevant here and leads to the important second theme of discussion outlined above, that is, the use of compromise to overcome conflicts of interest.

CONSTRAINTS ON THE USE OF ENFORCEMENT INSPECTION: THE ROLE OF COMPROMISE

It was argued in discussing the role of the police in enforcement that for many crimes, and especially serious crimes, there was a large degree of public support for a tough enforcement policy. It is by no means so clear that such support is as strong when it comes to many of the road traffic laws. No doubt flagrant examples of dangerous driving arouse hostility and demands for the police to take strict enforcement action, but other aspects of the road traffic laws create more difficult conflicts of interest. The law on excessive drinking before driving provides an example.

The connection between consumption of alcohol and safety of driving is well know. But equally well known are the powerful social habits which accept, even if they do not condone, the fact that many people drink more than is safe before setting out to drive. The conflict between the interests of safety on the roads and the strength of established social practices presents the police with a dilemma in seeking to enforce the law. Too strict enforcement may bring unpopularity and make their difficult job more difficult; failure to enforce strictly enough may bring criticism that they are not doing all that they should to promote road safety. The temptation is to compromise by seizing on the most obvious cases and to seek to deter and to influence attitudes, as by having regular patrols on certain stretches of road.

A situation where there is no obvious and universal public support for a strict enforcement policy is one which commonly confronts inspectors. The dilemma facing them is often at least as acute as that which faces the police in seeking to enforce the law on drink and driving. The criticism that they are identifying too closely with those whom they are supposed to be regulating, and thus failing to do their job, may be countered by the criticism that by pursuing too narrowly and single-mindedly the enforcement of the statutory provisions with which they are concerned they may be doing damage to other equally important interests. The constraints which this may put on the activities of inspectors is illustrated by the recent example of fire precautions in residential and public buildings. Following a series of fire tragedies, the Fire Precautions Act 1971 was passed with the object of making more effective provision for fire prevention in such premises. A major step to this end was the requirement in the Act that residential and public buildings must apply for a fire certificate, to be issued by the local fire authority only if it was satisfied that certain specified rules relating to the use of the building, means of escape and so on had been met. Inspectors would enforce these provisions.

When these new regulations were applied there were protests from the Chairman of the Royal Fine Art Commission and others that they were being interpreted too rigorously, with the result not only that they imposed an excessive financial burden but in some cases also conflicted with other safety requirements.[22] On the strict view of the inspector's role he should ignore such protests. His job is simply to see that the regulations are carried into effect, and if the consequences are unacceptable that is a matter for Parliament, which made the rules, and not for him. This is the implication of the view that the inspector should see himself as acting, as far as possible, like a policeman enforcing the criminal laws.

The question is, however, whether one can reasonably expect the inspector to act in this way; and whether in any case such a course either represents what Parliament intended or is necessarily the most effective way of securing fire protection for these buildings. Certainly the fire authority has the responsibility for seeing that the regulations are carried into effect,[23] but that is not necessarily the end of the matter. The fact that Parliament has legislated on fire precautions indicates a measure of agreement that more resources should be devoted to this object, but those regulations have to be applied in a variety of circumstances. It may be that a strict interpretation of the regulations would destroy the character of some historic buildings or mean that they would have to be closed to the public. These are considerations which have to be weighed against the necessity for some strengthening of fire precautions. As the director of the Fire Protection Association argued:

> I am sure that all those who have some influence in this field could get together with fire authorities to work out a satisfactory solution.[24]

This need for compromise is clearly a key element in any discussion of the future role of enforcement inspection. One can identify four factors which might incline inspectors to seek compromises rather than simply to adopt a role of strict enforcement:

(1) lack of whole-hearted public support for strict enforcement;
(2) identification with the interests of those inspected;
(3) lack of resources to achieve strict enforcement;
(4) the ethos of British public administration.

Of these, the first is the one which has been discussed both in relation to the police and to inspection for fire prevention purposes. It is a constraint which clearly operates much more in some areas than others, but it is a factor which cannot be ignored in any application of inspection for enforcement purposes.

The second factor is one heard in criticisms of certain inspectorates. It is most commonly countered by inspectors themselves in terms of the third factor. The argument broadly is that strict enforcement would provoke resistance and unwillingness to comply with the law, which would mean that far more inspectors would be needed for enforcement. The argument is often put in the form that since there are not and can never be enough inspectors to carry out strict enforcement a persuasive approach is in any case necessary. Whether either or both of these factors operates in the case of any particular inspectorate is important for which of the two contrasting views of enforcement inspectorates is adopted. However, this depends far more than in the case of the other two factors on an assessment of the results of inspection, and this is a point which will be considered later.

The fourth factor is by its nature more imprecise. It draws attention to the fact, however, that there is much in the tradition of British public administration which attaches importance to negotiation and compromise. Whether in the preparation of legislation or its implementation, public servants spend much time in the search for a workable way, and preferably one which can secure a reasonable degree of acceptance by the interests involved. Reasonableness is indeed a key concept in much of this work. It does not by any means follow that all the activities of public servants are characterised by compromise. The coercive element is evident in, for example, the activities of customs and excise officers or special investigators of the Department of Health and Social Security. Revenue collection and investigation of suspected fraud are by their nature activities which do not permit a high degree of negotiation and compromise.[25] Even so, this does not necessarily mean that officials engaged in these activities can simply pursue their aims without regard to other consequences. The outcry against the allegedly high-handed behaviour of some customs and excise officers concerned with the collection of VAT is a recent example. Given the constraints under which inspectors in any case operate as a result of the first factor identified above, the general tradition of compromise acts as a reinforcing factor in this direction. Not only are inspectors aware of this tradition, but frequently, as expert advisers of governments, they are drawn into the negotiating process itself. One of the most characteristic features of enforcement inspectors, their belief that most people are ready to comply with the law and that failure to do so arises from ignorance or error rather than reluctance or defiance, derives its force mainly from the combination of these two factors.

Nothing in this discussion should be taken as a denial of the dangers of inspectors identifying themselves too closely with the interests of those whom they inspect. It is still a significant question to ask, as the previous chapter showed, where the balance between strict enforcement and reliance on persuasion and advice should be drawn. That question needs to be examined in relation to the work of individual inspectorates, and especially to an assessment of the effectiveness of each inspectorate in achieving the aims for which it was established. Something will be said on this and particularly on the lack of objective means of assessment of the work of inspectorates in the concluding part of this chapter. The discussion here has emphasised that arguments about the need for a strict enforcement policy in relation to particular inspectorates have to be seen against a wider background – the inherent tendency to some degree of compromise in the operations of enforcement inspectorates in British society.

An important conclusion which follows from this discussion is that there are definite limits to what enforcement inspection can be expected to achieve. The kind of strict enforcement which we expect from the police in dealing with serious crime is not appropriate to the circumstances in which, by and large, enforcement inspectorates operate. Even those who look to fundamental changes in areas of regulation where inspectors work, and see them at least in part as being brought about by stronger enforcement policies on the part of inspectors, acknowledge the strength of the factors operating against such action by inspectors, including:

It was not intended by Parliament that they should operate in this way.
It would not be practical without far more resources being devoted to inspection.
It is not what public opinion wants.[26]

Before considering the implications of this conclusion for the future of inspection, it is necessary to examine a general question to which it leads, that is, whether there is any alternative to the use of inspection for enforcement purposes. It should not be assumed automatically that the objects of legislation in the specific area of influencing modes of behaviour can only or best be achieved by employing inspectors to enforce it. In particular we need to consider, first, whether other means exist for ensuring that standards are achieved and maintained apart from their imposition by statutory regulation; and, secondly, whether the underlying objectives at present sought by the imposition of standards can be achieved by some other means.

ALTERNATIVES TO INSPECTION

Self-regulation

To rely on voluntary means for the attainment and maintenance of standards is rarely likely to be satisfactory. The main reason is the one discussed earlier as being crucial to arguments for the use of enforcement inspection, that where there is a conflict of interests some kind of pressure will be needed to make sure that everyone conforms. There may be a general acceptance of the need for standards, and the great majority may be prepared to observe them in a voluntary system, but there will always remain the problem of the minority who, in pursuit perhaps of their own short-term interests, will ignore or breach any voluntary code. Clearly the seriousness of such a situation will depend on the importance attached to a high degree of conformity to standards in the individual area for which they are devised. Since we are concerned here with areas with which government is concerned, it may be assumed that they are all ones in which a high degree of conformity is desirable, since otherwise government involvement would not be necessary. Voluntary schemes thus do not provide an alternative to the imposition of standards by statutory regulation.

In practice, therefore, any alternative must be a form of regulation, an internal system as opposed to the external system represented by statutory regulation. Self-regulation is of course a common feature of many activities with which government has little concern. Professional football clubs, for example, must conform to the rules laid down by the Football Association if they wish to take part in organised football competitions, and can be penalised if they breach the rules. This combination of incentive and penalty is characteristic of schemes of self-regulation. Perhaps the nearest equivalent in the statutory sphere is the kind of scheme run by the Agriculture Marketing Boards.[27] In areas where government is concerned particularly with standards of conduct there are again many examples of bodies set up specifically to try to ensure that certain standards are met and maintained. The Advertising Standards Association, for example, was set up by the trade in 1962 with the object of promoting and enforcing the highest standards of advertising throughout the country; similarly, the Takeover Panel set up by the City of London financial institutions seeks to ensure that a code of practice is observed by bodies involved in takeover bids. As a detailed study of one such regulating body (the National Housebuilding Council) makes clear, the choice between statutory and self-regulation is a matter of political and practical convenience. Government often finds it convenient to operate through private groups and interests to whom it can offer 'semi-official status'.[28] It is often a feature of such self-regulation that it is introduced under the fear or threat that if the interests concerned do not themselves take effective action government will introduce statutory requirements.[29]

The existence of this alternative is relevant to the future of inspection in that before new inspectorates are established the advantages and disadvantages of doing so as compared with introducing some form of self-regulation ought to be closely examined. There seems less scope for the abandonment of existing inspectorates for a system of self-regulation. It seems doubtful, for example, whether organisations of wholesalers and retailers could devise an effective means of ensuring accurate weights and measures. It is of course true that the Robens Committee laid great stress on the development of an effective self-regulating system in industry and commerce to deal with health and safety hazards, but this was rather a change of emphasis than an entire replacement of statutory regulation: not only did they propose additional administrative powers for inspectors (prohibition and improvement notices), but there seems little prospect of less need for inspectors under the HSW Act, as over the years some have hoped.[30] The truth is that in any case health and safety at work is such a politically sensitive area that any government would find it difficult if not impossible to abandon statutory regulation and thus lay itself open to the charge of being insufficiently concerned with the hazards of health and safety at work. In other areas (such as horticultural marketing) statutory regulation has been introduced because existing organisations were unable or unwilling to operate an effective system of self-regulation.

Use of incentives
If the scope for applying standards by more reliance on self-regulation and less on statutory regulation seems limited, a more fundamental question is whether application of standards is the only or best means of achieving the ends for which it is at present designed. In particular, the scope for using incentives rather than specifying requirements – the carrot rather than the stick – needs to be examined. The most positive incentive is usually financial. Such incentives do not, however, necessarily remove the need for some form of inspection. The most obvious example is the government grant or subsidy. This can clearly provide a powerful inducement. Large sums of money, for example, have been expended under the Industry Act 1972 as regional development grants towards the cost of new machinery, plant and buildings for firms in the development areas. Similarly various grants and subsidies have been provided over the years by the agricultural departments as inducements to farmers to improve their buildings and equipment as well as the quality of their land. But the corollary of the provision of funds by government for these purposes is that there should be a check on their use to ensure that they are in fact applied to

the purposes for which they were provided in accordance with any terms or conditions which may have been specified. To this end the use of inspection as a device for ensuring conformity may be necessary, as in the examples of regional development grants or farm capital grants. However, the important point about such inducements is that they do not represent a conflict of interests but rather an additional reason for moving in a particular direction favoured by government. A firm wishing to expand might find the additional incentive provided by a grant a telling reason for doing so in an assisted area rather than moving elsewhere. Similarly, it is difficult to see other positive financial incentives such as tax relief applying to many of the situations in which inspectorates are now used. One might conceivably provide tax reliefs for certain limited and specific purposes, say, the installation of safer types of machinery, but this hardly seems appropriate to maintaining the accuracy of weighing machines or preventing the overcrowding of houses. There are, in other words, some things which it is desirable to encourage and for which financial incentives may be appropriate, but there are other things which it is desirable to prohibit entirely and where therefore financial incentives are unlikely to achieve their effect

Of greater importance in this context are what may be thought of as negative rather than positive financial incentives. They depend for their effect not on the positive inducement of the financial advantage to be gained from following one course of action rather than another but on the costs or penalities incurred by not taking action in the desired direction. Thus it has been argued that if firms had to pay the full costs of all work-related accidents improvement of safety would be more effectively achieved than it is under the present arrangements under the HSW Act 1974.[31]

The basis of this argument is that under the present arrangements firms are not usually aware of the full costs of accidents, but only of the immediate costs, such as the lost production if machinery has to be stopped. Although therefore they may make some response to such pressures as inspectors can bring, they are not likely to take really determined steps unless they have to bring the full costs of accidents into the reckoning. This might be brought about through the deterrent effect of strict enforcement and legal penalties, that is, on the assumption that breaches of the rules would be quickly detected and would attract severe penalties. A more likely means of bringing home the true costs of accidents would, however, be through financial mechanisms, such as the rate of charging insurance premiums, which might be related to the risk or record of accidents.[32] There is clearly force in the argument, and this has been indirectly acknowledged by the way in which the factory, and even more the alkali, inspectorates take account of the cost of safety measures in their dealings with particular firms or industries. For what the argument draws attention to is the large part played by economic considerations in determining how much effort is devoted to safety questions. The difficulty in the inspectorates' position is that they can only recommend steps which add to the costs of production; and these costs are not sufficiently offset by the reduction in costs from accidents, as they are at present calculated.

Quite apart from whether there are other areas in which incentives of this kind could operate effectively, the argument does bring out a general point of great importance. Assuming for the moment that a system of economic incentives was more effective in reducing accidents than regulation through inspectors, other consequences would still have to be taken into account – some increased unemployment, for example, and higher prices.[33] Thus the argument comes back once more to value-judgements. Everybody is in principle in favour of reducing accidents or ill-health at work, or for that matter air pollution or insanitary housing. But judgements still have to be made about how much reduction and at what cost, whether measured by unemployment, higher costs of goods, fewer houses or whatever it may be.

At the moment some inspectorates have fairly precise targets, like the river quality objectives to which pollution control officers of RWAs work, whereas others, like the factory inspectorate, are for obvious reasons not able to set targets in terms of percentage reduction of accidents, for example; rather they seek to improve the situation in a general and less well defined way. Critics of the factory inspectorate may well agree with them therefore that more should be done to promote safety and health at work, and may accept that there is a conflict between the interests of production and those of safety: but they may seek solutions in radically different ways:

> Any fundamental and solidly based improvement in safety and health at work must depend on a shift of the power to control production to those who are now getting hurt, the men and women on the shop floor.[34]

If this argument were followed the consequences of putting safety before production could well be much more far-reaching than using economic incentives as a means of increasing the resources devoted to safety. The point is not to argue whether such a course would be right but to emphasise the political nature of the decisions which have to be taken if government is to continue to seek ways of reducing accidents and ill-health resulting from work activities. And similar considerations would apply in the case of other areas at present regulated by inspectorates.

Greater public participation

It was earlier pointed out that laws designed to influence modes of behaviour do not always provide for specific enforcement responsibilities but sometimes rely for their effectiveness on the incentives provided to those who may be adversely affected by failure to comply with the law. It is possible to widen this approach and to see scope for greater action by interested individuals and groups in the implementation of legislation. The starting-point here is that individuals and groups with a direct interest in the success of the legislation have a positive incentive to take action to see that it is complied with. Thus angling clubs in the past often brought successful actions against river polluters, especially where the local authorities lacked the resources or the will to use their inspection powers effectively. How far one could extend this idea, and how far in particular it could replace inspection rather than supplement it are matters for debate.

In the first place, it seems more appropriate to some areas than others. It is difficult, for example, to see how it could be applied to the control of dangerous drugs, whereas it is clearly much more appropriate in the field of pollution. Again, in an area like fire precautions it is by no means certain that the incentives provided by increased opportunities for affected interests to participate would result in a balanced approach to fire protection measures. The second important consideration in considering this issue is in fact how far participation would result in a satisfactory resolution of priorities, a sufficient attention to legislative requirements but not an excessive one having regard to other interests involved. And there would be practical questions to be resolved such as means of overcoming the difficulties and expense which individuals and groups encounter at present in trying to take action. As with the discussions of financial incentives, however, the aim here is not so much to pronounce on the value of greater participation or establish whether it is or can be more effective than inspection. It is rather to draw attention to the fact that alternatives do exist to inspection, that much more needs to be done to examine them systematically, and that we should not assume that some form of inspection is the only or necessarily the best way of ensuring that legislative provisions are carried out.

There remains, therefore, a good deal of scope for further inquiry and research. This would be illuminating not only for its relevance to the relatively narrow area of enforcement but for the much wider concern with the factors which contribute to success and failure in the implementation of policies. The limits to inspection on the one hand and increased pressure for participation on the other are both very relevant to this wider concern.

THE FUTURE OF ENFORCEMENT INSPECTION

The discussion in this chapter so far as it relates to enforcement inspectorates has ranged widely since its object was to establish the main characteristics of inspection work which could have a bearing on its future role. To summarise the discussion, one may say

first, that enforcement by inspectors differs from enforcement by the police even though in some areas, notably the road traffic laws, there are some close parallels;

secondly, that this difference is closely related to the fact that strict enforcement of the laws against crime and especially serious crime attracts much stronger public support than strict enforcement of what are mainly regarded as administrative requirements;

thirdly, that the constraints represented by public attitudes are one of a number of factors inclining enforcement inspectors to a policy of persuasion rather than strict enforcement, and of compromise to resolve conflicting interests;

fourthly, that there are possible alternatives to the use of inspection to achieve the aims of legislation, but little has been done to explore them in any detail.

Apart from this last point, the discussion has assumed that there is still a need for enforcement inspection and that the main questions therefore arise in relation to the ways in which inspectors should operate. But this leaves unanswered the question by what criteria we decide exactly what part enforcement inspection should play in the future. As in the earlier discussion of efficiency inspectorates the question can be brought into focus by considering in the light of the preceding discussion whether and if so for what purposes inspectors are still needed. The 18,000 inspectors identified in this study may represent well under 1 per cent of the total of civil servants and local government officers. They nevertheless represent a distinct commitment of a small part of government resources to certain specific purposes.

Taxpayers and ratepayers are therefore entitled to ask whether the employment of these officials is justified, meaning ultimately whether the results achieved by their activities are worth the resources devoted to them. The answer to this question has proved elusive, for reasons which are closely bound up with the history and development of inspectorates in this country and which need to be further explored in any attempt to assess the future of inspection.

For reasons which have already been given, the question will be discussed largely in relation to enforcement inspection. The need for inspecting powers by central government in its relations with local government formed a central part of the earlier examination of the future of efficiency inspection. Here the concern is with the much more numerous enforcement inspectorates and the arguments have only a limited application to efficiency inspectorates.

Two reasons in particular point to the difficulty of arguing the need to justify the use of enforcement inspectorates. The first is that for the most part inspectorates, once created, have largely been left to get on with their job; Parliament has not instituted any special mechanism of review beyond, that is to say, such normal irregular external investigations as may be provided by committees of inquiry or select committees. Secondly, it has become a common assumption not only that there is a need for inspectors but that if anything more rather than less inspecting is needed.

Taken together, these two factors imply an almost unquestioned faith in the value of inspection. They largely account for the fact that the work of few inspectorates has come under close public scrutiny, and for the lack of any general pressure to justify their use. But within this general acceptance of the use of inspection for enforcement purposes there have developed two opposing tendencies. The assumption that more inspecting is desirable seems to be based largely on the view that the purpose of inspection is strict enforcement. The reality of the practical operation of inspection has been in the direction of using persuasion and advice rather than strict enforcement to achieve the ends of legislation. This divergence between the supposed true end of inspection and the reality of their operation in practice has become clear in the case of those few inspectorates which have been challenged over their methods of operating and have not found it easy to answer the criticisms. But it should also be of concern for all enforcement inspectorates and not simply those which happen to have come under public scrutiny.

Moreover, there are reasons for thinking that there is more rather than less need for examining the need for inspection in present circumstances. Against the long-standing tendency towards the persuasive and advisory mode of behaviour, should be set the fact of the increasing volume of government intervention. Much of that intervention is in areas, such as equality of treatment of the sexes or racial discrimination, which do not directly affect the work of inspectors. The problem rather, so far as their work is concerned, is more that of extension beyond fairly well-established frontiers either into unfamiliar territory or for purposes which are less easily defined in traditional terms. Consumer protection and the control of pollution not simply for health reasons but for reasons of general environmental protection as well are two examples. It is no longer, therefore, simply a question of whether inspection is still fulfilling a worthwhile purpose in relation to its traditional spheres of activity but whether it is appropriate to these newer and extended spheres of government intervention.

There can be little doubt that the nineteenth-century approach of laying down specific statutory requirements and then sending inspectors round to see that they were observed was an effective device of administration in the conditions which then prevailed. It certainly helped to ensure that order was introduced into the use of weights and measures where previously there had been chaos, that some of the worst excesses and abuses in factory conditions were curbed, and that many of the worst insanitary conditions in the industrial towns were eliminated. Yet the very success of this device in nineteenth-century conditions creates problems in its application in the twentieth century. When the evils which legislation sought to correct were both easily identifiable and widespread, specific curbs, where they could be applied, might have a spectacular effect. The sharp decline in death rates in the coal mines in the latter half of the nineteenth century provide an obvious example. But once the initial drive has made its impact, what then? Of course it may be necessary to use inspectors to see that standards are maintained, but how much inspection work then remains essential, and, more especially, to what extent does inspection remain the most appropriate means to make further progress, perhaps in areas of government intervention far removed from those originally calling for enforcement inspection?

The question may be asked, for example, what part strict enforcement of specific statutory requirements can play in protecting consumers against unfair trading practices. The fairly simple kinds of dishonesty practised by those using false weights and measures in the nineteenth century were relatively easy to detect; and although technical advances in this century have necessarily made weights and measures work more complex and more demanding in terms of the professional competence of inspectors there has been no essential change in the work itself. More extensive government involvement in the consumer protection field raises sharply the question how appropriate traditional inspection is in this wider field. The rationale of this increased intervention is that modern techniques, both of producing and selling goods, make the ordinary person more vulnerable to positively dishonest or merely sharp practices. However, the very fact that there was uneasiness among weights and measures inspectors about being seen to be exclusively protectors of consumers underlines the point that one needs to look closely at the need for inspection. Dealing firmly with rogue second-hand car dealers is one thing and very much in line with traditional inspection work; arguing with national manufacturing companies whether something is a misleading trade description is quite another thing, and not necessarily seen so obviously as a part of inspection.

The question to what extent inspection is still necessary has both theoretical and practical dimensions. One need not doubt that sending people out on visits of inspection armed with powers of entry and with the backing of criminal sanctions has some effect on behaviour and standards. Most visits will discover something wrong[35] and the consequences of action taken by inspectors will in most cases lead to the wrong being put right – at least for the time being. What is far from clear is the cost-effectiveness of such visits, more particularly when it is not simply specific requirements which are the object of the inspector's visits. Sending round inspectors on regular, routine visits is necessarily a time-consuming and relatively expensive process. One may note, for example, that in 1963, before the great expansion of the work, 900 weights and measures inspectors were needed to carry out what was essentially a routine task, making millions of checks to discover a limited number of errors and even fewer contraventions leading to prosecution. Even allowing for the deterrent effect of the mere existence of inspectors' visits one may ask whether it is all worth while, meaning not only whether inspectors are being deployed to best advantage but also whether there is any better way of achieving the end in view. The question is raised more acutely where the end in view is not simply conformity to a limited number of rules but some much broader end such as the improvement of health and safety at work. We simply do not know for the most part either whether inspection for the strict enforcement of specific requirements or the use of inspectors for broader purposes can be justified in terms of effectiveness or in terms of the efficiency of the means in general.

Given this situation one suspects that the demand for more inspection and stricter enforcement is somewhat analogous to the recurrent demand for stronger action against social security 'scroungers'. Both may be hard to justify in terms of the results achieved for the effort devoted to them but both seem to imply a political commitment, in the one case to achieving fairness in the use of taxpayers' money, in the other to ensuring that laws are complied with. Politically indeed there is much to be gained from demonstrating that inspectors mean business, for a policy of strict enforcement seems to raise no doubt that effective action is being taken, and that, in Owen Hartley's words, government is measuring up to one of the 'hallmarks of a truly democratic regime'.[36]

This essentially political demand has nevertheless to be set against the tendency of inspectors, working as has been stressed within the British empirical tradition, to move away from strict enforcement and detection and towards advice and prevention. Who is right remains an open question. If it is not clear whether it is justifiable to employ a relatively large number of people to carry out routine checks to ensure a high standard of compliance, it is equally unclear whether using inspectors to monitor attempts at self-regulation is likely to prove the most effective way of improving health and safety at work. In any case both sides have increasingly difficult problems to face. Those who put their trust in more strict enforcement must face the fact that the increased number and complexity of requirements to be enforced means that more and more resources will need to be devoted to inspection on the assumption that this continues to be based on regular visits; and if, on the other hand, to counter this problem more selective visiting is undertaken, can the commitment to strict enforcement be maintained? Equally those who see inspection less and less in terms of enforcing specific requirements and more and more in terms of promotion, monitoring and advice will have increasing difficulty in demonstrating the results achieved and the value of this kind of inspection.

The difficulty arises largely because of the lack of effective public debate and attention to the fundamental issues raised by inspection and this in turn means that the question of accountability has become blurred. For without a clearer idea of the relation between the purposes for which inspectorates have been established and the ways in which they operate, and between those purposes and their effectiveness in terms of the resources devoted to inspection it is hard to pin down to whom exactly the inspectors are accountable.

How should these problems be tackled? Some might argue for a new piece of administrative or political mechanism, a watchdog body, a kind of inspectorate of inspectors, on the analogy of a body like the Council on Tribunals, which keeps under review the constitution and working of the various administrative tribunals. Is something similar needed for at any rate enforcement inspectorates? Or should we be content with something more modest such as the simplification and co-ordination of inspection arrangements which has been advocated[37] and of which the creation of HSC and HSE might be seen as one example?

The fashionable faith of the 1960s in the restructuring of the institutions of government to produce greater efficiency seems to have waned somewhat. But in any case it seems doubtful whether new administrative machinery is what is needed, at least until more fundamental questions have been resolved. These, as this study has suggested, are essentially political questions about the scope and rationale of inspection in the modern world. One possibility is a more positive approach to the problems of inspection by those who have some concern and responsibility for them. One can distinguish three groups.

Inspectors themselves can hardly be expected to initiate a debate on the fundamental issues of inspection. As has been suggested, they see themselves for the most part as practical men with an important job to do, and they aic much more likely to be worried at not having the resources to do what they honestly and conscientiously believe needs to be done than about whether some alternative arrangement might be more effective than inspection in achieving the objects of legislation. Nevertheless, one of the points raised by the study has been that although few inspectorates have so far been in the limelight there is no guarantee that this will always be so. The critical pressures which have operated in the area of safety at work and pollution control may well be directed at other areas in the future. Since one aspect of such critical scrutiny is a degree of misunderstanding about the role of inspectors it is surely in the interests of inspectors themselves that, if only for defensive purposes, they should pay more attention to the relation between their aims and methods, and to means of assessing their effectiveness. They need to develop a greater degree of critical self-awareness than most of them have at the moment, particularly in the crucial area of the degree to which strict enforcement or persuasion can be demonstrated to produce better results.

Government departments have the responsibility for the legislation under which enforcement inspectors operate. Existing legislation needs to be reviewed from the point of view of whether there is a continuing need for the specific statutory requirements which are to be enforced by inspectors. But in addition, to the extent that inspectors operate not by enforcing specific requirements but more broadly, there is a need to examine whether the best use is being made of inspectors or more generally whether the same or better results might be obtained in some other way. Clearly these questions would need to be examined in consultation with inspectors themselves, who of course in many cases are part of the departments although in others they are in local authorities or other bodies. Finally, it is necessary to examine critically, in the light of such reviews of existing legislation, proposals for the use of inspectors to enforce new legislation to make sure that inspection is indeed the best way of achieving enforcement and if so to provide the necessary means of monitoring the work of inspection from this point of view.

Parliament should also take a more critical look at the need for inspection in new legislation, or for more inspection or stricter enforcement by inspectors when some particular issue comes up for debate. But if it is to probe more effectively into these questions as well as the possibilities of alternative approaches it will need to press for more information. In particular, the present regular reports of inspectorates, where they make them, would need to be strengthened by more analytical information about the effectiveness of inspection.

Numbers of inspections carried out, prosecutions instituted, unfit carcases of meat condemned or accidents investigated certainly have their uses, as have technical accounts of how particular hazards may be avoided. But it is largely impossible at the moment to form any idea of what inspectors really achieve for the resources devoted to inspection.

If action along these lines were taken it should not only help to avoid the kind of mutual misunderstandings which have entangled the alkali inspectorate but should also help to illuminate some more basic issues which lie behind the use of inspectors. Is there, for example, a fundamental conflict between the needs of production and the needs of safety at work which can only be resolved by radical changes in industry – or society – as some believe; or can the two be reconciled – is it in fact the case that efficient and successful firms tend also to be the ones with the best safety records, as HSE argue?[38]

Greater public awareness of and debate about the issues raised by inspection would at least help to put questions such as these in perspective. The truth is that enforcement inspection occupies a rather ambiguous position in British administration. Its origins in distinctive nineteenth-century conditions, when the state was feeling its way towards regulating the new conditions and problems presented by the rapid growth of industrialisation, coupled with its survival and indeed continued growth into the very different conditions of the late twentieth century make it an obvious candidate for opposing views. There is first the vitality view: survival shows the continuing strength of the original concept and the adaptability of inspectors pursuing essentially the same goals but varying the means they employ to take account of changing circumstances. In contrast is the self-interest view: survival shows how inspectors have been concerned too much with pursuing their own interests, accommodating themselves to the interests of those whom they are supposed to regulate rather than pursuing the public interest which should be their concern.

Neither view quite fits the developments which have taken place so far as it is possible to generalise about such a disparate group as enforcement inspectorates. The argument over the degree to which strict enforcement is less appropriate now is to draw attention to one set of pressures on inspectors – changing social circumstances which make it harder to operate simply by telling people what to do, and which make persuasion and advice more acceptable modes of behaviour for inspectors as for others. To argue that without strict enforcement administration becomes lax is to view these pressures rather differently. Unwillingness to accept without question what the inspector thinks should be done here becomes unwillingness to accept the inspector's view that as much is being achieved as can reasonably be expected to be achieved. Paradoxically, such an anti-authoritarian view leads to demands for a more authoritarian approach by inspectors, at least towards those whom they inspect. There is a degree of confusion and misunderstanding on both sides. Those claiming that inspectors have shown their adaptability to changing circumstances have not sufficiently thought out or shown how it is possible to meet reasonable expectations of achieving the law's ends by this means. Those who insist on a greater exercise of their powers by inspectors have not paid sufficient attention to the consequences: what would be the reaction of those inspected, how many more inspectors would be needed? – the limits to inspection may be both social and practical. Inspectors may not always have seen the dangers to their own credibility in the argument that too much prosecution would be counter productive, but their critics equally have often failed to see the difficulties in a get-tough policy in a society which finds it increasingly hard to make get-tough measures effective.

It can be said therefore that in the 1970s enforcement inspection continues to flourish largely because nobody has seriously explored – and certainly not in any systematic way – either the limits or the alternatives to inspection. Hence the impact of characteristically late-twentieth-century pressures, anti-authoritarian, pro-participation, reliance on market incentives, has chiefly been to induce confusion and misunderstanding. And hence the main conclusion of the present study must be that we cannot begin to determine the role of enforcement inspection in the future until we have clarified our ideas both about enforcement as a means of implementation and about what can reasonably be expected in consequence from the use of inspection in enforcement. What has been said here will, it is hoped, provide the groundwork and stimulus to greater public awareness and debate about the issues raised by what until now has largely remained an obscure and to some degree an almost forgotten corner of government.

NOTES: CHAPTER 8

1 J. Bentham, *Constitutional Code*, Vol. 9 of *Works*, ed. John Bowring, 1843, p.257.
2 See Appendix 1, p. [231].
3 The position in Scotland is somewhat different: see Appendix 2, p. [273].
4 Powers of Criminal Courts Act 1973, ss. 49, 50: SI 1976, no. 626.
5 For example, the auditor must satisfy himself as to the correctness or completeness of the abstract of accounts which is open to the inspection of local government electors (SI 1974, no. 1169, Reg. 15(8)).
6 Local Government Act 1972, pt VIII, especially ss.157, 161: for the position in Scotland, where there are no district auditors but auditors acting under the Commission for Local Authority Accounts operate in a broadly similar way, see Appendix 2, p. [272].

7 See especially the paper by W.B. Utting, director of the SWS, 'The role of the social work service', presented to a meeting of the Association of Directors of Social Services, York, 1977 (*Social Work Service*, 16 July 1978).

8 *Report of the Committee of Inquiry into the Care and Supervision Provided in Relation to Maria Colwell* (HMSO, 1974); *Report of the Social Work Service of DHSS into certain aspects of the management of the case of Stephen Menhenniott* (HMSO, 1978).

9 *William Tyndale Junior and Infants Schools Public Inquiry: A report to the Inner London Education Authority by Robin Auld, QC* (ILEA, 1976); *Sutton Centre Community School* (DES, 1978).

10 Evelyn Sharp, *The Ministry of Housing and Local Government* (RIPA/Allen & Unwin, 1969), p.215.

11 On this see J.A.G. Griffith, *Central Departments and Local Authorities* (RIPA/Allen & Unwin, 1966), especially pp. 515–28.

12 Griffith, op. cit., p.514.

13 *First Report*, Cmd 7870, 1950; *Second Report*, Cmd 8421, 1951.

14 *Central Government Controls over Local Authorities* (Cmnd 7634, HMSO, 1979).

15 F. Pethybridge, 'The case for a National Health Service advisory authority'. I am indebted to Mr Pethybridge, regional administrator, North West Regional Health Authority for letting me see this unpublished paper.

16 Sex Discrimination Act 1975, ss. 63–5; in many cases the complaint would be handled by a conciliation officer without the need for a formal hearing before an industrial tribunal (s.64).

17 Motor Vehicles (Construction and Use) Regulations 1973 (SI 1973, no. 24), regs 79, 81, 88.

18 cf. Theo Nichols and Pete Armstrong, *Safety or Profit* (Falling Wall Press, Bristol, 1973), esp. pp. 13–20.

19 See *Road Haulage Operators' Licensing* (HMSO, 1979), para. 3.27.

20 T.A. Critchley, *A History of Police in England and Wales* (Constable, rev. edn, 1978), p.203.

21 cf. R.M. Jackson, *Enforcing the Law* (Macmillan, 1967), pp. 27–34.

22 See correspondence in *The Times*, 8 September 1978 and subsequently. It was alleged for example that the swing doors which had to be installed for fire prevention purposes were too difficult for many old people to open (letter from John Ticehurst, 26 September); and that many minor accidents to children had resulted from the use of such doors (letter from John Herbert, 3 October).

23 cf. letter from Chief Fire Officer, Cambridgeshire, *The Times*, 12 September 1978.

24 N.C. Strother Smith, letter to *The Times*, 16 September 1978.

25 But it is also worth pointing out that even here prosecution is not necessarily automatic; far more contraventions of the income tax laws are settled by agreed payments by the offender than by prosecution.

26 cf. Cranston, op. cit., p. 109; Beaumont, op. cit., p. 216.

27 See Appendix 2, p. [275].

28 Anthony Barker, 'Self-regulation and consumer power', in D.C. Hague, W.J.M. Mackenzie, A. Barker, *Public Policy and Private Interests* (Macmillan, 1975), pp. 327–55.

29 ibid., pp. 329, 349.

30 cf. Chapter 4, p. [69].

31 Jenny Phillips, 'Economic deterrence and the prevention of industrial accidents', *Industrial Law Journal*, vol. 5, no.3, 1976, pp. 148–63.

32 ibid., esp. pp. 157–9.

33 ibid., pp. 162–3.

34 Nichols and Armstrong, op. cit., pp. 29–30.

35 cf. Law Commission 'Strict Liability and the Enforcement of the Factories Act 1961', op. cit., para. 27.

36 See above, Chapter 7, p. [189].
37 Hartley, op. cit., p.464.
38 *Health and Safety: Manufacturing and Service Industries 1977* (HMSO, 1978), para.
    9.

APPENDIX 1
INSPECTORS AND PUBLIC INQUIRIES

———◆———

The Public Health Act of 1848 which established the General Board of Health gave the Board power to appoint 'Superintending Inspectors'. They were to have specific powers and duties under the Act and generally were to assist in its 'superintendence and execution' under the direction of the Board. On a petition from a place by at least one-tenth of the ratepayers (or in limited circumstances on their own initiative) the Board could direct a Superintending Engineering Inspector to visit the place.

> and to make public inquiry, and to examine witnesses as to the sewerage, drainage . . . the number and sanitary conditions of the inhabitants . . . the nature drainage areas, and the existing municipal . . . boundaries . . . and as to any other matters in respect whereof the said Board may desire to be informed. . . .

Furthermore, the inspector was to give fourteen days' notice of his intention to hold an inquiry, and of the time and place where he was prepared

> to hear all persons desirous of being heard before him upon the subject of such inquiry.[1]

Such inquiries have to be seen in the context of one of the main objects of the Act, which was to secure its adoption in as many localities as were able and willing to appoint local boards of health for the improvement of water supplies, sanitation, etc. The procedure was that following the inspector's inquiry he made a report to the Board, which if all went well could then apply the Act by means of either an Order in Council or a Provisional Order. In this case then the appointment of inspectors was neither to secure compliance with the provisions of an Act of Parliament nor to control standards of efficiency, but rather to assist in the establishment of more effective means, as it was hoped, of dealing with public health problems. This, however, raises two further questions, first about the nature of the inquiries which the superintending inspectors carried out, and secondly about other functions which they performed.

Two distinct kinds of inquiry seem to be included in the duties of the 1848 inspectors. There is first a purely fact-finding inquiry – going to the area and finding out about the water supply and the drains and so on; secondly, there is the more formal business of sitting in a room listening to what people have to say and questioning them, which is likely to go beyond fact-finding since it will involve hearing those who object to the petition as well as those who support it. The inspector in other words was concerned not simply with investigating the facts of the situation but with assessing the arguments for and against the adoption of the Act in the particular area.

The Act does not make the clear distinction drawn above between general inquiries and public inquiries. Yet the distinction was present as can be seen both from the activities of the medical inspectors of the Board, and from the instructions given to the superintending inspectors. As to the first, it was not long after the Board had started work that an investigation of a cholera outbreak in Whitechapel was undertaken, the medical inspector being instructed

> to inquire into the facts of the outbreak, and to report to the Board on the steps necessary to be taken.[2]

In contrast to this are the detailed instructions issued by the Board to the superintending inspectors. They were first to make contact with people in the area who were most likely to be able to give reliable information about its sanitary condition, then to carry out a detailed physical inspection leading to the drawing up of detailed plans and proposals for the necessary works, etc., but specifically in relation to the hearing of views by interested parties they were told:

> Your examination is mainly one as to works, or as to engineering appliances for the removal of the evils in question, and you will conduct the inquiry according to your own professional views and methods of investigation: and when you deem it necessary to examine witnesses, it will be inexpedient that you should attempt to adopt the technical procedure of the courts of law, which is instituted for the determination of questions as to matters of fact with a view to legal decisions. You alone will be responsible for all inquiries, and you only are authorized to conduct them. The statute gives no authority for incurring the expense of hearing counsel and attorneys. It will be your duty to put such questions to witnesses as may appear necessary.[3]

These instructions seem to foreshadow the kind of public inquiry work which was later carried out by the engineering inspectorate of the Local Government Board and its successors, and later still by the Planning Inspectorate. But in what sense was this inspecting work, and what was the significance of calling the people who did it inspectors and, more especially, *superintending* inspectors?

Part of the answer can be found by looking at the reform of local Poor Law administration under the 1834 Act. That reform was in two stages: (1) investigation by Assistant Poor Law Commissioners, one of whose main tasks was to examine in detail the administration of poor relief in each parish within their districts with a view in most cases to recommending the union of parishes to form more effective units of administration under elected Boards of Guardians; (2) supervision of the work of the Guardians once they had assumed responsibility for local administration in the new Unions. The first, the investigation of existing administration and its reorganisation, was a necessary preliminary to the second, inspection of the work of the new authorities to see that they were operating efficiently.

The public health reforms of 1848 were to some extent modelled on the

Poor Law reforms, but the General Board of Health had much weaker powers than the Poor Law Commission. The 1848 Public Health Act represented a compromise between the views of Edwin Chadwick and the Health of Towns Commission of 1843–5 on the one hand, and of those who opposed the assumption by central government of responsibility for matters which were held to be purely a matter of local concern on the other. The former sought a stronger central authority with the power to ensure that works undertaken for sewerage, water supplies and drainage were properly planned and carried out; for this, superintending inspectors would have matched their titles.[4] As it was, the inspectors under the Act were not even permanent officials but, nominally at least, hired at a fee of up to £3 3s a day plus expenses to carry out their duties. Of more importance, the Act gave no power to the General Board to take action once the machinery of Provisional Orders had been set in motion and completed, other than the power of approving applications for loans by local boards – and even that power was nearly lost during the passage of the Bill through Parliament. The power of action was firmly with the local boards.

The General Board itself drew attention to the 'want of means' to

send Superintending Inspectors to visit Local Boards in order to aid them with such advice as their knowledge and experience might enable them to afford.[5]

Thus superintending inspectors who conducted inquiries under the 1848 Act were only halfway to being inspectors. They carried out the inquiries as an essential preliminary to the establishment of local authorities for public health purposes, but that was all. As Tom Taylor, assistant secretary of the General Board of Health in 1850 and later secretary of the Local Government Act Office under the 1858 Act, argued twenty years later, the main defect of the legislation was:

the want of all powers of the Secretary of State for inspection. We can give powers, but we have no means of seeing how those powers are carried into effect or that they are working for the good or ill of the district in which they are in force. We are totally without inspecting powers . . . it seems to me that we have only powers for doing half our work.[6]

It was not until, following the Royal Sanitary Commission's report, the Local Government Board was established in 1871 bringing together central government responsibilities for the poor law and medical and sanitary work that an engineering inspectorate was created with powers both of investigation and inquiry, and of supervisory or general inspection such as the Poor Law inspectors had long had.[7]

Before the late 1840s the title for someone who was sent out from the centre to hold inquiries and consider objections to proposals was usually Commissioner, as under the Inclosure Acts.[8] The association of the holding of public inquiries with the title of inspector can be dated from the Poor Law Act 1847[9] and the Public Health Act 1848. The essential point is that the public inquiry represented at that stage a form of control over the activities of local authorities in certain contexts. It was to that extent a specialised form of the public inquiry which had been developed to hold hearings on proposals in connection with the enclosure of land. Before the central authority could act in relation to local authorities it needed information not only about the facts but about the views of interested parties and their relative strength in particular localities, and this the public inquiry gave. It has to be remembered that although a considerable number of central government departments were set up, particularly in the years 1833–54, with powers over local authorities, the powers were nearly always limited and the intention was in most cases that the local authorities should have more power than the central.[10] To hold a public inquiry on proposals which a central department was anxious to carry was both a means of eliciting information and, through the publicity and questioning to which it gave rise, a means of preparing the way for changes.[11]

Thus, when the Charity Commission was established by an Act of 1853, its inspectors had two main tasks: (1) to inquire into the administration and finances of individual charities, for which purpose they could require the trustees and other persons to appear before them for questioning on oath and to produce necessary documents; (2) to hold a local inquiry in cases where the Commission (acting very largely on an inspector's information from his preliminary inquiries) were proposing a new scheme of administration for the charity. For this purpose inspectors could 'take and receive any evidence and information and hear and inquire into any objections or questions relating to the scheme or charity in question' and were to report back to the Commission the results of the inquiry and whether in their view the scheme should be approved.[12]

Thus although the association of inspectors with the holding of public inquiries is closely bound up with inspection as a means of control of local authorities and similar bodies it was only in the case of the General Board of Health that inspectors were appointed with this as practically their sole function. Nevertheless the title inspector for one who holds public inquiries became firmly established in England and Wales even when those inquiries had little or nothing to do with control of local authorities, as is the case with planning inspectors today.

NOTES: APPENDIX 1

1 11 and 12 Vict. cap. 63, VI, VIII, IX.
2 Minutes of General Board of Health, 19 December 1848 (PRO MH 5/1).
3 *Report of the General Board of Health on the administration of the Public Health Act . . . from 1848 to 1854* (PP 1854, vol. XXXV), p. 101.
4 cf. R.A. Lewis, *Edwin Chadwick and the Public Health Movement 1832–1854* (Longman, 1952), p.96; David Roberts, 'Jeremy Bentham and the Victorian administrative state', *Victorian Studies*, vol. II, 1959, p.204.
5 *Report of General Board of Health . . .*, p.43.
6 *First Report of Royal Sanitary Commission*, Minutes of Evidence question 206 (PP 1868–9, vol. XXXII).
7 But still not as extensive as those of poor law inspectors (cf. M.R. Maltbee, *English Local Government of Today*, New York, 1897, p. 87).
8 cf. R.E. Wraith and G.B. Lamb, *Public Inquiries as an Instrument of Government* (Allen & Unwin, 1972), p. 20.

9 The Act replaced the Poor Law Commissioners by the Poor Law Board and the assistant commissioners became inspectors.

10 cf. Roberts, *Victorian Origins*, pp. 106–18, esp. pp. 112, 114.

11 That Chadwick saw things in this light seems evident, cf. Lewis, op. cit., pp. 96–7, 102.

12 16 and 17 Vict. cap. 137, XII, LIV, LVII, LVIII. It is incidentally a mark of the difficulty of drawing boundary-lines that whereas assistant Poor Law Commissioners became inspectors in 1847, inspectors of the Charity Commission were renamed 'assistant commissioners' in 1887.

APPENDIX 2
THE INSPECTORATES

---◆---

This appendix is in three parts. Part 1 includes all those inspectorates which fall reasonably clearly within the definitions of enforcement or efficiency inspectorates discussed in Chapter 1. For each inspectorate, information is given as far as possible on origin, development, functions, powers, recruitment and numbers, with in some cases additional information. Numbers are generally given at the latest convenient date, but they are subject to fluctuation and in some cases are only approximate. These inspectorates form the main subject of the present study. The total number of inspectors in Part 1 is just under 18,000, made up of approximately 17,300 enforcement inspectors and 600 efficiency inspectors. Of these, central government inspectors (defined as inspectors employed by government departments and HSE) total about 3,700 (3,100 enforcement, 600 efficiency), or approximately 0.7 per cent of the 567,000 non-industrial civil servants. Local government inspectors, all of whom are enforcement, total about 13,500, or approximately 0.6 per cent of the 2,300,000 local government employees (or 1 per cent if manual workers – about 1,000,000 – are excluded). There are in addition just over 600 inspectors, all enforcement, employed by other bodies (RWA/RPB, CAA, GB).

Part 2 is designed to illustrate the difficulty of precise definition and includes examples of (i) inspectorates in which inspection for enforcement or efficiency purposes forms a relatively small part of their functions as compared with non-inspecting work; (ii) inspectorates whose enforcement or efficiency inspection activities overlap other categories, especially internal or checking inspection, to which on the whole it seems more appropriate to assign them. The first group in particular raises boundary problems (e.g. why include sea fisheries here and fire precautions in Part 1?) which could only be resolved by detailed investigation of every inspectorate to establish the relative weight to be given to each function or set of functions. Brief notes are given on each inspectorate in Part 2.

Part 3 provides some examples of checking inspectorates which are to some extent analogous to enforcement inspectorates.

SUMMARY TABLE

PART 1

Title of inspectorate	Date of origin	Appointing authority*	Number of inspectors
Enforcement inspectorates			
1 anatomy	1832	DHSS	1
2 factory	1833	HSE	958
3 trading standards/consumer protection	1835	CC/LB/RC	1,500

4	railways	1840		D Trans	22
5	mines and quarries	1842	(1850)	HSE	116
6	environmental health	1848		DC/LB	5,750
7	mercantile marine				
	superintendents	1850		D T	50
8	surveyors of ships	1854		D T	300
9	gas examiners, gas meter				
	examiners, gas engineers	1859		D En	50
10	alkali and clean air	1863		HSE	47
11	explosives	1875		HSE	15
12	building control	1875		DC/LB	4,110
13	cruelty to animals	1876		HO	15
14	river pollution	1876		RWA/RPB	420
15	plant health and seeds	1877		MAFF	75
16	electricity engineering	1882		D En	6
17	ships' provisions	1892		D T	11
18	wages	1909		D E	150
19	civil aviation (safety)	1920		D T/CAA	180
20	drugs	1920		HO	11
21	agricultural wages	1924		MAFF	36
22	road vehicle examiners	1930		D Trans	638(1,028)
23	petroleum engineering	1934		D En	12
24	egg marketing	1941		MAFF	40
25	agriculture (health and				
	safety)	1952		HSE	189
26	fire precautions	1959		CC/RC	2,180
27	radiochemical	1960		DOE	6
28	nuclear installations	1960		HSE	106
29	pipelines	1962		D En	6
30	horticultural marketing	1964		MAFF	140
31	gaming	1968		GB	37
32	diving	1975		D En	5
33	Scottish agricultural			DAFS	106
34	industrial pollution			SDD	9

Efficiency inspectorates

1	education (England and Wales)	1840	DES	452
2	education (Scotland)	1840	SED	116
3	police (England and Wales)	1856	HO	6 + 4
4	police (Scotland)	1857	SHHD	2
5	fire services (England and			
	Wales)	1947	HO	16 + 19
6	fire services (Scotland)	1947	SHHD	2 + 4

PART 2

Enforcement Inspectorates

Title of	*Appointing*
inspectorate	*authority**
a veterinary officers (slaughterhouses)	MAFF
b sea fisheries	MAFF/DAFS
c Forestry Commission	FC
d ancient monuments and historic buildings	DOE
e planning (enforcement) inspectors	CC/RC/DC/LB

Efficiency inspectorates

a auditors of local authority accounts	DOE/CLAA
b social work service (England and Wales)	DHSS
c social work services (Scotland)	SED
d probation	HO
e registration	RG

PART 3

1 Agricultural Development and Advisory Service	MAFF
2 regional development grant examiners	D I
3 white fish	WFA
4 agricultural marketing	AMB

* Abbreviations used in this column:

AMB	Agricultural Marketing Boards
CAA	Civil Aviation Authority
CC/LB/RC	County councils and London boroughs (England and Wales); regional and islands councils (Scotland)
CLAA	Commission for Local Authority Accounts
DC/LB	District councils and London boroughs (and islands councils in Scotland)
DAFS	Department of Agriculture and Fisheries for Scotland
DE	Department of Employment
D En	Department of Energy
DES	Department of Education and Science
DHSS	Department of Health and Social Security
D I	Department of Industry
DOE	Department of the Environment
D T	Department of Trade
D Trans	Department of Transport
FC	Forestry Commission
GB	Gaming Board of Great Britain
HO	Home Office
HSE	Health and Safety Executive
MAFF	Ministry of Agriculture, Fisheries and Food
RG	Registrar General for England and Wales; Registrar General for Scotland

RWA/RPB   Regional water authorities (England and Wales); river purification
          boards (Scotland)
SDD   Scottish Development Department
SED   Scottish Education Department
SHHD   Scottish Home and Health Department
WFA   White Fish Authority

ENFORCEMENT INSPECTORATES

1 Anatomy Inspector (Her Majesty's Inspector of Anatomy

Origin

The *Anatomy Act 1832* was passed to regulate the conditions under which bodies were used to teach anatomy to medical students. Three inspectors were appointed, one each for England, Scotland and Wales. A further Act in 1871 introduced certain modifications.

Functions

The inspector (there is only one now) is responsible for enforcement of the Acts and regulations, especially those relating to the use of donated bodies in medical schools. He is also involved in an advisory and supervisory role in the planning of new teaching hospitals.

Powers

Apart from the power to visit and inspect places licensed to practice anatomy (1832 Act, s. 5) the inspector's supervisory function derives from the fact that he must be notified of the use of bodies for anatomical examination (s. 9, 10).

Recruitment
Number

Inspectors are qualified medical practitioners.

1.

2 Factory Inspectorate (Her Majesty's Inspectorate of Factories)

Origin
and
Development

Four inspectors were appointed in 1833 under the *Factories Regulation Act* of that year to ensure that the provisions of that Act, mainly relating to the hours of employment of children, were observed. Successive Factories Acts extended the scope of the work up to the *Factories Act 1961*. Under the *Health and Safety at Work [etc] Act 1974* the inspectorate became part of the Health and Safety Executive, and that Act now governs its activities.

Functions

Under the 1974 Act the HSE may appoint inspectors to carry into effect the 'relevant statutory provisions', that is, the 1974 Act and regulations made under it together with certain existing Acts, of which the most important so far as the factory inspectorate is conned is the *Factories Act 1961*. Broadly speaking, the job of the factory inspectorate is to ensure that the legislation relating to health, safety and welfare in factories is observed.

Powers

The powers of inspectors under the 1974 Act include (i) powers of entry to specified premises; (ii) powers of examination and investigation on such premises, of taking measurements or samples and, in certain circumstances, of ordering tests of articles or substances; (iii) power to question people on matters relevant to their inquiries; (iv) power to require the production of necessary books and documents (s. 20(2)). Inspectors also have power to require specified improvements to be carried out in the case of a contravention of the statutory provisions ('improvement notices', s. 21); or to prohibit activities which he believes involve a risk of serious personal injury ('prohibition notices', s. 22). If he thinks an article or substance is a cause of imminent danger he can have it seized and destroyed or otherwise made harmless (s. 25). Inspectors can, in England and Wales, both institute proceedings for an offence under the relevant statutory provisions, and, in certain circumstances, prosecute in a magistrates' court (ss. 38 and 39). Prosecutions numbered 1,478 in 1977, when 4,833 improvement and 1,927 prohibition notices were issued.

Recruitment

Mainly from university graduates, but also from those with technical qualifications and industrial experience.

Numbers

958 (1979).

NB See Chapter 4 for a detailed discussion of the factory inspectorate.

3 *Trading Standards Officers/Consumer Protection Officers*

Origin
and
Development

The *Weights and Measures Act 1835* provide for the appointment of inspectors of weights and measures by the local justices throughout the country, but it was not until later in the century that a uniform and regular system was established, notably with the *Weights and Measures Act 1878* and modifications in Acts of 1889 and 1904. The *Weights and Measures Act 1963* is now the principal Act relating to inspection of weights and measures. County councils and London boroughs in England and Wales, and region and island authorities in Scotland, are now weights and measures authorities. Since 1960 there has been a considerable increase in legislation enforceable by weights and measures authorities, especially the *Trade Descriptions Act 1968*.

In addition, there is other legislation traditionally enforced by weights and measures inspectors, e.g. parts of the *Food and Drugs Act 1955* (in Scotland, the *Food and Drugs (Scotland) Act 1956*). The great increase in the volume of legislation and changes in its nature were major factors in decisions in the 1970s to change the title of inspectors to consumer protection or, more usually, trading standards officers.

Functions

The primary task of trading standards officers is to ensure that the various Acts with which they are concerned and regulations made under them are complied with. Many trading standards departments also carry out non-mandatory functions in the provision of advice to consumers.

Powers

Under the 1963 Act an inspector has the power to inspect and test weighing and measuring equipment, inspect goods, seize articles and documents and enter premises (other than dwelling-houses) where he thinks equipment may be kept (s. 48). Somewhat similar powers but including the power to require the production of books or documents relating to a business are in the 1968 Act (s. 28) and other legislation, but there are important qualifications to some of these powers such as seizing goods or documents which can only be exercised if the inspector has reasonable cause to suspect that an offence has been committeed. The power to institute proceedings where an offence is detected belongs to the local authority, subject, in some cases, to their notifying the central department of their intention beforehand.

Recruitment

The traditional route for weights and measures inspectors was recruitment as school-leavers by the local authority, and after experience and study taking the Board of Trade (now Department of Trade) examination to become a qualified inspector. With the widening of the work a Diploma in Trading Standards will become the basic qualification but it is unlikely that the source of recruitment will change much.

Numbers

Approx. 1,500 (1977).

NB See Chapter 3 for a detailed discussion and further information about trading standards officers.

4 Railway Inspectorate

Origin and Development

Under the *Railway Regulation Act 1840* an inspector general and two inspecting officers of railways were appointed to inspect new railways and report on their construction and equipment. An amending Act of 1842 gave them power to postpone the opening of a new railway if it was found unsatisfactory or unsafe. Companies were also required to report accidents, and these were investigated by inspectors although they had no statutory power to do so until the *Regulation of Railways Act 1871* (still the governing statute for this purpose). The main inspecting work is now carried out under the *Road and Rail Traffic Act 1933*.

The *Railway Employment (Prevention of Accidents) Act 1900* gave the Board of Trade power to appoint assistant inspecting officers (now called railway employment inspectors) to investigate the more serious accidents to employees, although again this work had previously been done to some extent on a non-statutory basis by the inspecting officers. Four inspectors were appointed for this purpose. This side of the work has increased greatly since the *Health and Safety at Work* [etc]. *Act 1974*, and is now carried on under an agency agreement between the inspectorate and the Health and Safety Commission.

Functions

There are two main functions of the inspecting officers:
(i) inspection of new works such as electrification schemes or the introduction of new signalling; under the 1933 Act a railway company (now the British Railways Board) is required to obtain the Minister's approval before bringing new works into operation, for which purpose he may order an inspection (s. 41);
(ii) investigation of accidents under the 1871 Act.

In addition the inspecting officers provide the Department generally with expert advice on railway matters, e.g. in relation to railway investment plans.

Under the agency agreement, the railway employment inspectors are responsible for enforcing all safety legislation on BR and other railway premises (except railway workshops).

Powers

Under the 1871 Act inspecting officers have the power to inspect stations, works, stock, plant, etc.; to summon and make inquiries of employees, managers, etc.; and to require the production of books, documents, etc. (ss. 3 and 4; no specific powers are provided under the 1933 Act. Under the 1900 Act railway employment officers had a general power to inspect for the purposes of ensuring compliance with the Act or rules made under it (s. 13). The agency agreement with HSC now gives them the wider powers of inspectors under the 1974 Act (see factory inspectorate). There is no direct provision for instituting proceedings as a result of the work of inspecting officers, but investigation of accidents may lead to criminal charges, e.g. manslaughter; such cases are referred to the Director of Public Prosecutions. Railway employment inspectors rarely prosecute; there has been only one case, against the British Railways Board, since 1974; it was unsuccessful.

Recruitment

Inspecting officers have always since 1840 been recruited from officers of the Royal Engineers (although for many years appointments have been subject to a civil service open competition). Employment inspectors are mainly chartered engineers with railway experience.

Numbers

5 inspecting officers (including chief), 17 employment inspectors (1979).

5 *Mines and Quarries Inspectorate (Her Majesty's Inspectorate of Mines and Quarries*

Origin and Development

Although an Act of 1842 provided for the Home Secretary to appoint an inspector to examine and report on collieries, mines inspection effectively began with the *Mines Act 1850*. Under it four inspectors were appointed to inquire into the safety arrangements in coalmines. Successive Acts widened the powers of inspectors, notably the *Coal Mines Regulation Act 1872*, and gave them responsibilities in mines other than coalmines and, from 1894, in quarries too. Further regulation of mines and quarries in the interests of the health and safety of those employed there has continued in the twentieth century. The *Mines and Quarries Act 1954* was the principal legislation until under the *Health and Safety at Work* [etc]. *Act 1974* the inspectorate became part of the Health and Safety Executive.

Functions

Under the 1974 Act the Mines and Quarries Act 1954 1954 became part of the 'relevant statutory provisions' to be enforced (see notes on factory inspectorate). Broadly speaking, the job of the inspectorate is to ensure that the legislation relating to health, safety and welfare in mines and quarries is observed.

Powers

As for factory inspectors. Three prosecutions were instituted in 1977 (one in relation to a fireclay mine, two in relation to quarries); one prohibition notice was issued against a quarry owner.

Recruitment

From mining engineers with experience in the industry.

Numbers

116 (1979).

NB See Chapter· 4 for further discussion and information about inspection of mines.

6 *Environmental Health Officers*

Origin,
Development and
Functions

The *Public Health Act 1848* made provision for local Boards of Health to appoint inspectors of nuisances. The *Nuisances Removal and Diseases Prevention Act 1855* specified their duties as being to notify their employing authority of the existence of nuisances in the area, and to inspect food offered for sale. Later nineteenth-century Acts, notably the *Sanitary Act 1866* and the *Public Health Act 1875*, elaborated on what constituted a nuisance and on the procedure for dealing with nuisances. By the end of the century inspectors were generally known as sanitary inspectors. The twentieth century has added to the range of responsibilities. From the original preoccupation with housing conditions (e.g. provision of drains, fitness for habitation, overcrowding) and food hygiene inspectors have been drawn into control of smoke and noise pollution, safety, health and welfare of workers in offices and shops, and numerous lesser enforcement areas (e.g. conditions in pet shops). Among the main pieces of legislation with whose enforcement they are concerned are the *Public Health Act 1936*, a variety of *Housing Acts*, the *Food and Drugs Act 1955*, the *Clean Air Acts 1956 and 1968*, the *Offices, Shops and Railway Premises Act 1963* the *Control of Pollution Act 1974* and the *Health and Safety at Work* [etc.] *Act 1974*. Sanitary inspectors became public health inspectors in 1956 and environmental health officers in 1974.

Powers

Inspectors as such have the normal specified powers of entry and inspection in the great variety of circumstances provided by the range of legislation, including those under the HSW Act 1974 (see factory inspectorate). Much of the legislation confers additional powers on the local authority (district council or London borough in England and Wales, district council or islands authority in Scotland) to take action as a result of inspection, e.g. impose a closing order on a house. Environmental health officers administer such provisions, and take action on other matters within their sphere of responsibility, e.g. dealing with food condemned as unfit, instituting proceedings for breaches of the Offices, Shops and Railway Premises Act.

Recruitment

Normal local government recruitment followed by specific instructions and training leading to the Diploma in Environmental Health, the basic qualification.

Some graduates are recruited, certain degrees giving exemption from the need for a diploma.

Numbers   Approx. 5,000 (E & W), 750 (S).

NB Scottish legislation differs in detail from that for England and Wales. See especially *Public Health (Scotland) Acts 1897 and 1945; Food and Drugs (Scotland) Act 1956.*

7 Mercantile Marine Superintendents

Origin, Development and Functions   The *Mercantile Marine Act 1850* provided for Local Marine Boards to be established with local offices, each under the charge of a superintendent. Their main purpose was to ensure that properly certificated masters were in charge of ships and that the terms of agreement, accommodation, etc., required under the Act for the crew had been observed. Local boards were soon abolished and superintendents are now Department of Trade officials operating from twenty mercantile marine offices in the major ports of the United Kingdom. The inspection of ships' documents to ensure that they comply with the statutory requirements is a major part of the work. They may also hold inquiries into the death of any person who dies in a ship registered in the UK. The work of superintendents is mainly governed by the *Merchant Shipping Act 1970*.

Powers   Superintendents have power to board and inspect a ship, its equipment, articles on board and documents at all reasonable times (1970 Act, s. 76.). Wider powers (e.g. to summon witnesses) are given for the purpose of carrying out inquiries into deaths (1970 Act, s. 61; Merchant Shipping Act 1979, s. 27).

Recruitment   Superintendents are executive officers and higher executive officers of the Department of Trade.

Numbers   Approx. 50 (1979).

8 Surveyors of Ships

Origin, Development and Functions   The *Merchant Shipping Act 1854* provided for the appointment of inspectors for various purposes, and these provisions were repeated in the *Merchant Shipping Act 1894* which superseded the 1854 Act. Both Acts provided for the appointment of surveyors. Surveyors carry out surveys of ships to ensure that they meet the requirements for passenger and safety certificates and safety equipment certificates; they investigate casualties, conduct random general inspections and carry out various other functions. The principal legislation governing their work is contained in the *Merchant Shipping Acts 1894 to 1979*.

Powers

Surveyors have power to board and inspect a ship, its equipment, articles on board and documents at all reasonable times (1970 Act, s. 76). Wider powers (e.g. to enter premises or to require the production of documents) may be given for specific cases, and also for the investigation of serious accidents and casualties (1894 Act, ss. 728, 729; also s. 465).

Recruitment

Surveyors of ships must have served as master or engineer on a foreign-going ship and possess Extra Certificates of Competency or they may be naval architects with appropriate experience.

Numbers

Approx. 300 (1978).

9 Gas Examiners, Gas Meter Examiners, Gas Engineers

Origin and Functions

An Act of 1859 (22 and 23 Vic. cap. 66) concerned with the regulation of the measures used in sales of gas by meter provided for the appointment of inspectors by justices for the purpose of testing meters. *The Gasworks Clauses Act (1847) Amendment Act 1871* provided for the appointment of gas examiners, by local authorities in the case of private companies supplying gas, by justices in the case of local authority gas undertakings. It was not until the twentieth century that these regulatory functions were gradually taken over by central government; for example, the *Gas Regulation Act 1920* provided for the appointment of gas referees and a chief gas examiner by the Board of Trade for testing the quality of gas. The present system dates from nationalisation under the Gas Act 1948 and is now governed by the *Gas Act 1972*. The Department of Energy now employs three sets of people to see that safety and other regulations under the Act are observed. Gas examiners are responsible for testing gas at terminals and other British Gas Corporation installations to see that it conforms to prescribed standards of pressure, quality, etc. Gas meter examiners test the design of gas meters, each of which has to be stamped before it can be used, and investigate complaints from consumers who are in dispute with the BGC over the quantity of gas used. Gas engineers carry out investigations of installations, piping, etc., on consumers' premises, mostly at the request of the BGC, to see whether they comply with the regulations relating to gas safety. Gas engineers also investigate serious incidents, e.g. where there has been loss of life.

Powers

Gas examiners and gas meter examiners have specific powers of entry to installations, premises, etc., for the explicit purposes for which they are appointed (1972 Act, ss. 26, 30, and regulations made under these sections, e.g. Gas Quality Regulations 1972, No. 1804; Gas (Meter) Regulations 1974, No. 848). Gas engineers have in addition the power to disconnect premises from the gas supply in order to avert danger (1972 Act, s. 31).

Numbers

Approx. 50 people are employed on these duties.

10 *Alkali and Clean Air Inspectorate (Her Majesty's Alkali and Clean Air Inspectorate)*

Origin and Development

Under the *Alkali Act 1863* an inspector was appointed by the Board of Trade to see that alkali works operated in conformity with the Act, and in particular that they secured the condensation (i.e. absorption) of at least 95 per cent of the hydrochloric acid given off by this manufacturing process. Later Acts extended the range of works and processes controlled, and did not confine the control to the emission of hydrochloric acid but to all 'noxious or offensive gases' emitted. The *Alkali* [etc.] *Works Regulation Act 1906* is the basic legislation governing the work of the inspectorate, but like the factory and other inspectorates it became a constituent part of the Health and Safety Executive under the *Health and Safety at Work* [etc.] *Act 1974*. It was not however fully integrated into HSE, pending examination by the Royal Commission on Environmental Pollution of the whole question of air pollution control. The Commission recommended (5th Report, Cmnd 6371, 1976) that the inspectorate should cease to form part of HSE and be reconstituted as a pollution inspectorate concerned with industrial pollution affecting water and land as well as air. The government has not yet (1979) announced a decision on this recommendation.

Functions

Under the 1974 Act regulations can be made specifying the processes which are to be subject to control. It is the duty of those in charge of works carrying on such processes to use the 'best practicable means' to prevent the emission into the atmosphere of 'noxious or offensive' substances and to render harmless or inoffensive any substances which are emitted (1974 Act, s. 5(1)). The task of the inspectorate is to enforce this provision. Originally, the inspectorate was responsible for works and processes throughout Great Britain. Separate arrangements now apply to Scotland (see industrial pollution inspectorate).

Powers   Inspectors now have all the powers of inspectors under
                      the 1974 Act (see factory inspectorate).

Recruitment   Inspectors must have a degree in chemistry, chemical
                      engineering or other relevant subject and at least five
                      years' experience in industry.

Numbers   47 (1979).

                      NB See Chapter 6 for further information and discus-
                      sion of the alkali inspectorate.

                      11 *Explosives Inspectorates (Her Majesty's Inspectorate
                      of Explosives)*

Origins and   The *Explosives Act 1875* provided for the regulation of
Functions   the manufacture and storage of explosives in the
                      interests of safety. The Home Secretary was
                      empowered to appoint inspectors for the purposes of
                      the Act. The basic function remained essentially
                      unchanged until under the *Health and Safety at Work*
                      [etc.] *Act 1974* the inspectorate became a constituent
                      part of the Health and Safety Executive; as part of HSE
                      it is now effectively an arm of the factory inspectorate,
                      concerned not only with the enforcement of the par-
                      ticular provisions relating to explosives but more
                      widely with other dangerous products.

Powers   Inspectors now have all the powers of inspectors under
                      the 1974 Act (see factory inspectorate).

Recruitment   Originally and traditionally inspectors were recruited
                      from officers of the Royal Artillery; more recently
                      recruitment has included those with the necessary
                      scientific qualifications with civilian experience.

Numbers   15 (1979).

                      12 *Building Control Officers*

Origin,   Apart from arrangements in London dating back to the
Development   eighteenth century (where inspectors were and still are
and Functions   known as district surveyors and operate under the
                      GLC Building Acts), the origin of building control
                      inspection may be regarded as the *Public Health Act
                      1875*, and corresponding Scottish legislation. There
                      had earlier been byelaws designed to prevent unsafe or
                      unhealthy building construction, including inadequate
                      foundations, lighting and ventilation. The 1875 Act
                      was followed by other legislation culminating in the
                      Public Health Act 1936 (and corresponding Scottish
                      legislation) which gave local authorities the power to
                      make building byelaws based on Model Byelaws. The

work of building control officers is now mainly governed by the building regulations made under the *Public Health Act 1961* and the *Building (Scotland) Act 1959*, but it should be noted that Part III of the *Health and Safety at Work* [etc]*Act 1974* considerably extended the scope of the regulations. Broadly speaking, the function of building control officers is to ensure that all new, altered and extended buildings comply with the regulations. These are detailed and complex and cover such matters as materials, damp resistance, structural stability, insulation, ventilation and height of rooms, and drainage. Schedule 5 of the 1974 Act extends the regulations to include services, fittings and equipment, access, etc.

Powers

Apart from the usual powers of inspectors to enter premises and sites, to require plans and particulars to show compliance with the regulations, and to enforce the regulations, there is also power to carry out, or have carried out, tests on materials and components, including soil tests (1974 Act, s. 68).

Recruitment

Recruitment is normally of school-leavers, who as trainees do practical work in a local authority building control department and at the same time are released for studies to HNC or HTC level with additional studies to qualify them to take professional examinations, especially those of the Institution of Building Control Officers.

Numbers

3,750 (England and Wales); 360 (Scotland).

13 *Cruelty to Animals Inspectorate*

Origin and Functions

The *Cruelty to Animals Act 1876* imposed restrictions on the conducting of experiments on live animals; those wishing to perform such experiments required a licence from the Home Secretary, and places where experiments were to be conducted had to be registered. The Home Secretary was to have all registered places visited from time to time by inspectors to secure compliance with the Act. The 1876 Act still governs the activities of the inspectorate. Inspectors make recommendations on the suitability of applicants for licences and of places proposed for registration. Most licensees are in universities. Registered places are visited without prior notice at varying intervals to see that the conditions under which licences have been granted are being observed.

Powers

No specific powers other than those of visiting and inspecting (1876 Act, s. 10), but during a visit an inspector may order the painless killing of an animal found to be suffering severe pain.

Recruitment

Inspectors must have medical or veterinary qualifications; some are former licensees recruited in their forties.

Numbers

15 (1979).

14 River Pollution Inspectors

Origin and Development

The *Rivers Pollution Prevention Act 1876* made it an offence to pollute rivers with sewage or solid or liquid wastes from industrial processes; local sanitary authorities were to enforce the Act so that effectively the job fell on sanitary inspectors. Responsibility for river pollution control was transferred to river boards in England and Wales in 1951 (*Rivers (Prevention of Pollution) Act 1951*) and to river purification boards in Scotland except for the most sparsely populated areas where county councils continued to have responsibility (*Rivers (Prevention of Pollution) (Scotland) Act 1951*). Inspectors appointed by river boards (after 1963 river authorities) or by river purification boards did not necessarily do the work full-time but might combine it with other functions. In 1974 regional water authorities in England and Wales took over responsibility for river pollution control as well as for water supply and sewage disposal (*Water Act 1973*). In Scotland river purification boards continue to be responsible; they now cover the whole country.

Functions

The main function of inspectors continues to be to ensure that the statutory provisions relating to river pollution are observed. Control is now exercised through a system of individual consents to discharge. Inspectors are involved in the determination of the conditions to be attached to consents, and in inspecting to see that the conditions are complied with.

Powers

The legislation does not specifically provide for either the appointment or powers of inspectors, but 'duly authorised' persons have power to enter any land for the purpose of performing any functions of regional water authorities, they may take equipment with them and may take away samples of effluent for analysis (*Water Resources Act 1963*, ss. 111–113; *Water Act 1973*, s. 9). Similar provisions apply in Scotland.

Recruitment

The great majority of inspectors are recruited as school-leavers and qualify as inspectors after taking the examination of the Institution of Water Pollution Control.

Numbers

Approx. 370 (England and Wales), 50 (Scotland); but the work is frequently combined with other functions.

NB See Chapter 6 for further information and discussion of river pollution inspection.

15 *Plant Health and Seeds Inspectorate (England and Wales)*

Origin and Development

Under the *Destructive Insects and Pests Act 1877* local authorities (county councils and the larger boroughs) were to enforce orders made under the Act for controlling Colorado beetle and other pests, e.g. American gooseberry mildew, potato wart disease. The work was taken over by the Board of Agriculture in 1914 as part of the work of the general inspectorate of the Board (later Ministry). The sale of seeds was first regulated by the *Seeds Act 1920* which, for example, prohibited the sale of seeds containing more than a prescribed percentage of injurious weeds; this too was enforced by the general inspectorate. With the development of the National Agricultural Advisory Service after the war and the growth in the work of controlling pests and diseases a separate plant health and seeds inspectorate was established to enforce the Acts and regulations made under them. The main items of legislation governing the work now are the *Plant Varieties and Seeds Act 1964* and the *Plant Health Act 1967*.

Functions

The inspectorate is responsible for enforcement of orders made by the minister in relation to plant health prohibiting the landing from abroad of plants, trees, etc., affected by disease or pests, and preventing the spread of disease or pests discovered in this country, e.g. by the destruction of crops (1967 Act, ss. 2 and 3). They are responsible for certification of seed potatoes, for cereal certification, certification of plants, fruit and vegetables for export, and enforcement of the seeds regulations.

Powers

Through orders made under the Acts, inspectors have power in specified circumstances to enter premises, examine material, request information and by means of a statutory notice require plant material to be destroyed, treated or disposed of in a specified way, and require the treatment of land, equipment and premises.

Recruitment

Inspectors are expected to have a degree in science or an equivalent qualification and usually have some agricultural or horticultural background. They may be recruited from within or outside the ministry.

Numbers

75 (1978).

NB For Scotland see Scottish agricultural inspectorate; and for plant health in relation to trees see Forestry Commission inspectorate.

16 Electricity Engineering Inspectorate

Origin and
Functions

The *Electric Lighting Act 1882* provided for the licensing and regulation of electricity undertakers, who were to be subject to inspection. Since nationalisation of the electricity industry in 1947 the main purpose of regulation remains to secure the regular and efficient supply of electricity and the protection of the public from danger. This remains prominent in the work of the inspectorate and its members enforce regulations relating to such matters as the materials and design of overhead power lines, height of overhead line conductors above ground, underground cables, enclosure of open-air sub-stations, variations in supply voltage and alternating current frequency, and standards of consumers' installations. An important part of their work is the investigation of accidents which have caused, or might have caused, injury. Perhaps their major function is the conduct of public inquiries and hearings, following objections to proposals by electricity boards for new power stations or overhead lines.

Powers

Inspectors with due authorisation are empowered at all times to inspect and to make examination and tests of the works and circuits of electricity boards. Powers in relation to public inquiry work are broadly similar to those of DOE planning inspectors.

Recruitment

There are no specified sources of recruitment to the inspectorate, although it is important for candidates to have wide experience in electricity supply. They must have appropriate professional qualifications.

5.

Numbers

NB This inspectorate acts for the Scottish Economic Planning Department also in the enforcement of safety regulations.

17 Inspectorate of Ships' Provisions

Origin and
Functions

The *Merchant Shipping Act 1892* provided for the inspection of provisions and water for the crews of long-distance ships to see that they were fit for use. Inspectors were to be appointed by the Board of Trade. The functions of inspectors remain broadly the same but include responsibility generally for ensuring that regulations relating to food hygiene are observed. They also perform allied functions, e.g. investigating complaints about food from crew members. The *Merchant Shipping Act 1970* now governs the activities of inspectors.

Powers   Inspectors have the general powers of inspection under the Merchant Shipping Act 1970, s. 76 (see surveyors of ships).

Recruitment   Inspectors are generally recruited from the food industry.

Numbers   11 (1979).

18 *Wages Inspectorate*

Origin   Under the *Trade Boards Act 1909* the Board of Trade had power to appoint officers to investigate whether employers were paying the minimum wages agreed by trade boards set up by the Act for certain industries where wages were low and the workers poorly organised. Inspectors are now appointed under the *Wages Councils Act 1979*.

Functions   The function of the inspectorate remains to ensure that the statutory minimum wages in certain industries and services are paid. All complaints are investigated, and in addition routine inspections are carried out of between 5 per cent and 10 per cent of known establishments annually.

Powers   Inspectors have power to require the production of wages sheets and other records kept by employers, to enter the premises of employers at all reasonable times and to question workers. They also have power to institute and conduct proceedings, and may also institute civil proceedings on behalf of a worker who has been underpaid (1979 Act, s. 22). Inspectors can also require employers to provide information by means of a questionnaire (1979 Act, s. 24).

Recruitment   Inspectors are selected from executive officers of the Department of Employment, and given several months' training before going out on their own. There is no recognised career structure in the inspectorate, and for most inspectors this is merely one of a number of jobs which they may do in the course of a civil service career.

Numbers   150 (1978).

Statistics   Detailed statistics of numbers of inspections, arrears of wages paid, etc., are published annually in the *Depart-*

ment of Employment Gazette. In 1978 nearly 32,000 establishments were inspected out of 391,000 on the department's list, and arrears were paid to nearly 23,000 workers of nearly £1½ million (*DE Gazette*, May 1979, p. 455). Numbers of prosecutions in recent years:

1972	0	1976	0
1973	0	1977	7
1974	2	1978	16
1975	2		

19 Civil Aviation (Safety) Inspectorates

Origin and Development

The *Air Navigation Act 1920* marked the beginning of attempts to regulate civil aviation in the interests of the safety of passengers and of people on the ground. This has always consisted of a number of elements including the airworthiness of aircraft, controls over the crews of aircraft and investigation of accidents. From the beginning there has also been a tendency to share the work between central departments and other bodies. For example, in the 1920s and early 1930s a Joint Aviation Advisory Committee did much of the work on the renewal of certificates of airworthiness which were required for all aircraft; this was replaced by the Air Registration Board, which was responsible for all the work on certification of airworthiness until 1971. The creation of the Civil Aviation Authority under the *Civil Aviation Act 1971* took this tendency a good deal farther; effectively the CAA is the authority responsible under the Act for the enforcement of regulations relating to safety except for the investigation of accidents, which remains the responsibility of the Accidents Investigation Branch of the Department of Trade.

Functions

Inspecting functions of the CAA are governed in particular by the Air Navigation Order 1974 (SI 1974, No. 1114). They cover three aspects: (i) the flight operations inspectorate has the task of ensuring that crew training requirements are observed, that air operations certificates have been obtained, proper operating manuals are used, etc.; (ii) airworthiness inspectors are concerned with testing new aircraft for airworthiness, issuing air engineer licences, ensuring that maintenance is carried out according to agreed schedules, etc.; (iii) the aerodromes inspectorate is concerned with the licensing and inspection of aerodromes to ensure that they comply with requirements relating to such matters as hazards to aircraft and provision of fire-fighting equipment.

The work of the DT Accidents Investigation Branch is governed by the Civil Aviation (Investigation of Accidents) Regulations (SI 1969. No. 833). The main function is to determine the circumstances and causes of accidents.

Powers

CAA inspectors have powers under the 1974 Regulations of entry and inspection, and also power to require the production of certificates, licences and other documents. DT inspectors under the 1969 Regulations have wider powers to summon and examine witnesses and take statements as well as powers to require the production of books and documents and to examine aircraft involved in accidents.

Recruitment

Professional qualifications and experience are required for all these inspectorates; for example, flight operations inspectors are recruited from pilots with long experience, including experience in command of aircraft; airworthiness engineers must have professional engineering qualifications, and at least ten years' experience, and are recruited from the airline industry; aerodromes inspectors are mainly recruited from RAF officers with substantial recent aircrew experience.

Numbers

Approx. 180 altogether, of whom 12 are DT inspectors.

20 Drugs Inspectorate

Origin and Functions

Under the *Dangerous Drugs Act 1920* the manufacture, export and import of certain drugs such as opium and morphine were made subject to a licensing system, and their sale and use regulated. Inspectors were appointed to ensure that the Act's requirements were complied with. The system is still essentially the same, although the range of drugs controlled has been extended. The *Misuse of Drugs Act 1971* now governs the activities of the inspectorate of the Drugs Branch of the Home Office. The main task of inspectors is to visit the premises of manufacturers, suppliers and distributors of controlled drugs, examine the records they are required to keep under the Act and inspect any stocks of drugs which are kept. They also check on the records kept by medical practitioners and other authorities to handle drugs for possible misuse.

Powers

Inspectors have power to enter premises of producers or suppliers of drugs, require the production of books and documents, and inspect stocks (1971 Act, s. 23).

Recruitment

Recruitment is from higher executive officers of the Home Office.

Numbers

11 (1978).

21 *Agricultural Wages (England and Wales)*

Origin and Development

The *Agricultural Wages (Regulation) Act 1924* provided for the making of orders specifying minimum wages for agricultural workers to be enforced by the Ministry of Agriculture. Until the war inspectors who carried out this work formed part of the general agricultural inspectorate of the ministry. A separate wages inspectorate was set up in 1948 and became part of a combined safety and wages inspectorate in 1957. Since 1962, when wages inspectors' work was transferred to Treasury class executive officers there has been no separate wages 'inspectorate'. The *Agricultural Wages Act 1948* governs the work of the inspectors.

Functions

The basic function of inspectors is to ensure compliance of employers with the 1948 Act and with orders made under it by the Agricultural Wages Board. This is done largely through investigation of complaints and test inspections on farms.

Powers

Inspectors have power to inspect and take copies of wages sheets and other records of wages and conditions of employment, to enter premises at all reasonable times, and to require workers and employers to give information with regard to workers' employment. They also have power to institute and conduct proceedings (1948 Act, s. 12).

Recruitment

Inspectors (who are appointed by the Minister) (1948 Act, s. 12) are selected from executive officers of the Ministry of Agriculture, Fisheries and Food.

Numbers

36 (1978) but in many cases the work is only part-time and is combined with other functions.

Statistics

The minister (jointly with the Secretary of State for Wales from 1978) is required to make an annual report to Parliament. In 1978 4,627 holdings received test inspections on 83 of which (1.9 per cent) infringements of the Act or orders were found; of 218 cases investigated as a result of complaints, underpayment was established in 71. The total amount of arrears recovered was about £12,000. (*Report on Wages in Agriculture 1978*, HMSO, 1979, paras 34,35.) Numbers of prosecutions in recent years:

| 1975 | 1 | 1977 | 4 |
| 1976 | 5 | 1978 | 4 |

NB For Scotland see Scottish agricultural inspectorate.

22 Road Vehicle Examiners

Origin and
Development

The *Road Traffic Act 1930* introduced statutory checks on public service vehicles for safety purposes. These were to be carried out by vehicle examiners of the Ministry of Transport. Checks on goods vehicles were brought in by the *Road and Rail Traffic Act 1933*, and on private cars, small goods vehicles and motor-cycles by the *Road Traffic Act 1956*. The nature of the checks and the part played by Department of Transport examiners varies according to the type of vehicle involved, but the primary purpose of all the procedures is to ensure that vehicles in use on the roads conform to the regulations specifying safety standards. The *Road Traffic Acts of 1956, 1960* (for public service vehicles) and *1972* now chiefly govern the activities of vehicle examiners.

Functions

For *public service vehicles*, i.e. buses and coaches, no specific statutory method of inspection is laid down, apart from an initial test when new to ensure that they qualify for a certificate of fitness; this test is, however, carried out by professional engineering staff of the Department of Transport and not by vehicle examiners. In practice, examiners carry out two kinds of inspection: (i) annual inspections of all vehicles by arrangement with the owners; (ii) random spot checks on vehicles without notice.

For *heavy goods vehicles*, examiners (i) carry out spot checks either at the roadside (in conjunction with the police) or at operators' premises; (ii) carry out annual inspections at Department of Transport testing stations.

For *passenger cars, etc.*, annual inspection of vehicles over three years old is undertaken by commercial garages under authorisation from the department: vehicle inspection staff make checks on the garages to ensure that standards are maintained. In addition, vehicle examiners carry out spot checks on vehicles on the road (in conjunction with the police).

Powers

Powers of vehicle examiners in relation to public service and heavy goods vehicles include the power to enter and inspect any vehicle coming within the statutory categories, and power to enter premises where vehicles are kept. There are certain supplementary powers (1960 Act, s. 128: 1972 Act, s. 56). Examiners have power under certain conditions to prohibit the use of public service or heavy goods vehicles until defects found at inspection have been put right (1960, s. 133: 1972, ss. 57, 58). They also have power to enter premises where second-hand goods vehicles are sold and test inspect them to make sure that they are roadworthy (1972, s. 61).

There are powers to inspect vehicles, premises and records in connection with the testing of passenger cars, etc. (1972, s. 43); to test motor vehicles on the road (1972, s. 53); to inspect premises, etc., of an applicant for or holder of a haulage operator's licence (Transport Act 1968, s. 82); and to enter premises where second-hand motor vehicles are sold and test and inspect them for roadworthiness (1972, s. 61).

Recruitment
Professional and technical staff are recruited from those with appropriate qualifications (Institution of Mechanical Engineers, HNC, etc.): goods vehicle testers are recruited without qualifications and trained as testers.

Numbers
1,028. Of this number 390 are goods vehicle testers at Department of Transport testing stations, and 638 professional and technical staff (excluding those at headquarters). Testers are classified as industrial staff, and it is doubtful how far they should be regarded as enforcement inspectors since their main task is checking the physical condition of goods vehicles.

Statistics
In recent years, inspections of PSV have averaged under 100,000 a year and approximately 5 per cent of inspections have resulted in suspensions because of defects. Inspections of HGV have averaged around 150,000 a year but the number of inspections resulting in prohibitions has fallen sharply from over 40 per cent in the mid-1960s to around 15 per cent.

23 Petroleum Engineering Inspectorate

Origin and Development
The *Petroleum (Production) Acts of 1918 and 1934* first attempted to regulate the search for and production of petroleum on land by means of a licensing system; inspection powers were mainly concerned with the inspection of plans in relation to the sinking of boreholes, and the work was carried out by the mines inspectorate. But although 1934 may be taken as the starting-point of a petroleum production inspectorate the work only became significant and led to the establishment of a separate inspectorate with the development of North Sea oil and gas. The *Continental Shelf Act 1964*, which applied the provisions of the 1934 Act

to undersea oil, marked the beginning of a new and greatly expanded role for the inspectorate. In addition to work on petroleum production the inspectorate became responsible for safety regulations under the *Mineral Workings (Offshore Installations) Act 1971.* There were five inspectors in 1970 and these have now grown to twelve, but because of the expansion of the work these no longer constitute solely a petroleum production inspectorate but, together with supporting staff, form the Operations and Safety Branch of the Petroleum Engineering Division of the Department of Energy.

Functions 　'As the name of the branch implies, the work of the inspectorate falls into two categories: (i) concerned with production: this is mainly governed by the Petroleum (Production) Regulations 1966 (SI 1966, No. 898) and 1976 (SI 1976, No. 1129) and includes the approval of all well-drilling and abandonment programmes; the inspectorate also verifies the measurement of the quantities of oil and gas produced offshore for Petroleum Revenue Tax purposes; (ii) concerned with safety: this has two aspects (a) safety of offshore installations – for example, the inspectorate monitors the activities of authorities appointed by the secretary of state to certify installations as fit for use (Offshore Installations (Construction and Survey) Regulations, SI 1974, No. 289); it also carries out routine safety inspections on offshore installations; (b) safety of those working on installations: this includes the investigation of accidents (Offshore Installations (Inspectors and Casualties) Regulations, SI 1973, No. 1842; and under an agency agreement with the Health and Safety Commission the inspectorate is now responsible for enforcing the provisions of the *Health and Safety at Work* [etc.]*Act 1974* on offshore installations.

These somewhat complex responsibilities indicate that in terms of the categories used in Chapter 1 the inspectorate has both enforcement and checking responsibilities, but the former is a significant part of the whole, particularly with the development of occupational safety responsibilities.

Powers 　Inspectors naturally have somewhat different powers according to their differing responsibilities, but under the 1971 Act they include: power to board and obtain access to all parts of offshore installations, obtain information, and inspect and take copies from logbooks and other documents; power to test and, in certain circumstances, dismantle, etc., equipment;

power to require the carrying out of procedures and tests by those specifically designated in regulations (1971 Act, Schedule).

Recruitment

Recruitment is from professionally qualified engineers with experience in a relevant industry (e.g. oil, construction engineering).

Numbers

12 (1978).

24 *Egg Marketing Inspectorate (England and Wales)*

Origin and Development

Wartime regulations under the Defence Regulations laid down quality and weight standards for eggs and required packers and wholesalers to be licensed. These regulations were administered by area egg officers. Various schemes operated after the war and were administered from 1957 to 1971 by the British Egg Marketing Board, but were mostly related to checking quality in connection with egg subsidy schemes. An egg marketing inspectorate was set up in 1973 to enforce the EEC Egg Marketing Regulations adopted in that year. The Eggs (Marketing Standards) Regulations 1973 (SI 1973, No. 15) made under the *European Communities Act 1972* (s. 2) govern the work of inspectors.

Functions

The main function of inspectors is to make spot checks on egg packers and wholesalers to ensure that they are conforming to the regulations relating to such matters as grading for quality and weight and labelling.

Powers

Inspectors have power to enter and inspect land and premises where regulated activities are carried on, to take samples of eggs and to require the production of books and documents; they can also take more specific action, e.g. they can require that a container which does not comply with EEC regulations should comply before it is marketed (SI 1973, No. 15, reg. 4).

Recruitment

Recruitment is from within the ministry: successful applicants are given specialised departmental training before officially undertaking inspection duties.

Numbers

40 (1978).

NB For Scotland see Scottish agricultural inspectorate.

25 *Agriculture (Health and Safety) Inspectorate (Her Majesty's Agricultural Inspectorate)*

Origin and Development

The *Agriculture (Poisonous Substances) Act 1952* made provision for the agriculture Ministers of both England

and Wales and Scotland to make regulations for protecting agricultural workers against the risk of poisoning from toxic pesticides, and for the appointment of inspectors to enforce them. The *Agriculture (Safety, Health and Welfare Provisions) Act 1956* extended these powers to safety, health and welfare generally and among other things required an employer to provide sanitary facilities for employees; there was also power to make regulations, e.g. for reporting accidents and keeping records. In England and Wales enforcement was carried out by a combined safety and wages inspectorate from 1956 until 1962 when wages work was replaced with other functions in connection with land, pests and subsidies. In Scotland, enforcement formed part of the work of the Scottish agricultural inspectorate. Under the *Employment Protection Act 1975* responsibility for health and safety in agriculture was transferred to the Health and Safety Commission and Executive from 1 March 1976. A full-time inspectorate in England and Wales was formed in January 1975 and transferred to HSE in March 1977. Scottish inspectors were transferred to HSE in September 1976 but retained wages work until November 1977.

Functions
The extant provisions of the 1952 and 1956 Acts and regulations made under them are 'relevant statutory provisions' under s. 53 of the HSW Act 1974 (see note on factory inspectorate). The main functions of the inspectorate are advice, education and enforcement of the statutory provisions relating to health and safety in agriculture and some new entrant activities, in accordance with the 1974 Act.

Powers
Inspectors have the powers of inspectors under the 1974 Act (see note on factory inspectorate). In 1978, 2,097 improvement notices and 793 prohibition notices were issued and 295 convictions obtained in the courts.

Recruitment
The present inspectorate has been largely recruited from the staff of the agricultural departments previously engaged on health and safety work; future recruitment will be by open competition through the Civil Service Commission.

Numbers
189 (1979).

26 *Fire Precautions Inspectorate*

Origin and Development
Two distinct strands can be seen in the work of fire prevention. There is, first, the provision of advice by fire brigade staff on fire prevention matters, including

advice to enforcing authorities; the general duty of fire
authorities to give advice when asked on fire prevention is contained in the *Fire Services Act 1947* (s.
1(1)(f)). Secondly, there is the obligation on fire
authorities to enforce specific statutory provisions in
relation to fire prevention and for this purpose to
appoint inspectors; the *Factories Act 1959* was the first
to impose this duty, which has since grown considerably, notably under the *Offices, Shops and Railway Premises Act 1963* and the *Fire Precautions Act
1971*, which is now the principal Act for this purpose.
It can be said that (i) fire prevention work became a
significant part of the work of fire authorities from the
date of operation of the 1947 Act, i.e. 1948; (ii) that
inspection and enforcement has become a relatively
more important part of fire prevention work since
1959. At the same time, it must be remembered that (i)
advisory work still occupies a good deal of the time of
fire prevention officers: (ii) fire prevention work is not
itself an exclusive function and in many fire brigades
officers engaged on the work also have operational
duties. For the purpose of this note the fire precautions
inspectorate is taken to consist of those officers of fire
brigades who are engaged exclusively or primarily on
fire prevention work, but the limitations of this
definition must be borne in mind in considering what
follows.

Functions

Under the 1971 Act fire authorities are required to
appoint inspectors to enforce various statutory provisions relating to fire safety, especially (i) fire safety
precautions in offices, shops and other premises
covered by the 1963 Act; (ii) means of escape in case of
fire in premises covered by the Factories Acts; (iii) fire
safety in premises covered by the 1971 Act. Certain
types of premises designated by the Secretary of State
under the 1971 Act require fire certificates issued by
fire authorities dealing with use of the building, means
for fighting fires, means of escape, etc. Among the
types of premises intended to be brought within the
scope of the Act are those with public access and those,
like hotels or old people's homes, which provide
sleeping accommodation (1971 Act, ss. 1, 6, 8, 12, 18).

Powers

Under the 1971 Act inspectors have power to enter and
inspect premises, make examinations and inquiry to
see that the Act and regulations are being complied
with, question employees and require facilities and
assistance to be given them to carry out their duties (s.
19).

Recruitment   Inspectors are not recruited as such, generally speaking, but are drawn from the ranks of fire brigade officers, for whom specialist training is available at the Home Office Fire Service Technical College.

Numbers   Approx. 2,000 (England and Wales); 180 (Scotland).

NB Fire authorities are counties (England and Wales) and regions and islands (Scotland).

27 Radiochemical Inspectorate

Origin and Development   The *Radioactive Substances Act 1960* strengthened the arrangements for dealing with radioactive wastes by requiring users of radioactive materials (except the UK Atomic Energy Authority) to be registered, and by requiring authorisations for the disposal of radioactive wastes. Inspectors could be appointed to assist the minister (now Secretary of State for the Environment) in the execution of the Act. The inspectorate now forms part of the Radioactive Waste (Professional) Division of DOE.

Functions   The main functions of the inspectorate under the 1960 Act are to advise the secretary of state on applications for registration and authorisation, and check by visits of inspection that those who receive registration or authorisation are complying with the conditions under which these have been granted (ss. 1, 6, 12). The inspectorate will also be closely involved in work arising from the expanded role of DOE in radioactive waste management following the Sixth Report of the Royal Commission on Environmental Pollution (e.g. in ensuring that the handling and treatment of wastes is carried out with due regard to environmental considerations).

Powers   Inspectors may enter the premises of those registered, authorised or exempt under the 1960 Act, carry out tests and inspections and require the occupier to provide information or documents; they may also under certain circumstances exercise these powers on premises not registered under the Act if they have reasonable grounds for believing that radioactive materials are kept or used there (1960 Act, s. 12 and Second Schedule).

Recruitment   Inspectors are professionally qualified.

Numbers   6 (1979, but under review and likely to be increased).

28 *Nuclear Installations Inspectorate (Her Majesty's Nuclear Installations Inspectorate)*

Origin and Development

The *Nuclear Installations (Licensing and Insurance) Act 1959* provided that those wishing to use a site for the installation or operation of a nuclear plant must first obtain a licence from the Minister of Power; conditions might be attached to any licence granted, designed to secure safety both for workers and the general public in the design, siting, construction, installation, operation and maintenance of nuclear plants; the minister had power to appoint inspectors to assist him in the execution of the Act. The specific provisions are now contained in the *Nuclear Installations Act 1965*, but under the *Health and Safety at Work* [etc.] *Act 1974* the inspectorate became a constituent part of the Health and Safety Executive which is now the licensing authority under the 1965 Act.

Functions

The main work of the inspectorate consists of safety assessments in connection with the granting of licences and subsequent visits of inspection to ensure that the conditions of licences have been complied with (1965 Act, s. 4). The inspectorate also carries out all safety inspection, i.e. under the Factories Act as well as the Nuclear Installations Act at major nuclear installations, especially power stations, advises on development proposals in the neighbourhood of nuclear power stations and is involved in international collaboration in nuclear safety matters particularly through the EEC (Euratom Treaty) and the International Atomic Energy Agency.

Powers

Inspectors have the power to enter licensed premises at all reasonable times, to carry out tests and inspections and to require the production of information and documents by the licensee, together with all other powers of inspectors under the 1974 Act (see note on factory inspectorate).

Recruitment

Inspectors are qualified engineers and scientists from various disciplines associated with the nuclear field. They were originally recruited mainly from the UK Atomic Energy Authority, but now include many with other industrial experience.

Numbers

106 (1979).

29 *Pipelines Inspectorate*

Origin and Development

The *Pipelines Act 1962* first made specific provision for the regulation of the construction and use of pipelines in the interests of safety. Under the Act the Minister of

Power (now Secretary of State for Energy) had power among other things to issue notices requiring the examination, repair and testing of pipelines and the notification of accidents, for which he could direct a public inquiry to be held. He could also appoint inspectors to assist him in the execution of the Act. The *Petroleum and Submarine Pipelines Act 1975* extended broadly the same provisions to North Sea pipelines.

Functions

The main function of the inspectorate is to see that safety provisions under the two Acts are observed; these concern both those working on the construction or maintenance of lines and the general public. The inspectorate also has an advisory role in relation to pipelines for both government departments and local authorities.

Powers

Inspectors have the power under the 1962 Act to inspect and test pipelines, take samples of anything being conveyed by pipeline, inspect pipeline works and require the production of documents (s. 42). There are additional powers under the 1975 Act to conform with the special conditions of underwater pipelines; for example, inspectors have power to enter vessels and installations used in connection with pipelines (s. 27). The 1962 Act is a 'relevant statutory provision' under the *Health and Safety at Work* [etc.] *Act 1974* so far as it relates to the safety, health or welfare of those working on the construction or maintenance of pipelines. The inspectorate acts as the agent of the Health and Safety Commission in enforcing these provisions and corresponding provisions in the 1975 Act and in that connection inspectors have the powers of inspectors under the 1974 Act (see note on factory inspectorate).

Numbers

6 (1978).

30 *Horticultural Marketing Inspectorate (England and Wales)*

Origin

The *Agriculture and Horticulture Act 1964* (Part III) made provision for the Minister of Agriculture, Fisheries and Food to make regulations relating to the grading, packaging and labelling of fresh horticultural produce. Provision was also made for persons authorised by the Minister to carry out inspections. The statutory scheme, which replaced the previous system of voluntary grading, covered five products and was applicable at wholesale level only. It was intended to promote higher quality and greater uniformity of home produce and improve its competitiveness against imported supplies. The statutory grades were, like those of the EEC, based on the international standards recommended by ECE and OECD. Since 1973 the EEC grading regulations have been applicable in the UK and are legally effective by s. 2(1) of the European Communities Act 1972. The authority for enforcing the rules contained in the regulations is contained in Part III of the 1964 Act as amended by the Grading of Horticultural Produce (Amendment) Regulations 1973. They apply at all stages of distribution to a wide range of fresh fruit and vegetables.

Functions

Inspectors carry out spot checks at ports, pack-houses, wholesaler markets and, to a limited extent, retail shops to ensure that the regulations are being observed.

Powers

Inspectors have the power to enter premises, inspect and take samples of any regulated product found on the premises, and seize and detain certificates or labels used in connection with such produce (1964 Act, s. 13 as amended).

Recruitment

Inspectors are mainly recruited from the fruit and vegetable trade.

Numbers

140 (1979).

NB For Scotland see Scottish agricultural inspectorate.

31 Gaming Inspectorate

Origin and Function

The Gaming Act 1968 established a Gaming Board for Great Britain to regulate gaming facilities particularly through a system of registration and licensing of gaming premises. The Board had power to appoint inspectors under the Act. Enforcement of the gaming laws had previously been entirely the responsibility of the police. The effect of the Act was intended to be to leave the primary responsibility of enforcement to them with the inspectorate having a supervisory role in relation to clubs and other places where gaming was carried on. There was also emphasis on the advisory role of the inspectorate in relation to clubs and other aspects of gaming, e.g. suppliers of gaming machines. As is indicated in the annual reports of the Board, inspectors frequently issue warnings to licensees as a result of what has been discovered at an inspection visit, but they also pass on much information to the police for them to take action either by way of caution or prosecution.

| Powers | Inspectors may enter licensed premises at any reasonable time, and inspect them, and inspect machines or other equipment, books and documents to see whether there has been any contravention of the Act or regulations made under it (1968 Act, s. 43). |

Recruitment — Inspectors are usually former police officers.

Numbers — 37 (1979).

32 Diving Inspectorate

Origin and Functions — The *Mineral Workings (Offshore Installations) Act 1971* provided that the Secretary of State for Energy could make regulations for the safety, health and welfare of those working on offshore installations and appoint inspectors to carry out the functions specified in the regulations, or generally assist in carrying out the Act. The *Offshore Installations (Diving Operations) Regulations 1974* (SI 1974, No. 1229) lay specific duties in connection with safety of diving operations on various people, such as installation managers, and make various rules for this purpose (e.g. imposing restrictions on the number of hours a diver may be under water). The main functions of the diving inspectorate are to carry out inspections to ensure that the regulations are observed and to investigate accidents. They have similar functions in relation to diving on pipelines under the *Petroleum and Submarine Pipelines Act 1975* and the *Submarine Pipelines (Diving Operations) Regulations 1975* (SI 1975, No. 823).

Powers — Inspectors have the powers specified in the 1971 Act (see note on petroleum engineering inspectorate).

Numbers — 5 (1979).

33 Scottish Agricultural Inspectorate

Organisation and Functions — The agricultural inspectorate of the Department of Agriculture and Fisheries for Scotland combines what were identified as two separate inspectorial functions in Chapter 1. It is responsible for checking on the use of grants and subsidies under the various statutory schemes applying to Scottish agriculture, such as those for farm capital grants. In England and Wales this work is carried out by the Agricultural Development and Advisory Service of MAFF. It also has responsibility for enforcing legislation, which in England and Wales is the responsibility of separately organised enforcement inspectors, especially:

(i)   agricultural wages (under the *Agricultural Wages (Scotland) Act 1949*);

      (ii)   plant health and seeds (*Plant Health Act 1967,* etc., as for England and Wales);

      (iii)   horticultural marketing (*Agriculture and Horticulture Act 1964* and EEC Regulations, as for England and Wales);

      (iv)   egg marketing (EEC Regulations, as for England and Wales).

For the purposes of enforcement Scottish inspectors have identical powers of entry and inspection, etc., under the legislation as those in England and Wales.

Numbers

The total staff of the inspectorate numbered 296 in 1978, and of these 106 had the designation inspector (or assistant inspector). However, for the reasons given above it is not possible to be precise about the number of inspectors as more narrowly defined for the purposes of this study, that is, those who are solely or mainly engaged on the enforcement of statutory provisions.

34 Industrial Pollution Inspectorate (Scotland) (Her Majesty's Industrial Pollution Inspectorate)

Origin and Development

The *Alkali Act 1863,* which established the alkali inspectorate applied to the whole of the United Kingdom. In 1920 administration of the Alkali Acts in Scotland was transferred to Edinburgh and a chief inspector for Scotland appointed. The *Alkali* [etc.] *Works Regulation (Scotland) Act 1951* enabled the secretary of state to make separate provision for the scheduling of works in Scotland and for extending or amending the list of noxious or offensive gases. In 1971 the inspectorate was renamed and received its present title.

Functions

In addition to its function under the Alkali Acts, which correspond to those of the alkali and clean air inspectorate, the inspectorate is responsible for inspection in Scotland under the *Radioactive Substances Act 1960* which is performed in England and Wales by the radiochemical inspectorate. It also has advisory functions in relation to (a) air pollution (Clean Air Acts, Control of Pollution Act 1974, etc.); (b) industrial effluents and other industrial wastes (Rivers (Prevention of Pollution) (Scotland) Acts, Deposit of Poisonous Wastes Act 1972, etc).

Numbers

9.

EFFICIENCY INSPECTORATES

1 *Education Inspectorate (England and Wales) (Her Majesty's Inspectorate of Schools, etc).*

Origin and Development

Inspection of schools was originally introduced in 1840 as a condition of the giving of grants by the government to voluntary bodies which were willing to provide schools for elementary education purposes. Inspection was gradually extended to secondary schools and to institutions for further and higher education. Its statutory basis is now the *Education Act 1944.*

Functions

Although the basic reason for the introduction of inspection was the need for government to be satisfied that the conditions of grant were being met, there has always been much debate about the functions of the inspectorate. Two other functions in particular have long been associated with the inspectorate: the provision of information to the central authority or department, and the provision of advice to teachers and those responsible for running schools and other educational institutions. Nothing is specified in the legislation, which merely requires the secretary of state to cause inspections to be made, and allows him to appoint inspectors for this purpose.

Powers

Inspectors have the right to enter schools and other educational institutions and carry out inspections but have no other specific powers under the legislation except in relation to the special provisions for schools which are not part of the state system.

Recruitment

Inspectors are mainly recruited from former teachers in schools, technical colleges, etc.

Numbers

404 (England), 48 (Wales) (1978). The authorised complement for England is 430.

NB See Chapter 5 for further discussion and information about inspection in schools.

2 *Education Inspectorate (Scotland) (Her Majesty's Inspectorate of Schools, etc., for Scotland)*

Origin and Development

Although inspection of schools began in 1840 as it did in England and Wales, and although, again as in England and Wales, the legislation (now *Education (Scotland) Act 1962*) merely requires the secretary of state to cause inspections to be made, there has been a distinctively Scottish development of the inspectorate corresponding in some degree to the distinctive character of the Scottish educational system. For this reason alone it is not possible to say that the discussion in Chapter 5 applies broadly to Scotland as it does to England and Wales. There are of course some basic similarities: reliance on direct contact with schools and other educational institutions as the foundation of the work, importance of the information-providing role to the secretary of state, etc. But the way in which the role of the inspectorate operates in practice would require separate study, for example, of the relation between the Scottish Education Department and the local education authorities in Scotland which, at least until the 1975 reorganisation of local government, probably differed significantly from that in England and Wales. Although, therefore, the summarised information in the preceding section is broadly applicable to the Scottish education inspectorate, it is very far from being the whole story. It is probable, for example, that formal inspections play a greater part in Scottish than in English inspection: in 1977, 300 primary schools (out of a total of 2,500) were formally inspected, largely on an area basis, and 70 secondary schools (out of a total of 460) had team inspections (*Education in Scotland 1977*, Cmnd 7246, 1978, para. 37).

3 Police Inspectorate (England and Wales) (*Her Majesty's Inspectorate of Constabulary*)

Origin and Development

The *Police (Counties and Boroughs) Act 1856* provided for the appointment of inspectors to inquire into the state and efficiency of police forces. (The Metropolitan Police were and have remained excluded from these provisions.) The statutory provisions governing the appointment and work of inspectors are now contained in the *Police Act 1964*.

Functions

Under the legislation inspectors have the duty of inspecting and reporting to the Home Secretary on the efficiency of police forces, and also of carrying out other duties as directed by the Home Secretary aimed at furthering police efficiency. The chief inspector must make an annual report (1964 Act, s. 38). Regular visits to police forces form the major part of the work of inspectors.

Powers

There are no specific powers of an inspector under the legislation, but in practice he has wide scope for examining the work of police forces, obtaining information seeking to satisfy himself that the force is generally well run (e.g. he can provide opportunities for private discussion with any police officer who has a grievance).

Recruitment	Inspectors are recruited from former police officers, mainly chief constables.
Numbers	6 (and 4 assistant inspectors).

4 Police Inspectorate (Scotland) (Her Majesty's Inspectorate of Constabulary for Scotland).

Origin and Development

The appointment of inspectors of constabulary in Scotland dates from the *Police (Scotland) Act 1857*. They are now appointed under the *Police (Scotland) Act 1967* to inquire into the state and efficiency of police forces, their buildings and equipment (s. 33). In most respects the inspectorate is broadly comparable with that for England and Wales. There are at present 2 inspectors.

5 Fire Services Inspectorate (England and Wales) (Her Majesty's Inspectorate of Fire Services)

Origin and Development

The *Fire Brigades Act 1938* gave the Home Secretary power to prescribe standards of efficiency and to appoint inspectors, but these provisions did not become effective as a result of the outbreak of war and the creation of the National Fire Service. When, under the *Fire Services Act 1947*, the service was returned to the local authorities, provision was again made for the appointment of inspectors and assistant inspectors but with the limited object of obtaining information about the work of fire authorities.

Functions

The only duty specifically laid on inspectors by the 1947 Act is to provide the Home Secretary with information about the manner in which fire authorities carry out their functions under the Act, and also about technical matters (s. 24). In practice, through regular visits to fire brigades and inspections they aim to co-ordinate the activities of fire authorities; for example, they provide authorities with technical information and advise the Home Office on the operational, technical and organisational aspects of fire service matters.

Powers

No specific powers are provided in the 1947 Act.

Recruitment

Inspectors are recruited from former fire brigade officers.

Numbers

16 (and 19 assistant inspectors).

6 Fire Services Inspectorate (Scotland) (Her Majesty's Inspectorate of Fire Services for Scotland)

The 1947 and 1971 Acts apply also to Scotland and a

separate inspectorate is responsible to the Secretary of
State for Scotland. There are at present 2 inspectors
and 4 assistant inspectors.

PART 2

ENFORCEMENT INSPECTORATES

(a) *Inspection of slaughterhouses by veterinary officers of MAFF*
Veterinary officers of the Ministry of Agriculture, Fisheries and Food constitute the Veterinary Service, one of the five arms of the Ministry's Agricultural
Development and Advisory Service. Their functions are wide, including the
investigation of new diseases and animal productivity and welfare. Thus the
main aims of the Veterinary Service, as indeed of ADAS as a whole, are
promotional and advisory, and enforcement work is a relatively small part of
their task. One may sum up by saying that the veterinary service is responsible
for certain enforcement inspection including that in connection with standards of hygiene in slaughterhouses but that it does not constitute an inspectorate (see also Chapter 1, p.14).

(b) *Sea fisheries inspectorates*
These are examples of borderline inspectorates in the sense that although they
have definite enforcement tasks going back to nineteenth-century attempts to
regulate fishing rights within certain limits between this country and France,
they now have a preponderance of tasks which have little or no connection
with enforcement inspection.

The two inspectorates (one for England and Wales and one for Scotland)
have enforcement powers and duties under the *Sea Fisheries Act 1968*, the *Sea
Fish (Conservation) Act 1967* and the *Fisheries Limits Act 1976*. Much of this
work relates to conservation (e.g. enforcement of regulations relating to the
size of nets or the size of fish permitted to be caught), and to fishing limits,
where the inspectorates work closely with the Royal Navy. However their
many functions include the administration of licensing and quota
arrangements, general liaison with the fishing industry and the provision of
information and advice to the departments about the industry.

There are 19 designated inspectors in England and Wales and 10 in Scotland, recruited from the merchant navy or Royal Navy.

(c) *Forestry Commission inspectorate*
This is an example of inspecting powers being conferred on a body other than
a central department or local authority for limited and specific purposes. The
Plant Health Act 1967 makes the Forestry Commission the competent
authority for making orders for preventing the introduction of pests into
Great Britain so far as trees are concerned (the agriculture ministers are
responsible for orders other than those relating to trees), and also provides
that orders may enable inspectors to enter land, make inquiries and remove or
destroy seeds, plants, etc. Under the *Foresty Act 1967* the Commission has
general powers of entry and inspection for the purpose of their responsibilities

under the Act. The enforcement work (e.g. to prevent illegal movement of elm timber under the Dutch elm disease regulations) is, however, a part-time activity of Commission staff with other duties. On this basis 78 staff are designated inspectors.

(d) *Inspectorate of Ancient Monuments and Historic Buildings*
Inspectors were first appointed under the *Ancient Monuments Protection Act 1882* to report to the Commissioners of Works on the condition of monuments and the best means of preserving them. Listing of historic buildings was begun under the *Town and Country Planning Act 1947*. The two types of work were brought together in 1972 when the chief inspector of ancient monuments became chief inspector of ancient monuments and historic buildings within the Department of the Environment. The principal legislation now is the *Ancient Monuments Act 1953* and the *Town and Country Planning Act 1971*.

Although inspection of sites is an important part of the work of ancient monuments inspectors, enforcement inspection in the sense in which it has been used in this study is not a major function. In the case of historic buildings this is equally true, but those who carry out the work are termed investigators and not inspectors; their main task is to discover, inspect and report on buildings of special architectural or historical interest and make recommendations about their preservation or listing. Similarly inspectors of ancient monuments are principally concerned with deciding on what measures should be taken to preserve particular monuments and giving advice to the owners of those which remain in private hands. An important part is played by a system of grants both for ancient monuments and historic buildings as an inducement to owners to take proper care. Where important sites are threatened by development, inspectors may excavate and record the findings.

In a sense therefore the inspectors does not fall clearly into any of the five categories identified in Chapter 1. It has some concern with checking where grants are paid, and it has some concern with enforcement (e.g. it is an offence under the Acts to destroy a monument which has been the subject of a preservation order). But its main task is an executive one of administering the legislation relating to preservation of monuments. The need for inspecting powers derives from the nature of the objects whose protection is sought. There are at present 43 inspectors for England, 8 for Scotland and 5 for Wales.

(e) *Planning (Enforcement) Inspectors*
The *Town and Country Planning Acts 1947* provided that local planning authorities could serve enforcement notices in cases where they believed that building had been carried out either without permission or not in accordance with the conditions under which permission had been granted. Persons duly authorised by the authority could enter land and survey it in connection with any proposal to serve a notice. Under the *Town and Country Planning Act 1971* and *Town and Country Planning (Scotland) Act 1972* this power to serve enforcement notices is extended to any case where the authority thinks there has been a breach of planning control. Many authorities, especially since local government reorganisation, employ specific members of their staff to carry out enforcement work, and these are often called planning inspectors. On the other hand, development undertaken without permission is not an offence, and there is not usually anything in the nature of regular surveys to detect

breaches of planning control; most exercises of the power to serve enforcement notices arise from complaints. The work of enforcement officers is therefore more in the nature of investigatory inspection so far as it relates to the preliminary investigation of complaints to see whether the issue of an enforcement notice would be justified. It is, however, an offence not to comply with an enforcement or other similar notice (e.g. a listed building notice), and to the extent that enforcement officers use their powers to seek to secure such compliance they are acting in much the same way as enforcement inspectors. On the whole, and particularly in view of the fact that there is little systematic attempt to secure that development is only carried out in accordance with planning control conditions, it is better to regard this as a borderline case.

EFFICIENCY INSPECTORATES

(a) *Auditors of Local Authority Accounts*
As discussed in Chapter 8, district auditors in England and Wales can only be regarded as being in part an efficiency inspectorate. Their origin lies in the *Poor Law Amendment Act 1844*, which provided for the appointment of auditors for districts of unions. From 1868 these auditors were appointed by the central authority and in course of time district auditors became responsible for the audit of all local authority accounts except for those boroughs which chose to exercise their statutory right to appoint their own auditors. The appointment and duties of district auditors are now governed by the *Local Government Act, 1972*, Part VIII. Their main functions are to see that accounts are properly prepared, that expenditure has been authorised by law, that there is an adequate system of internal financial control, and that there has been no fraud, waste or extravagance. For these purposes they have extensive powers to examine books and documents, and to question local authority officials; they can apply to the courts for a declaration if they find anything contrary to law; and they can certify a failure to include an item or a loss by wilful misconduct and take steps with the authority to recover the money.

The audit service has a strength of approximately 630, of whom about half are professionally qualified accountants, mostly recruited from executive officers of the Department of the Environment and given professional training, but some are recruited directly from qualified accountants or from university graduates who are then given professional training.

Auditors of local authority accounts in Scotland also function only in part as an efficiency inspectorate. The administrative arrangements have, however, always differed from those in England and Wales. Before the local government reforms of 1975, the secretary of state appointed auditors who were usually professional firms of accountants. Under the *Local Government (Scotland) Act 1973*, a Commission for Local Authority Accounts was appointed by the secretary of state to secure the audit of all local authority accounts, consider reports on these accounts and investigate them where necessary, and advise and make recommendations to the secretary of state (s. 97). Auditors are responsible to the Commission and may be employed directly by it or by firms of chartered accountants acting as agents of the Commission; the majority of Scottish local authority accounts are still audited by such firms. Auditors are required to satisfy themselves that accounts have been prepared in accordance with regulations under the Act and proper accounting practices observed (1973 Act, s. 99). There is also a general Code of Practice which is similar to that issued by the DOE. The Commission employs 30 auditors, of whom half are professionally qualified. Over 30 firms of chartered accountants are employed as agents.

(b) *Social Work Service (England and Wales)*
The Social Work Service of the Department of Health and Social Security was formed in 1971 by the amalgamation of the Children's Inspectorate of the Home Office and the Social Work Division of the DHSS. Although the latter were both comparatively recent creations of the postwar period they had long roots, so far as inspection work was concerned, in the nineteenth-century inspection of reformatory schools and the Poor Law inspectors. However, there are two reasons why there may be doubt about treating the SWS as an inspectorate:

(i) use of inspection powers is only one part of its functions;
(ii) inspection powers relate to only part of the work of local authority social service departments.

The main inspecting powers are:
(i) entry and inspection of old people's homes, homes for the mentally disordered, etc. (*National Assistance Act 1948*, ss. 35, 39; *Health Services and Public Health Act 1968*, s. 12; *Mental Health Act 1959*, s. 21; and regulations made under these Acts).
(ii) children's homes, foster homes, etc. (*Children and Young Persons Act 1969*, s. 58).

The main function of the SWS, organised on a regional basis, has been officially described as being to 'advise and support' the social service departments of local authorities (DHSS Circular 22/71). It does this, for example, by stimulating and disseminating developments in practice and methods in the personal social services (DHSS Circular DSWS(79)1).
The strength of the SWS was approximately 125 in early 1979.

(c) *Social Work Services (Scotland)*
The Scottish Social Work Services Group (Scottish Education Department) is responsible for social work policies and for advising local authorities and other social work providers. Within the Group the Central Advisory Service, which was formed in 1967, broadly combines the functions performed in England and Wales by the Social Work Service (DHSS) and the probation inspectorate (Home Office). In Scotland the social work departments of the regional councils have the statutory responsibility for all social work including probation.
The main inspecting powers are now contained in s. 6 of the *Social Work (Scotland) Act 1968*. Under it authorised officers of the secretary of state may

enter residential and other establishments provided by local authorities or voluntary organisations, inquire into their state and management and into the condition and treatment of the persons in them, and inspect records and registers; they may also enter the offices of local authorities or voluntary organisations to inspect records and registers.

These inspecting powers are exercised by officers of the Central Advisory Service, but, as with the SWS and probation inspectorate in England and Wales, inspecting work forms only part of the work of the Service, which is broadly advisory and promotional in nature.

The staff of the Central Advisory Service numbered 35 in 1979.

(d) *Probation*
The probation inspectorate of the Home Office for England and Wales dates from 1936. It now operates under the powers of the Home Secretary to approve bail hostels, and probation hostels and homes, and to make rules for their regulation, management and inspection (*Powers of Criminal Courts Act 1973*, s. 49). The probation service in England and Wales is provided not by local authorities but by committees of local magistrates working in liaison with local authorities: for example, the local authority treasurer is also treasurer of the local committee and handles the payment of salaries of probation officers. The Home Office meets 80 per cent of the cost of the service. The probation inspectorate thus fits neither into the category of central inspectorates concerned with the efficiency of services provided by local authorities nor into the category of internal inspectorates. The position is different in Scotland, where probation is a local government service. See (c) Social Work Services (Scotland).

The formal powers of probation inspectors are limited to inspection of approved probation homes and hostels and bail hostels. In practice the inspectorate has a strongly promotional and advisory role through a regular programme of visits and inspections.

Inspectors, who are mainly recruited from those who have worked in the probation service, number 27.

(e) *Registration*
Registration of births, marriages and deaths is carried out by registration officers appointed and paid by local authorities. On the other hand, these officers are required to comply with instructions or directions given to them by the Registrar General for England and Wales or the Registrar General for Scotland. The direction of the registration service is thus in the hands of central government but the staff are not civil servants. Formally, inspectors (England and Wales) or district examiners (Scotland) are appointed by the Registrars General to inspect registers and other documents held by registration officers (the *Registration of Births, Deaths and Marriages Regulations 1968*, SI 1968, No. 2049, reg. 12: *Registration of Births, Deaths and Marriages (Scotland) Act 1965*, s. 34). In practice inspectors aim to ensure that registration officers are aware of and act in accordance with their duties, act as liaison officers with the local authorities, and carry out other field activities such as investigating complaints against the registration service. The inspectorates therefore have elements of both efficiency and internal inspection but do not fit exactly into either category.

There are 14 inspectors of registration together with 9 assistant inspectors; and 3 district examiners together with 2 assistant examiners.

PART 3

EXAMPLES OF CHECKING INSPECTORATES

1 The Agricultural Development and Advisory Service of MAFF, as its name implies, is largely concerned with the promotion of agriculture in England and Wales. It is largely responsible for administering the various statutory grant and subsidy schemes such as those for farm capital grants, and in connection with these it operates in both an advisory and checking capacity. The staff of ADAS is about 5,000, of whom about one-third are in the veterinary service, which also has some enforcement responsibilities (see p. 270 above).

2 Regional development grants are payable under Part I of the IndustryAct 1972 for approved capital expenditure (e.g. for machinery or buildings) to firms operating in the assisted areas. Department of Industry examiners have power under the Act to enter and inspect premises for which a grant has been made to ensure that the purposes and conditions of the grant have been met. Grant money may be recovered if they have not. About 20 examiners are employed on the work and are recruited from executive officers of the Department.

3 Under the Sea Fish Industry Act 1970 officers of the White Fish Authority who have been authorised for that purpose have the right to go on board vessels to see whether there have been contraventions of the regulations made under the Act or the terms of schemes. In effect these powers are mainly to ensure that the levy which the Authority is entitled to make is paid and that the conditions on which grants and loans are made (e.g. to build new vessels or improve existing ones) have been met. About 20 officials of the Authority are engaged on this work.

4 The difficulties of drawing precise boundaries between enforcement and checking are illustrated by another example from agriculture. Under the Agricultural Marketing Act 1958 (but with origins in the 1930s) schemes for regulating the marketing of agricultural products can be submitted by representatives of producers for the approval of the Minister of Agriculture, Fisheries and Food. The schemes may under s. 8 of the Act provide for powers of entry by officers of the Board established to run such schemes 'for the purpose of securing compliance with the scheme'; and Boards have power to impose fines in certain specified cases, e.g. a refusal to supply information required by a Board (s. 9). On the other hand, more serious breaches such as the selling of regulated products in contravention of the provisions of the scheme are matters for the courts and not the Boards (s. 6). (For an example of a scheme see Potato Marketing Scheme (Approval) Order 1955, SI 1955, No. 690.) The degree to which inspection can be regarded as for enforcement or checking purposes depends on the view taken of the nature of the schemes. If they are regarded as largely coercive, imposed on more or less unwilling producers, then enforcement is the main purpose; if on the other hand, one emphasises the voluntary

nature of the schemes, derived from the fact that they represent the view of the majority of the producers, then one could argue that the analogy was more closely with checking on the conditions under which grants are paid.

INDEX

Note: Page numbers in italic type refer to figures and tables
Page numbers in bold type refer to major references